The Reference Shelf

U.S. National Debate Topic 2008–2009

Alternative Energy

Edited by Paul McCaffrey

The Reference Shelf
Volume 80 • Number 3
The H.W. Wilson Company
New York • Dublin
2008

The Reference Shelf

The books in this series contain reprints of articles, excerpts from books, addresses on current issues, and studies of social trends in the United States and other countries. There are six separately bound numbers in each volume, all of which are usually published in the same calendar year. Numbers one through five are each devoted to a single subject, providing background information and discussion from various points of view and concluding with a subject index and comprehensive bibliography that lists books, pamphlets, and abstracts of additional articles on the subject. The final number of each volume is a collection of recent speeches, and it contains a cumulative speaker index. Books in the series may be purchased individually or on subscription.

Library of Congress has cataloged this serial title as follows:

U.S. national debate topic 2008-2009 : alternative energy / edited by Paul McCaffrey.
p. cm. — (The reference shelf ; v. 80, no. 3)
Includes bibliographical references and index.
ISBN 978-0-8242-1080-9 (alk. paper)
1. Renewable energy sources. 2. Energy development. I. McCaffrey, Paul, 1977–
II. Title: Alternative energy.

TJ808.U82 2008
333.79'4—dc22

2008015543

Cover:

Visit H.W. Wilson's Web site: www.hwwilson.com

Printed in the United States of America

Contents

Preface

With energy prices soaring, turmoil in the Middle East, and increased fears of global climate change, criticism of traditional fuel sources has reached a crescendo in recent years. Fossil fuels—coal, oil, and natural gas—have come in for particular scorn. Beyond their contribution to greenhouse gas emissions and air pollution in general, these energy sources each have other distinct shortcomings. Coal is dangerous to mine, and certain extraction methods—strip-mining for example—exact a terrible toll from the surrounding environment. Aside from the ecological devastation wrought by oil spills, our dependence on petroleum has a number of troubling political implications, forcing us to rely on and enrich potentially unstable, corrupt, and/or repressive regimes. Though considerably cleaner than coal and oil, natural gas has many of the same political drawbacks as oil. Furthermore, given a lack of infrastructure and increased demand, from China and elsewhere, natural gas is likely to grow increasingly expensive in the years to come. Finally, all these fuel sources are non-renewable: There is a finite amount of each and they could one day be used up. While coal reserves are expected to last for some time, how much untapped oil is left is uncertain and the subject of considerable debate.

Though their failings are obvious, fossil fuels have yet to be supplanted by other forms of energy. Despite their flaws, they remain the cheapest and most efficient energy options available. Of late some have suggested that nuclear energy might be an effective alternative. Though a more or less traditional fuel source, nuclear power does not contribute significantly to greenhouse gas emissions or air pollution. However, fears of nuclear disaster, especially in this age of terrorism, and the difficulties associated with nuclear waste disposal, not to mention the excessive upfront costs of building the actual plants, make a nuclear renaissance an unlikely scenario. This then leaves renewable sources, derived from biomass, solar energy, wind power, hydrogen fuel cells, hydroelectricity and wave power, and geothermal energy.

Meant to serve as a resource for those participating in the 2008–2009 National Debate Topic concerning whether the American federal government ought to expand alternative energy incentives, this edition in the Reference Shelf series examines renewable fuel sources, charting how they are obtained and used as well as their benefits and drawbacks. Of special interest is the question of their viability—

whether they have the potential for widespread, efficient, and cost-effective use.

Articles in the first chapter, "Fossil Fools: Climate Change, Traditional Energy Sources, and Their Drawbacks," explore a number of issues. Chief among them global climate change and the accompanying debate. Much of the argument over alternative energy depends on one's perception of global warming. Is it a real threat? And if so, is human fossil-fuel consumption to blame? Entries consider the science behind climate change as well as the arguments of global-warming skeptics. Oil, natural gas, coal, and nuclear energy are also profiled, with an emphasis on their strengths and weaknesses as sources of fuel and of pollution.

The subsequent chapters examine the various types of alternative energy, with entries in the second section, "Good Bye to Gasoline? Ethanol and Biodiesel," exploring the potential of fuel derived from crops like corn and sugarcane. Selections in the third chapter, "The Sun and the Wind: Renewable Twins?," focus on solar energy and wind power.

Perhaps no energy source shows as much transformative potential as hydrogen. Indeed, many anticipate that our carbon-fueled economy will some day be replaced with one driven by hydrogen power. The possibility of hydrogen energy is the focal point of pieces in the third chapter, "The Hydrogen Revolution: Is It Feasible?" Among the issues discussed are the technological obstacles that will need to be overcome if hydrogen is to emerge as the fuel of the future.

People have used energy generated by hydropower for centuries. Of all renewable energy sources, hydroelectricity is the most common. In "Hydroelectric and Wave Power: Viable Alternatives?," selections discuss this traditional renewable energy source, noting the environmental costs associated with it as well as the expanding promise of tidal power. Finally, entries in the last chapter, "Geothermal Energy," consider methods of accessing the heat stored in the Earth's crust for use as fuel.

In conclusion, I would like to thank the many publishers and authors who have kindly granted permission to reproduce their work in these pages. I would also like to extend my gratitude to those who have contributed their time, energy, and talent to this project, particularly Richard Stein and Christopher Mari.

Paul McCaffrey
June 2008

1

Fossil Fools?
Climate Change, Traditional Energy Sources, and Their Drawbacks

Editor's Introduction

The chief catalyst behind recent efforts to shift to renewable energy is global climate change. When fossil fuels are burned, carbon dioxide and other greenhouse gases are released into the Earth's atmosphere. As levels of these gases rise, it is theorized, more of the sun's heat, which would otherwise be released back into space is trapped in the atmosphere, causing temperatures to increase. What implications such temperature increases may have remains difficult to anticipate. Already, at the North and South Poles, ice caps are melting, leading to rising sea levels. Glaciers are retreating throughout the globe and much of the world is experiencing prolonged drought. If these trends continue, some believe that a "tipping point" will be reached and cataclysmic climate change will ensue. Among the hypothetical outcomes is the shutting off of the Gulf Stream, which could paradoxically cause a new ice age and render much of North America and Europe uninhabitable.

The articles in this chapter, "Fossil Fools? Climate Change, Traditional Energy Sources, and Their Drawbacks," explore the phenomenon of global warming and provide in-depth examinations of traditional energy sources. In "Carbon's New Math," Bill McKibben describes the mechanisms behind global warming and what will likely need to be done to impede the process. He believes that steep reductions in carbon emissions are required if catastrophic changes are to be forestalled. Any strategy, McKibben argues, would necessarily rely on alternative energy sources as well as conservation.

In contrast to McKibben, Thomas Sieger Derr, in his piece, "The Politics of Global Warming," contends that climate-change alarmism does us a disservice. He argues that the science behind human-influenced global warming is not as settled as McKibben and others would have us believe. "There are, of course, good reasons for controlling many emissions and finding alternative sources to fossil fuels . . . ," Derr remarks. "But stopping global warming is not one of them."

In "Can the United States Shed Its Oil Addiction," Josef Braml discusses the mixed blessings of petroleum. He evokes the extensive pollution associated with it as well as the many political and moral compromises that must be made in order to keep the oil flowing.

Michael T. Klare offers a bold prediction in "The Geopolitics of Natural Gas": "What oil was to the twentieth century, natural gas will be to the twenty-first."

This in turn poses a series of dilemmas. On one hand, countries like Russia and Iran are among the chief sources of natural gas, and their politics are not always in line with the United States and the West in general. Moreover, considerable infrastructure is required for the transport and delivery of the fuel. Pipelines already run throughout Europe, but transferring the fuel across the ocean requires specially designed container ships since a transatlantic pipeline is impractical.

Jeremy Main describes the recent resurgence of the coal industry in "Old King Coal Comes Back." Though fraught with environmental detriments, coal is cheap and plentiful and thus likely to remain a dominant factor in energy production for years to come, particularly if oil and natural gas prices continue to spike.

Is nuclear power poised for a comeback? Charles Petit considers this question in "It's Scary, It's Expensive, It Could Save the Earth," the final piece in this chapter. Given the challenge posed by global warming and the other environmental costs associated with fossil fuels, nuclear energy would seem an ideal alternative. Unfortunately, as Petit relates, the American public remains skeptical of the technology, particularly in light of past accidents. Nevertheless, countries overseas are already at work on building new plants.

Carbon's New Math*

By Bill McKibben
National Geographic, October 2007

To deal with global warming, the first step is to do the numbers.

Here's how it works. Before the industrial revolution, the Earth's atmosphere contained about 280 parts per million of carbon dioxide. That was a good amount—"good" defined as "what we were used to." Since the molecular structure of carbon dioxide traps heat near the planet's surface that would otherwise radiate back out to space, civilization grew up in a world whose thermostat was set by that number. It equated to a global average temperature of about 57 degrees Fahrenheit, which in turn equated to all the places we built our cities, all the crops we learned to grow and eat, all the water supplies we learned to depend on, even the passage of the seasons that, at higher latitudes, set our psychological calendars.

Once we started burning coal and gas and oil to power our lives, that 280 number started to rise. When we began measuring in the late 1950s, it had already reached the 315 level. Now it's at 380, and increasing by roughly two parts per million annually. That doesn't sound like very much, but it turns out that the extra heat that CO_2 traps, a couple of watts per square meter of the Earth's surface, is enough to warm the planet considerably. We've raised the temperature more than a degree Fahrenheit already. It's impossible to precisely predict the consequences of any further increase in CO_2 in the atmosphere. But the warming we've seen so far has started almost everything frozen on Earth to melting; it has changed seasons and rainfall patterns; it's set the sea to rising.

No matter what we do now, that warming will increase some—there's a lag time before the heat fully plays out in the atmosphere. That is, we can't stop global warming. Our task is less inspiring: to contain the damage, to keep things from getting out of control. And even that is not easy. For one thing, until recently there's been no clear data suggesting the point where catastrophe looms. Now we're getting a better picture—the past couple of years have seen a series of

* Article by Bill McKibben from *National Geographic*, October 2007.

reports indicating that 450 parts per million CO_2 is a threshold we'd be wise to respect. Beyond that point, scientists believe future centuries will likely face the melting of the Greenland and West Antarctic ice sheets and a subsequent rise in sea level of giant proportion. Four hundred fifty parts per million is still a best guess (and it doesn't include the witches' brew of other, lesser, greenhouse gases like methane and nitrous oxide). But it will serve as a target of sorts for the world to aim at. A target that's moving, fast. If concentrations keep increasing by two parts per million per year, we're only three and a half decades away.

So the math isn't complicated—but that doesn't mean it isn't intimidating. So far only the Europeans and Japanese have even begun to trim their carbon emissions, and they may not meet their own modest targets. Meanwhile, U.S. carbon emissions, a quarter of the world's total, continue to rise steadily—earlier this year we told the United Nations we'd be producing 20 percent more carbon in 2020 than we had in 2000. China and India are suddenly starting to produce huge quantities of CO_2 as well. On a per capita basis (which is really the only sensible way to think about the morality of the situation), they aren't anywhere close to American figures, but their populations are so huge, and their economic growth so rapid, that they make the prospect of a worldwide decline in emissions seem much more daunting. The Chinese are currently building a coal-fired power plant every week or so. That's a lot of carbon.

Everyone involved knows what the basic outlines of a deal that could avert catastrophe would look like: rapid, sustained, and dramatic cuts in emissions by the technologically advanced countries, coupled with large-scale technology transfer to China, India, and the rest of the developing world so that they can power up their emerging economies without burning up their coal. Everyone knows the big questions, too: Are such rapid cuts even possible? Do we have the political will to make them and to extend them overseas?

The first question—is it even possible?—is usually addressed by fixating on some single new technology (hydrogen! ethanol!) and imagining it will solve our troubles. But the scale of the problem means we'll need many strategies. Three years ago a Princeton team made one of the best assessments of the possibilities. Stephen Pacala and Robert Socolow published a paper in *Science* detailing 15 "stabilization wedges"—changes big enough to really matter, and for which the technology was already available or clearly on the horizon. Most people have heard of some of them: more fuel-efficient cars, better-built homes, wind turbines, biofuels like ethanol. Others are newer and less sure: plans for building coal-fired power plants that can separate carbon from the exhaust so it can be "sequestered" underground.

These approaches have one thing in common: They're more difficult than simply burning fossil fuel. They force us to realize that we've already had our magic fuel and that what comes next will be more expensive and more difficult. The price tag for the global transition will be in the trillions of dollars. Of course, along the way it will create myriad new jobs, and when it's complete, it may be a much more elegant system. (Once you've built the windmill, the wind is free; you don't need to guard it against terrorists or build a massive army to control the countries from which it blows.) And since we're wasting so much energy now, some of the first tasks would be relatively easy. If we replaced every incandescent bulb that burned out in the next decade anyplace in the world with a compact fluorescent, we'd make an impressive start on one of the 15 wedges. But in that same decade we'd need to build 400,000 large wind turbines—clearly possible, but only with real commitment. We'd need to follow the lead of Germany and Japan and seriously subsidize rooftop solar panels; we'd need to get most of the world's farmers plowing their fields less, to build back the carbon their soils have lost. We'd need to do everything all at once.

As precedents for such collective effort, people sometimes point to the Manhattan Project to build a nuclear weapon or the Apollo Program to put a man on the moon. But those analogies don't really work. They demanded the intense concentration of money and intelligence on a single small niche in our technosphere. Now we need almost the opposite: a commitment to take what we already know how to do and somehow spread it into every corner of our economies, and indeed our most basic activities. It's as if NASA's goal had been to put all of us on the moon.

Not all the answers are technological, of course—maybe not even most of them. Many of the paths to stabilization run straight through our daily lives, and in every case they will demand difficult changes. Air travel is one of the fastest growing sources of carbon emissions around the world, for instance, but even many of us who are noble about changing lightbulbs and happy to drive hybrid cars chafe at the thought of not jetting around the country or the world. By now we're used to ordering take-out food from every corner of the world every night of our lives—according to one study, the average bite of food has traveled nearly 1,500 miles before it reaches an American's lips, which means it's been marinated in (crude) oil. We drive alone, because it's more convenient than adjusting our schedules for public transit. We build ever bigger homes even as our family sizes shrink, and we watch ever bigger TVs, and—well, enough said. We need to figure out how to change those habits.

Probably the only way that will happen is if fossil fuel costs us considerably more. All the schemes to cut carbon emissions—the so-called cap-and-trade systems, for instance, that would let businesses bid for permission to emit—are ways to make coal and gas and oil progressively more expensive, and thus to change the direction in which economic gravity pulls when it applies to energy. If what we paid for a gallon of gas reflected even a portion of its huge environmental cost, we'd be driving small cars to the train station, just like the Europeans. And we'd be riding bikes when the sun shone.

The most straightforward way to raise the price would be a tax on carbon. But that's not easy. Since everyone needs to use fuel, it would be regressive—you'd have to figure out how to keep from hurting poor people unduly. And we'd need to be grown-up enough to have a real conversation about taxes—say, about switching away from taxes on things we like (employment) to taxes on things we hate (global warming). That may be too much to ask for—but if it is, then what chance is there we'll be able to take on the even more difficult task of persuading the Chinese, the Indians, and all who are lined up behind them to forgo a coal-powered future in favor of something more manageable? We know it's possible—earlier this year a UN panel estimated that the total cost for the energy transition, once all the pluses and minuses were netted out, would be just over 0.1 percent of the world's economy each year for the next quarter century. A small price to pay.

In the end, global warming presents the greatest test we humans have yet faced. Are we ready to change, in dramatic and prolonged ways, in order to offer a workable future to subsequent generations and diverse forms of life? If we are, new technologies and new habits offer some promise. But only if we move quickly and decisively—and with a maturity we've rarely shown as a society or a species. It's our coming-of-age moment, and there are no certainties or guarantees. Only a window of possibility, closing fast but still ajar enough to let in some hope.

The Politics of Global Warming*

By Thomas Sieger Derr
First Things, August/September 2007

With the virtual apotheosis of Al Gore, talk of global warming has become pervasive—and pervasively one-sided. Churches of all varieties have signed on as a moral cause. Corporations, including former doubters, have adopted anti-warming language, either from new conviction or convenient public image. Politicians, with few exceptions, dare not openly deny that there is a problem, though their responses may vary.

Through it all, one would never know there are dissenters of distinguished credentials in the scientific community. Even where their existence is admitted, they are thoroughly marginalized, accused of being in the pay of the oil companies (Gore slyly and meanly implies this in his movie, *An Inconvenient Truth*), or dismissed as over-the-hill retirees out of touch and perhaps a bit senile. Their articles are denied publication in *Science* and *Nature*, those two so-called flagship science journals of high reputation despite some embarrassing lapses.

When dissenters do speak and publish, the majority who embrace the prevailing theory that humans are causing global warming try to silence them on the grounds that, because they are in error, they must not be allowed to be heard. Newspapers who seek balance in their reporting are told that they are doing a disservice to the public, to truth, and to the survival of the human race. The Weather Channel, a full-bore promoter of global-warming alarm (which feeds its appetite for newsworthy disaster), has, through its chief climate expert Heidi Cullen, even said that weather reporters who don't accept the reigning thesis should be decertified by the American Meteorological Society—in other words, believe our way or lose your job. When British television producer Martin Durkin made a counter-movie to Gore's, the head of the Royal Society declared that he should not be allowed to show it.

The result is that anyone who finds the dissenters persuasive—including me—

is suspected of being a right-wing extremist, making politics determine science. In vain do we point out that dissenters from established scientific consensus have often been dramatically vindicated. Undeterred, some of our critics have even compared us to Holocaust deniers or urged that dissenters be tried as war criminals. Or maybe burned at the stake for heresy—for our religious critics do think of us as heretics and sinners.

This dismal state of affairs is made possible by an astonishing historical amnesia. It is indisputable that climate swings are a regular feature of our planet's life. Short-term changes lie within our personal memories: The current warming trend dates from only about 1975. Before that, a pronounced cooling period starting about 1940 led the scientific consensus of the 1970s to proclaim global cooling and perhaps the first signs of an ice age. Note that these swings do not correspond to the amount of CO_2 released into the atmosphere; 60 percent of global warming since 1850 occurred before 1940, while 80 percent of CO_2 was emitted after that date—and temperatures fell from 1940 until the turnaround in the late 1970s.

Going further back, we find the "little ice age" of the sixteenth and seventeenth centuries, when the Hudson and the Thames froze, crops failed, and disease was rampant, so that millions died. Before that, we come upon the "medieval climate optimum," when a prevailing warmth made life pleasant, grape vines grew in England, and the Vikings established settlements in Greenland and Newfoundland (which they called Vinland; the names are revealing) —settlements that lasted until the little ice age froze them out.

That period was, in turn, preceded by an unfavorable climate in the Dark Ages, and that by another warm stretch in Roman times. Using proxy records (tree rings, ice-core samples, ocean-bottom sediment), geologists have determined that such climate swings stretch back into prehistory. Fred Singer (who has impeccable credentials and experience as a climate scientist) and Dennis Avery have calculated that this swing-and-return pattern occurs roughly but regularly every 1,500 years. Obviously, the pattern has nothing to do with human activity. Nor does it correspond to the levels of CO_2 in the atmosphere. If anything, climate change appears to precede, not follow, increases in CO_2.

So what's going on? There is a significant body of scientific opinion that finds the sun to be the principal climate driver. The sun's output is variable and complex, more and less intense at different periods. A German team has shown an almost perfect correlation between air temperatures and solar cycles for the past 150 years. A Danish team likewise has constructed a multi-era match of solar activity (measured by sunspots) to global temperatures. Nigel Weiss of Cambridge University, a mathematical astrophysicist and past president of the Royal Astronomical Society, also correlates sunspot activity with changes in the earth's climate. Because solar activity is cyclical, he expects that a downturn is coming and will usher in a cooling climate for earth in, maybe, three decades. Actually, global average temperature seems to have plateaued since 2000, though it is probably too soon to expect the downturn to have begun. Still, Richard Lindzen, a distinguished atmospheric physicist at MIT and a leading doubter that human activity is driving warming, thinks the odds are about 50 percent that the earth will be cooler in twenty years—due to natural cycles. It may or may not be significant, but it is suggestive, that NASA's instruments calculate that Mars, Jupiter, Pluto, and the Titan moon of Neptune are warming, suggesting a solar-system-wide phenomenon. To be sure, this is not hard evidence; other factors (axis tilt and wobble on Mars, for instance) may be a cause. Still, it may be a clue to what is happening here on our planet.

Some caveats are in order. Human activity may add something to the natural cycle, though how much is hard to tell. I have seen a paper that estimates the human contribution at 3 percent and another that gives it at 0.28 percent, for an almost undetectable effect on climate. The principal greenhouse gas, some 97 percent of the total, is water vapor, which leaves little [room] for CO_2 and other trace gasses. Scott McIntosh, of the Southwest Research Institute in Boulder, says that warming caused by CO_2 compared to the effect of solar magnetic fields is like a flea's contribution to the weight of an elephant.

We do know, however, that atmospheric emissions can affect climate—for example, the serious consequences of the ash cloud thrown up by volcanic eruptions; so perhaps there is something to the greenhouse-gas theory. People can also argue about the historical record and try to modify the data that shows natural climate cycles. There may be problems with the sun theory; climate is also affected by ocean currents, meteor impact, the tilt of the earth's axis, cosmic rays, precipitation systems, and other factors. And so on. Those of us who are doubters will not complain when we in turn are doubted. Debate is healthy and must not be choked off.

Nevertheless, the large, rough historical record should be enough to awaken the critical instincts and make anyone take a long second look at the claims of the global-warming alarmists—and alarmists they certainly are, deliberately and unabashedly so.

They've claimed, for example, that the glaciers will melt in Greenland and Antarctica and raise the oceans so much that low-lying cities and countries will be submerged and the Gulf Stream will shut down and plunge Europe into an ice age.

As it happens, while there is edge-melting in Greenland and along the peninsula of Antarctica that stretches toward South America, snow is accumulating in the interior of Greenland and in most of Antarctica. The warming peninsula there is just 2 percent of the continent; the other 98 percent is cooling. The Larson B ice shelf, which collapsed, was 1/246 the size of the West Antarctic ice shelf, which has been retreating slowly anyway for thousands of years. As for the Gulf Stream threat, oceanographers debunk it. Even the Intergovernmental Panel on Climate Change (IPCC), the U.N. body that puts out huge periodic reports warning of climate disaster, has backed down from its earlier estimates of sea rise, from three feet for the next century to seventeen inches—and many scientists think even that is too high.

Speaking of glaciers, the alarmists point out that they are melting everywhere. Kilimanjaro will be bare in a few years, and the Alpine glaciers will be but pale shadows of themselves, and so on around the globe. But Claude Allègre, a distinguished French climate scientist, has recanted his earlier support for the IPCC's conclusions, and says of Kilimanjaro specifically that its snow cap is retreating from natural causes having to do with moisture from the Indian Ocean. Alpine glaciers, like most everywhere, grow and retreat often through their lives. In 2003, as the Schnidenjoch glacier in Switzerland was retreating, a 4,700-year-old archer's quiver was exposed; that pass has been open to human travel many times since the last ice age.

On and on, the alarms go. Perhaps you've seen the claim that the Arctic sea ice is disappearing and that polar bears are threatened with extinction because they can't hunt from ice floes any more. But Arctic sea ice, like the glaciers, grows and retreats in natural cycles. Gore's computer simulation of the drowning polar bear may look sad, but, of course, it's fake. Canadian wildlife biologists say most populations of the bears are actually increasing.

Or perhaps you've heard that storms on land and sea will increase in number and intensity, and we can expect more Katrinas. In fact, there has actually been a downward trend in the number of the bigger, detectable tornadoes since 1950; we detect more because better reporting picks up more small ones. New evidence shows that hurricane intensity does not correlate with ocean temperature.

Maybe you've read that tropical diseases such as malaria will spread into now-temperate zones, higher latitudes, and higher altitudes—Nairobi, for example. But Nairobi was built when malaria was already endemic there. It was repelled with better insecticide, especially, in Africa, DDT. The current resurgence of malaria comes not from global warming but from the ban on DDT spraying, growing resistance to drugs, and poverty.

You've also been told that failing to curb our greenhouse-gas emissions will cause irreparable economic damage to the poorer nations, as the Stern Report insisted. But the report was savaged by economists. William Nordhaus of Yale is among those who fault Stern for using a near-zero social-discount rate, which would charge current generations for problems not likely to occur for two or three centuries hence.

In fact, one can make the opposite case from Stern's with greater plausibility: Economies would be wrecked by adoption of the Kyoto targets. Even a moderate stabilization of greenhouse-gas emissions would require something like a 60 to 80 percent reduction in fossil-fuel use, and standards of living would drop through the floor. Poor countries would have a nearly impossible time rising out of their poverty. Is it any wonder that China and India and other developing nations will have none of Kyoto-style proposals, and are loudly and clearly telling the developed nations to proceed without their participation? Naturally, they are much more interested in Bush's proposal to bypass the useless Kyoto framework and substitute technological changes and voluntary goals for the binding targets championed by the Europeans.

One of the goofiest ways of raising consciousness about global warming has been the lectures we've received about purchasing carbon offsets. As it happens, the purchase of carbon offsets allows the buyer to continue his merry energy-guzzling ways, his sins having been forgiven for a cash payment. The process has the ring of a medieval indulgence sale, as many critics have gleefully noted. Gore buys carbon offsets so he can justify living in a mansion with huge electricity use. And he can certainly afford that, as his $100,000 lecture fees and his relations with Internet companies and environmental businesses have made him extraordinarily wealthy.

Everywhere you go, you hear the news that we have only a few years to save the planet before we reach the point of no return, the tipping point, irreversible catastrophic climate change, and the end of civilization. Hyperbolic statements like these are meant mainly to scare people into acting and accepting the enormous sums required for the proposed reduction program. Sir John Houghton, the first chair of the IPCC, wrote in a 1994 book, "Unless we announce disasters, no one will listen."

A backlash against such exaggeration is growing, not least among scientists concerned for their own professional integrity. In any case, we need cooler heads to go with a warmer climate. Lindzen and Israeli astrophysicist Nir Shaviv calculate that a doubling of CO_2 in the atmosphere by 2100 would cause a temperature rise of 1 degree Celsius, which is only a little more than the rise from the late nineteenth century to the present has been. A 50 percent rise would yield a 0.5-degree-C. increase. There are, of course, good reasons for controlling many emissions and finding alternative sources to fossil fuels: pollution control, for instance, and freedom from economic fealty to some rather nasty oil-producing regimes. But stopping global warming is not one of them.

It almost seems as if the issue is not in science but in ideology and social psychology. Environmental alarmism is part of a systematic rejection of industrial civilization, of technology, consumerism, globalization, and what most of us think of as growth and progress, in favor of a return to local, simpler, largely agricultural societies—and, of course, fewer children, since humans are the ultimate pollution. Climate reversal has grown to become the latest focus of this way of thinking.

It is an issue that has acquired popular traction, even among people who do not share the radical goals of the larger movement, thanks to deliberate alarmism; and it is now firmly entrenched in our public discourse, especially in our politics. I suspect that it will stay there until the temperature starts to decline again, at which point, as in the 1970s, we'll hear more about the inevitable return of an ice age.

Can the United States Shed Its Oil Addiction?*

By Josef Braml
The Washington Quarterly, Autumn 2007

Since the 1950s, U.S. energy consumption, mainly driven by the transportation sector and fed by oil, has almost tripled. Because the cultivation of domestic resources has not been able to keep up with demand, the United States has become increasingly dependent on energy supplies from unstable regions of the world. The costs and risks to national security provide the first major incentive for a readjustment of U.S. energy policy. U.S. dependency on foreign energy creates immense economic challenges and vulnerabilities as well. One-third of the skyrocketing U.S. trade deficit can be attributed to increased costs of imported oil. This is not a critical problem as long as U.S. trading partners continue to reinvest their returns in the United States. If U.S. productivity and economic power were seriously harmed by a lack of supply or by soaring prices, however, investors might seek different havens for their investments. This shift would put the dollar and the U.S. economy under considerable strain. Finally, growing public awareness about climate change and its dire consequences for people and the economy is increasing the political pressure to find more efficient alternatives to an outdated economy that relies on fossil fuels.

In his 2006 State of the Union address, President George W. Bush highlighted what he called "a serious problem," namely the United States' addiction to oil, "which is often imported from unstable parts of the world."[1] Despite that statement, not much political capital has been spent on solving the problem. The pessimistic conventional wisdom in the United States is that the "prospects for serious energy security reform will remain weak, unless there is a serious shock of the international system."[2] Path dependencies of the political system have so far prevented an active development and use of renewable energy, despite substantial support among the American public on this issue. Security, economic, and environmental factors, however, give U.S. policymakers strong incentives to lead the

*Josef Braml, 'Can the United States Shed Its Oil Addiction? *The Washington Quarterly*, 30:4 (Autumn 2007), pp117–130.

country into a renewable-energy future. Instead of competing with rising powers for the scarce fossil energy resources of the past, the United States could put itself in a much stronger position by leading the way in cultivating the alternative fuels and energy technologies of the future.

THE COSTS OF OIL ADDICTION

With only 5 percent of total world population, the United States consumes almost one-quarter (22.5 percent) of global energy.[3] In the last 55 years, energy consumption in the United States has almost tripled, with this increasing demand being satisfied mostly by oil. In 2005, petroleum provided more than 40 percent of total U.S. energy consumption. Although the exploitation of gas and coal increased slightly in the 1970s, since the 1980s their contribution to energy consumption has remained constant at 25 percent and 20 percent, respectively.

Domestic oil production has not kept up with increased demand. Although the United States has managed to boost oil production from 5.9 million barrels per day in 1950 to 7.8 million barrels per day in 2005, this is not sufficient considering the daily need of 20.7 million barrels, two-thirds of which is consumed by the transportation sector.[4] Given the U.S. transportation system's dependency on liquid fuels and the time it would take to develop a market for new technologies, a Council on Foreign Relations task force predicted that "the United States will depend on imported oil . . . for at least several decades."[5]

The superpower's dependency on foreign oil has markedly increased during the past decades. In 1950 the United States was still self-reliant, running on its own resources. Fifty years later, more than 60 percent of the oil consumed in the United States is delivered from abroad, and the trend shows no signs of abating in the future. Reliance on foreign-sourced fossil fuels poses a threat to U.S. national security and creates economic vulnerabilities as well as environmental challenges.

RISKY GEOPOLITICS

If the United States continues its overreliance on fossil fuels, it will become increasingly dependent on producing nations that are unstable and that pose a risk to its interests and could come into conflict with other consumer states. Although the United States can still count on Canada and Mexico, which are its two most important petroleum providers, its tense relationship with Venezuela illustrates the challenges in securing energy resources even in its own backyard, let alone the Middle East and other volatile areas. Some observers of petropolitics go as far as to describe an "axis of oil" (Russia, China, and eventually Iran) at work that is "acting as a counterweight to American hegemony" and will deprive the United States of its oil supplies and strategic interests.[6]

The Persian Gulf, another region the United States used to dominate, has become very volatile and unreliable in terms of delivering energy resources. This region will continue to be vital to U.S. interests in reliable oil supply for at least the next two decades.[7] The U.S.–Saudi Arabian relationship in particular is well rooted in bilateral economic and political ties. The Saudi monarchy possesses the world's largest oil reserves and is one of the United States' main suppliers of oil. U.S. energy dependence, however, undermines the U.S. National Security Strategy's aim of fighting terrorism by demanding meaningful political reform from authoritarian regimes to become more democratic and market oriented.[8] Through interventions in the markets, Saudi Arabia has helped the United States to stabilize the price of oil, allowing oil consumers to enjoy relatively steady prices from the mid-1980s to 2003. Nevertheless, because oil production has not kept pace with increased worldwide demand for oil, especially from the United States and China, there has been a sharp increase in the price of oil over the past three years.

Although the cultivation of Saudi oil remains more or less under Riyadh's control, Saudi Arabia has been trying to attract foreign investors to exploit its gas reserves as well, which are estimated to be the world's fourth largest. The monarchy is fostering strategic partnerships, in particular with Russia, the holder of the world's largest proved natural gas reserves, and China, both of which are competing with the United States for regional and global influence.[9] On his last visit to Saudi Arabia, President Vladimir Putin emphasized that Russia and Saudi Arabia are the world's leading energy producers and exporters and that it would be "easy" for the two countries "to find common ground."[10] King Abdullah, for his part, pointed out that Russia and Saudi Arabia not only enjoy "huge economic potentials, vast natural resources, and a variety of investment opportunities" but also "huge political influence at the world stage," which will contribute to taking their "mutual cooperation to new heights within a strategic perspective." China's competition for access challenges the rules-based international order for energy trade and investment championed by the United States. Chinese and Russian engagement creates new commercial and security options for energy-exporting states in the Middle East, including regimes that are at odds with U.S. interests.

By eliminating Saddam Hussein's regime in 2003 and failing to control the situation in Iraq, the United States has not only weakened its regional dominance but also shot itself in the foot economically. Instability in Iraq prevents the exploitation of one of the world's best long-term, high-yield oil resources, which could have been helpful for that country's reconstruction and for stabilizing global oil prices.

Iran, bolstered by the disaster in Iraq, possesses the world's third-largest proven oil reserves and controls the Strait of Hormuz, an important strategic choke point. Iran has troops stationed on an island near the strait's entrance and could disrupt the transit of about 17 million barrels of oil per day, which amounts to 40 percent of the world's oil trade.[11] Iran's use of its oil weapon could cause a significant increase in oil prices and damage to Western and Asian economies. Tehran has also sought to cultivate economic and military ties with Russia and China. In March 2004, China signed a $100 million deal with Iran to import liquefied natural gas in exchange for Chinese investment in Iran's oil and gas exploration and pipeline infrastructure. According to an unclassified 2003 CIA report, "Ballistic missile-related cooperation from entities in the former Soviet Union, North Korea, and China over the years has helped Iran move toward its goal of becoming self-sufficient in the production of ballistic missiles."[12] Chinese and Russian economic and strategic interests have contributed to undermine U.S. efforts to impose meaningful sanctions by the UN Security Council to solve the Iranian nuclear issue.

Given these difficulties in the Persian Gulf region, it is no surprise that the United States has been looking for alternative providers of oil. As early as May 2001, the National Energy Policy Development Group, created by executive order and chaired by Vice President Dick Cheney, stated that "West Africa is expected to be one of [the] fastest-growing sources of oil and gas for the American market."[13] The 2002 National Security Strategy reiterated this interest: "We will strengthen our own energy security and . . . expand the sources and types of global energy supplied, especially in the Western Hemisphere, Africa, Central Asia, and the Caspian region."[14]

The U.S. military's Africa Command (AFRICOM) is expected to be established by September 2008. AFRICOM, for the time being a subunified command of European Command (EUCOM), will serve as another base in the global war against terrorism. There is a growing perception that its primary mission is to secure access to the oil and gas resources of African countries, which has been substantiated by EUCOM commander General Bantz Craddock, who told journalists in Washington, "You look at West Africa and the Gulf of Guinea, it becomes more focused because of the energy situation," with the result that protecting energy assets "obviously is out in front."[15]

The United States currently obtains 15 percent of its imported oil from sub-Saharan Africa, most of it from Nigeria, and intends to increase oil imports from Africa to one-quarter of its total imports by 2015. This significant increase seems plausible given that U.S. government projections estimate that the largest change in regional production will materialize for suppliers in Africa and the Middle East that are not members of the Organization of the Petroleum Exporting Countries (OPEC). These suppliers are predicted to increase their share of the world total from 6 percent in 2005 to 11 percent in 2030.[16]

Other powers with global aspirations are also aware of this potential, turning the African continent into another arena of global competition for fossil fuels. China is especially keen to lock up oil supplies with bilateral deals with countries such as Sudan. Beijing does not mix business with politics, and its engagement with African leaders is devoid of any discussion of human rights, rule of law, and other complications that might deter other countries.

Central Asia, previously seen as Russia's backyard, is now another region of great strategic significance to other great powers. Kazakhstan has increased its energy resource production markedly since the late 1990s, and in 2005 it delivered two-thirds of regional crude oil supply, followed by Azerbaijan (22 percent) and Turkmenistan (10 percent). The Caspian region produced 2 percent of total world oil output in 2005, which makes it a significant but not major supplier of crude oil to world markets.[17] In order to free hydrocarbon-rich Kazakhstan from Russia's infrastructure and dominance as well as to circumvent Iran, the United States pushed for the construction of the Baku-Tbilisi-Ceyhan pipeline, which routes Caspian oil through Azerbaijan, Georgia, and Turkey and began transporting oil in 2005.

During a visit in May 2006, Cheney expressed his admiration for what had been accomplished economically and politically in Kazakhstan. He embraced President Nursultan Nazarbayev as a personal friend, affirmed the "strong ties" between Kazakhstan and the United States, and expressed the United States' pride to be Kazakhstan's "strategic partner."[18] Given Kyrgyzstan's musings of giving in to Russian pressure to evict the United States from the Manas air base and to limit U.S. access to Kazakhstan's oil supplies, the United States is seeking to reaffirm its presence in Kazakhstan. China has meanwhile begun building a pipeline from the recently discovered Kashagan oil field in the Caspian Sea region.

In addition to its oil ambitions, China wants to avoid encirclement by U.S. forces. China is the biggest buyer of Russian military hardware, increasingly relies on Russian energy resources, and shares Russia's interest in rolling back U.S. influence in Central Asia. Since 2003, Moscow has been reasserting its power in its geopolitical backyard by cooperating with autocratic regimes in the region at the expense of U.S. democratization efforts and economic interests.

The United States has traditionally had a good relationship with Venezuela, due in no small part to Venezuela being the fourth-largest supplier of oil to the U.S. market. The U.S. government's relationship with President Hugo Chávez, however, has been quite tense, especially since 2005 when Venezuela cancelled its cooperation with the U.S. Drug Enforcement Administration and terminated a bilateral military-exchange program. On the domestic front, right after Chávez's election victory in 1998, the Venezuelan government tightened control by "renationalizing" its resources and has threatened at times, as it did in April 2004, to stop delivering oil to the United States. Venezuela has attempted to diversify its oil markets with Chinese buyers in mind.

Venezuela and Iran are close partners in the powerful OPEC, and Caracas has also cultivated a cooperative relationship with Beijing. Iranian experts reportedly assisted Petroleos de Venezuela, Venezuela's state oil company, to improve its access to Asian oil markets.[19] During Chávez's visit to Beijing in December 2004 and Chinese vice president Zeng Qinghong's visit to Venezuela in January 2005, China and Venezuela signed agreements that committed the China Petroleum Corporation to invest $410 million in developing Venezuelan oil and gas reserves. Placing his energy resources "at the disposal of the great Chinese fatherland," Chávez seeks to "free" his country from "100 years of domination by the United States."[20] In his visits to China, Chávez has promoted plans to rebuild a Panamanian pipeline to pump crude oil to the Pacific. Meanwhile, at the request of the Senate Foreign Relations Committee, the U.S. Government Accountability Office (GAO) is considering contingency plans in case of Venezuelan oil supply disruption.[21]

Eight of the top 10 countries with the largest proven oil reserves—Iran, Iraq, Kuwait, Libya, Nigeria, Saudi Arabia, United Arab Emirates, and Venezuela (Canada and Russia excepted)—are members of OPEC.[22] Both OPEC's and non-OPEC countries' oil production is expected to rise.[23] Although in the medium term, OPEC's share of world oil production is expected to remain at 40 percent, OPEC's power will be most significant in the long term when non-OPEC oil production declines, as OPEC controls 70 percent of today's proved reserves worldwide.[24] The United States thus has security and economic interests at stake when dealing with the OPEC cartel, many of whose members are not on particularly good terms with Washington. Combined with a rising worldwide demand, the decline of non-OPEC countries' production will give OPEC even more power and will cause prices to be much higher and more unstable in the future.

ECONOMIC VULNERABILITIES

The price for imports of crude oil has increased markedly since 2003, but demand has not waned in response. Due to higher oil prices, energy imports added about $70 billion to the U.S. trade deficit in 2005 and $50 billion in 2006.[25] They currently account for roughly one-third of the current trade imbalance. In the summer of 2005, Federal Reserve Board Chairman Alan Greenspan warned Congress that increased energy prices since the end of 2003 diminished U.S. economic growth by about one-half of a percentage point in gross domestic product in 2004 and by three-fourths of a point in 2005.[26]

High energy prices hurt energy-intensive sectors of the economy and have trickle-down effects on other sectors as well. Consumers have been hurt by rises in fuel prices. Feeling their reduced purchasing power, they cut back on spending, thus diminishing economic growth from the demand side. In a May 2007 poll, two-thirds of Americans reported that they have been affected financially in some meaningful way by higher gas prices. For 18 percent, it created a financial hardship, and an additional 49 percent indicated that high gas prices caused them to adjust their usual spending and saving habits in significant ways. Lower-income households and middle-income families have been especially affected.[27]

If consumer spending falters and business becomes more cautious about expanding, reassessing the profitability of investment projects in light of higher energy costs, the United States might slide into a recession, which would cause higher unemployment and slow private spending even further. Signals of a weakening U.S. economy may prevent trading partners from reinvesting their returns in the United States. If U.S. productivity and economic power were seriously questioned, investors might seek different havens to get a better return on their investments. This would put the U.S. economy under considerable strain and put the dollar in doubt as a safe harbor currency.

In the long run, however, U.S. markets may adapt to these challenges. Higher energy prices will provide strong market incentives to find alternative sources of energy, to develop new technologies, and to improve energy efficiency. For these effects, there is an additional driving force: increasing public concern about environmental damage caused by traditional forms of energy consumption.

THE AMERICAN PUBLIC GOES GREEN

Oil consumption accounts for about 40 percent of energy-related carbon dioxide emissions, which cause pollution, human health problems, and climate change. The past five years have shown substantial increases in the public's belief that the environment needs greater attention. Americans worry "a great deal" more about the "quality of the environment" than "the possibility of future terrorist attacks in the United States."[28] Moreover, they project that the environment will be the "most important problem" facing the United States 25 years from now. Strikingly, Americans are much less concerned about the lack of energy sources or an energy crisis, terrorism, social security, health care, or the economy in general.

Americans are not only concerned, they are ready to take and pay for action to reduce global warming. An overwhelming majority of U.S. citizens are prepared to spend "several thousand dollars" to make their homes energy efficient (78 percent), to ride mass transit such as buses and subways "whenever possible" (77 percent), to install a solar panel to produce energy for their homes (71 percent), and to buy a hybrid car (62 percent).[29] Only 36 percent, however, would support the construction of a nuclear energy plant near their homes.

In addition to their openness to personal sacrifices, Americans want their government to deal with the problem. About 80 percent of U.S. taxpayers favor spending government money to develop alternative sources of fuel for automobiles, set higher emissions and pollution standards for business and industry, more strongly enforce federal environmental regulations, spend more government money on developing solar and wind power, set higher emissions standards for automobiles, and impose mandatory controls on carbon dioxide emissions and other greenhouse gases.[30]

Interestingly, proposals reflecting these public concerns figured less prominently on the political agenda during Bush's tenure than other proposals that had the strongest public opposition, such as opening up the Arctic National Wildlife Refuge for oil exploration or expanding the use of nuclear energy (about one-half of Americans are opposed to each).[31] Is it just this administration, or can other factors help explain this distortion?

PATH DEPENDENCIES OF THE POLITICAL SYSTEM

Even though a broader analysis of security, economic, and environmental considerations strongly suggests a national interest in becoming less dependent on traditional fossil fuels, the status quo has proven to be more powerful than these pressing issues in determining the U.S. response to energy dependence.

One important factor is a lack of political leadership on the issue. The president and Congress have so far calculated that imposing costs on consumers and taxpayers would cost them politically. Bush has only recently and, so far, only rhetorically begun to act like a steward of the earth, mainly to appease part of his evangelical base, which has recently been emphasizing moral aspects of the environmental issue. Some evangelical leaders have decided to back the Evangelical Climate Initiative to fight global warming, proclaiming that "millions of people could die in this century because of climate change."[32] The National Association of Evangelicals, representing 45,000 churches and 30 million evangelicals, is also committed to "creation care," whereas the Southern Baptist Convention, another Republican stronghold representing 16 million people, warns its members not to align with "extreme environmental groups" or to rely on "questionable science."[33]

Coping with this somewhat tricky environmental cause of his flock, Bush has generally stressed the need to be "wise stewards of the environment" in his energy initiative.[34] During its tenure, the administration has routinely blocked any binding international efforts to significantly reduce greenhouse gas emissions, such as the Kyoto Protocol. Yet, Democratic aspirants for the White House also shy away from asking sacrifices from their voters. In the Democratic presidential debate in April 2007, Senator Joseph Biden (Del.), for example, did not really ask the average American to accept any "hard" solutions to global warming.[35]

Another important factor is established fossil fuel interests' access to policymakers. The Cheney energy task force is but one prominent, albeit not transparent, example of this. Because the group proceeded behind closed doors, critics charged that the energy industry was exercising undue influence over national energy policy. Congress, exercising its oversight authority, prompted the GAO, the investigative arm of Congress, to make the records of the task force public. The GAO filed a lawsuit against the Bush administration, but Judge John D. Bates, a recent Bush appointee, dismissed the case. The GAO dropped the case, and most of the activities of the energy task force have still not been disclosed to the public. Campaign contributions to Republicans and Democrats are another means by which the oil industry maintains its connections to the government.

The electoral system causes yet another misrepresentation. Because every state, regardless of its size and population, is represented by two senators, highly populated states, many of which bear the brunt of environmental problems, have arguably disproportionately smaller representation in the Senate on this issue than less populated rural states. For economic reasons, many farmers in these rural states are strongly opposed to environmental policies and could be counted on as reliable allies of the oil lobby. Even bills that have been promoted by prominent Republicans, such as Senator John McCain (Ariz.), have been voted down in the Senate in 2003 and 2005. Additionally, rules in the Senate enable individuals to block legislation through holds or filibusters. On June 21, 2007, for example, a Senate bill that would have provided tax incentives for alternative energies lacked the 60 votes necessary to end the filibuster.

A combination of these factors has led U.S. policymakers to adopt a business-as-usual approach, favoring traditional fossil energy interests and disregarding security, economic, and environmental concerns. What could change this dynamic?

AN OPPORTUNITY FOR ENTREPRENEURIAL LEADERSHIP

Sensing the pressure from state environmental initiatives, such as those in California, and anticipating mandatory federal controls over carbon emissions, entrepreneurial members of the business community have become involved in the U.S. Climate Action Partnership (USCAP). USCAP is a group of businesses and leading environmental organizations jointly calling on the federal government to enact national legislation to reduce greenhouse gas emissions. Automakers such as General Motors proactively help lawmakers to come up with legislation that emphasizes innovation and the role of new technologies. U.S. carmakers have been lagging behind foreign manufacturers technologically and losing market share to them as they have pioneered fuel-efficient vehicles and are ahead of the curve when it comes to hybrid cars. The Big Three U.S. automakers have a particular interest in flex-fuel technology that could burn various alternative fuels because it might give them an advantage over foreign automakers building hybrid cars. To provide an additional incentive for innovation, the government could help redirect the U.S. automakers' currently unsustainable path by assisting them in avoiding financial difficulty by covering the cost of their retired workers' health benefits if the companies invested in new technology.

The U.S. government has an important role to play in supporting innovation in the private sector.[36] New technologies require development efforts that the market alone cannot create. From an economic standpoint, alternative energy sources have been put at a disadvantage by the U.S. government's subsidies for the fossil fuel and nuclear industries since the 1980s.[37] To compensate for this and to remedy a market failure inherent to public goods such as innovation, the government should subsidize new research and development (R&D).

Renewable fuels, both corn- and sugar-based, and ethanol from cellulose sources such as switchgrass have particular market potential. They may one day displace fossil-based transportation fuels. For the time being, however, they still have to compete with traditional fuels, and technology to develop their full potential will take time. Although national subsidies could accelerate the use of ethanol in the short term, only international research cooperation to come up with new technologies and open markets will make this enterprise commercially viable in the long run.

The U.S. agricultural sector could choose to imitate best practices from other countries, such as Brazil, whose pioneering use of ethanol, biodiesel, and flex-fuel cars on a commercial scale has helped the country to run its transportation sector independently of foreign oil. U.S. farmers are protected by secondary tariffs of $0.54 per gallon on imported ethanol. If Washington removed those market barriers, U.S. refineries could take advantage of more efficient ethanol producers worldwide, notably in Brazil, the Caribbean, and Central America. In turn, competition would help U.S. farmers to become more efficient and competitive in producing ethanol and biodiesel.

In March 2007, the United States and Brazil entered into a bilateral energy partnership to develop biofuels. Because other nations also have an interest in alternative fuels and in technology development that meets the market test, there are incentives for multilateral action. As one cannot rule out competitors' free-riding on U.S. and Brazilian R&D, there is even more reason to create multilateral structures to conduct collective research efforts. Under a multilateral framework, scientists and economists worldwide could collaborate on new technologies and efficient marketing strategies.

As a protection against OPEC's interests and influence, innovation-oriented governments should establish countercyclical taxes on fossil fuels linked to the market price of oil.[38] These taxes would protect investors in new energy technologies against sudden OPEC-instigated drops in oil prices. In addition, the revenue generated by sustainable-energy security taxes should be used for supporting R&D in renewable energies.

With technological advances, the argument of a trade-off between environmental protection and the economy or "government against the market" rhetoric is increasingly losing legitimacy. A majority of Americans have come to realize that traditional fossil fuel–based thinking undermines U.S. security as well as its technological and economic leadership in the world.

Entrepreneurial political leaders may find economic opportunities for environmentally sound new technologies to be a winning issue in 2009. A nationwide survey among registered voters commissioned by the Center for American Progress found that a majority of Americans think that their country is falling behind (40 percent) or has fallen far behind (13 percent) the rest of the world in developing clean, alternative energy. At the same time, a solid majority of Americans believe that shifting to new, alternative energy production will help the U.S. economy and create jobs.[39]

Moreover, for 35 percent of respondents in a CBS News/*New York Times* survey, the environment is a make-or-break issue in the 2008 presidential election.[40] Only 15 percent of respondents indicated that they would be turned off by a presidential candidate who asked the American people to make sacrifices to protect the environment, while one-third said it would make them more likely to support that candidate.

GETTING SMART ON ENERGY

Political and public scrutiny of the security, economic, and environmental costs of the current U.S. energy policy compels the United States to embark on an alternative path toward a more efficient homegrown supply of renewable energy. Brookings Institution scholar David Sandalow suggests that "[a]n unusual political consensus and game-changing technologies give the next president a rare opportunity to address several of the nation's most important security, environmental, and economic challenges."[41] The future president and other political leaders, recognizing the critical mass of support that has emerged among the American public, should aggressively move forward on lessening U.S. dependence on traditional fuels.

The worldwide interest in renewable energies creates a unique chance for the United States to reclaim world leadership, spearheading international cooperation to solve the energy conundrum. Unlike limited fossil fuels, renewable forms of energy are to a large degree the result of unlimited and mobile brain power. Although U.S. hard power seems to have lost its effectiveness in securing America's energy security and economic prosperity, its technological and political leadership potential still holds a promising alternative for the next president, who would even be more likely to gain that office by promoting renewable energy alternatives as part of their campaign to seek an end to the U.S. addiction to oil.

NOTES

1. "State of the Union Address by the President," Washington, D.C., January 31, 2006, http://www.whitehouse.gov/stateoftheunion/2006/.
2. See Jan H. Kalicki and David L. Goldwyn, eds., *Energy and Security: Toward a New Foreign Policy Strategy* (Washington, D.C., and Baltimore: Woodrow Wilson Center Press and Johns Hopkins University Press, 2005), p. 7.
3. Energy Information Administration (EIA), Department of Energy, "Annual Energy Review 2005," July 27, 2006, p. 302, http://tonto.eia.doe.gov/FTPROOT/multifuel/038405.pdf.
4. Ibid., p. 163 ("Diagram 2. Petroleum Flow, 2005").
5. Council on Foreign Relations (CFR), "National Security Consequences of U.S. Oil Dependency," *Independent Task Force Report*, no. 58 (2006), p. 14.
6. See Flynt Leverett and Pierre Noel, "The New Axis of Oil," *National Interest*, no. 84 (Summer 2006): 62–70.
7. CFR, "National Security Consequences of U.S. Oil Dependency."
8. "The National Security Strategy of the United States of America," March 2006, http://www.whitehouse.gov/nsc/nss/2006/nss2006.pdf.
9. Karen Matusic, "Saudis Extend Geopolitical Base With Gas Deals," *Oil Daily*, February 2, 2004.
10. Flynt Leverett and Pierre Noel, "Ahead of the Curve: The New Axis of Oil," National Interest, February 13, 2007, http://www.nationalinterest.org/Article.aspx?id=13584.
11. Anthony H. Cordesman, "Iran, Oil, and the Strait of Hormuz," March 26, 2007, pp. 2, 7, http://www.csis.org/media/csis/pubs/070326_iranoil_hormuz.pdf.
12. Central Intelligence Agency, "Unclassified Report to Congress on the Acquisition of Technology Relating to Weapons of Mass Destruction and Advanced Conventional Munitions," January–June 2003, https://www.cia.gov/library/reports/archived-reports-1/jan_jun2003.htm.
13. National Energy Policy Development Group, "National Energy Policy: Report of the National Energy Policy Development Group," May 2001, pp. 8-11.
14. "The National Security Strategy of the United States of America," September 2002, http://www.whitehouse.gov/nsc/nss/2002/index.html, pp. 19–20.
15. John C. K. Daly, "Questioning AFRICOM's Intentions," *ISN Security Watch*, July 2, 2007, http://www.isn.ethz.ch/news/sw/details.cfm?id=17811.
16. EIA, "Annual Energy Outlook 2007," p. 71.

17. Bernard A. Gelb, "Caspian Oil and Gas: Production and Prospects," *CRS Report for Congress*, RS21190, September 8, 2006, pp. 1–2, http://www.au.af.mil/au/awc/awcgate/crs/rs21190.pdf (citing BP and EIA sources).
18. Office of the Vice President, "Vice President's Remarks in a Press Availability With President Nursultan Nazarbayev of the Republic of Kazakhstan in the Presidential Palace," Astana, Kazakhstan, May 5, 2006, http://www.whitehouse.gov/news/releases/2006/05/20060505-4.html.
19. Kerry Dumbaugh and Mark P. Sullivan, "China's Growing Interest in Latin America," *CRS Report for Congress*, RS22119, April 20, 2005, p. 4, http://fpc.state.gov/documents/organization/45464.pdf.
20. Juan Forero, "China's Oil Diplomacy Lures Latin America," *New York Times*, March 2, 2005, http://www.iht.com/articles/2005/03/01/business/oil.php.
21. Andy Webb-Vidal, "U.S. to Look Into Venezuela Oil Supply Reliance," *Financial Times*, January 13, 2005, http://search.ft.com/nonFtArticle?id=050113008494.
22. "Worldwide Look at Reserves and Production," *Oil & Gas Journal* 103, no. 47 (December 19, 2005): 24–25.
23. EIA, "Annual Energy Review 2005," pp. 5, 36.
24. "Worldwide Look at Reserves and Production," pp. 24–25.
25. James K. Jackson, "U.S. Trade Deficit and the Impact of Rising Oil Prices," *CRS Report for Congress*, RS22204, April 13, 2007, p. 1, http://ncseonline.org/NLE/CRSreports/07apr/RS22204.pdf.
26. Jeannine Aversa, "Oil Prices Said to Slow U.S. Economy a Bit," Associated Press, July 18, 2005.
27. Jeffrey M. Jones, "Oil Company Greed Seen as Major Reason for High Gas Prices," Gallup News Service, May 30, 2007, http://www.galluppoll.com/content/?ci=27709.
28. Lydia Saad, "Environmental Concern Holds Firm During Past Year," Gallup News Service, March 26, 2007, http://www.galluppoll.com/content/?ci=26971.
29. Joseph Carroll, "Americans Assess What They Can Do to Reduce Global Warming," Gallup News Service, April 24, 2007, http://www.galluppoll.com/content/?ci=27298.
30. Lydia Saad, "Most Americans Back Curbs on Auto Emissions, Other Environmental Proposals," Gallup News Service, April 5, 2007, http://www.galluppoll.com/content/?ci=27100.
31. Ibid.
32. Laurie Goodstein, "Evangelical Leaders Join Global Warming Initiative," *New York Times*, February 8, 2006, http://www.nytimes.com/2006/02/08/national/08warm.html?ex=1184299200&en=37788a3c967e1eb2&ei=507.
33. Bradford Plumer, "Inside the Evangelical War Over Climate Change," *New Republic Online*, March 15, 2007, http://www.tnr.com/doc.mhtml?i=w070312&s=plumer031507.
34. Office of the Press Secretary, The White House, "President Bush Discusses Energy Initiative," Wilmington, Delaware, January 24, 2007, http://www.whitehouse.gov/news/releases/2007/01/20070124-4.html.
35. "South Carolina Democratic Debate," April 26, 2007, http://www.msnbc.msn.com/id/18352397/.
36. CFR, "National Security Consequences of U.S. Oil Dependency," p. 8.
37. Nader Elhefnawy, "Toward a Long-Range Energy Security Policy," *Parameters* 36, no. 1 (Spring 2006): 101–114.
38. National Security Task Force on Energy, "Energy Security in the 21st Century: A New National Strategy," July 2006, p. 12, http://www.americanprogress.org/kf/energy_security_report.pdf.
39. Center for American Progress, "Americans Feel New Urgency on Energy Independence and Global Warming," April 18, 2007, http://www.americanprogress.org/pressroom/releases/2007/04/environmental_poll.html.
40. "Americans' View on the Environment," *New York Times*, April 26, 2007, http://www.cbsnews.com/htdocs/pdf/042607environment.pdf.
41. David Sandalow, "Ending Oil Dependence: Protecting National Security, the Environment, and the Economy," 2007, p. 17, http://www.opportunity08.org/Files/FD.ashx?guid=35206acc-10c0-41a2-8a64-a21dae54886d.

The Geopolitics of Natural Gas*

By Michael T. Klare
The Nation, January 23, 2006

In the high-stakes arena of energy geopolitics, natural gas is rapidly emerging as the next big prize. What oil was to the twentieth century, natural gas will be to the twenty-first. Consider these recent developments:

Item. As we went to press, Russia was restoring the flow of natural gas to Western and Central Europe after state-controlled Gazprom curtailed deliveries on January 1 in a bid to force Ukraine to pay the market price for gas previously supplied at subsidized rates. Although emphasizing the price issue, Russian officials apparently intended to constrict Ukraine's energy supplies as a way of punishing that country's pro-Western president, Viktor Yushchenko, architect of the Orange Revolution, for his overtures to NATO and the EU. Gazprom's pipelines to Western Europe (which buys a quarter of its gas from Russia) pass through Ukraine so it could siphon off some of the diminished supply, leaving very little for other customers and provoking fears of an energy crisis at the onset of winter.

Item. A dispute between China and Japan over the ownership of an undersea gas field in an area of the East China Sea claimed by both countries has grown increasingly inflammatory, with China sending warships into the area and Japan threatening "bold action" if the Chinese begin pumping gas from the field. The conflict has soured relations between Beijing and Tokyo and provoked a strong nationalistic response from the populations of both countries. The huge anti-Japanese demonstrations in Shanghai and other Chinese cities last April were prompted, in part, by Tokyo's announcement that it would permit drilling in the area by Japanese firms. A peaceful resolution of the dispute does not appear imminent.

Item. Ever since India announced plans more than a year ago to build a natural gas pipeline from fields in Iran to its own territory via Pakistan, the Bush Administration has been applying pressure on New Delhi to cancel the project, claiming

* "The Geopolitics of Natural Gas" by Michael T. Klare. Reprinted with permission from the January 23, 2006, issue of *The Nation*. For subscription information, call 1-800-333-8536. Portions of each week's *Nation* magazine can be access at *http://www.thenation.com*.

it will undermine US attempts to isolate Tehran and curb its nuclear efforts. "We have communicated to the Indian government our concerns about the gas pipeline cooperation between Iran and India," Secretary of State Condoleezza Rice announced after meeting with Indian Foreign Minister Natwar Singh on March 16. But the Indians have continued talks with Islamabad and Tehran over the pipeline plan.

The United States is becoming increasingly dependent on natural gas. This country now relies on natural gas for approximately one-fourth of its total energy supply, more than from any source except oil. As a result, the economy has become more and more vulnerable to fluctuations in gas supply and pricing—a vulnerability that should be especially evident this winter as gas prices hit record levels, with painful effects on the poor. Natural gas provides approximately 14 percent of the energy used to generate electricity in this country, 45 percent of home heating fuel and 31 percent of the energy and petrochemicals consumed by agriculture and industry. Gas is also used as a feedstock for the manufacture of hydrogen, a promising new entrant in the race to develop alternative fuels.

The United States currently relies on North American supplies for most of its gas, but with those reserves being depleted at a rapid pace and few untapped fields available for exploitation, need for gas from other regions is growing and energy plants seek more gas from foreign suppliers like Qatar, Nigeria and Russia. As with oil, America could become heavily dependent on foreign suppliers for essential energy needs, a situation fraught with danger for national security. Many of America's key allies, including the NATO powers and Japan, are dependent on imports.

As the global output of petroleum begins to contract in the decades ahead, industrialized nations will increasingly rely on natural gas. According to the Energy Department, the world's known gas reserves stood at 6,076 trillion cubic feet in 2004. In terms of energy output, this is equivalent to approximately 1,094 billion barrels of oil, or approximately 92 percent of known petroleum reserves. But because the world is consuming a smaller proportion each year of the remaining gas supply than it is of the remaining oil supply (1.5 percent as compared with 2.5 percent), gas should remain relatively abundant even after the supply of petroleum begins to contract. Considerable untouched gas is also believed to reside in remote "stranded" fields that could someday be added to the tally of proven reserves, further enhancing the fuel's role in the global energy equation.

Because natural gas is more environmentally friendly than oil or coal (it releases half as much carbon dioxide as coal for equal energy output, and a third less than petroleum), it is attractive to countries seeking to reduce their greenhouse gas emissions in accordance with the Kyoto treaty. In Europe gas's share of all fuels used in generating electricity is projected to rise from 18 percent in 2002 to 29 percent in 2030. A similar trend can be expected in the United States, if Congress or some future administration moves to reduce the nation's emissions of CO_2.

Developing nations like China, India and South Korea, increasingly aware of the environmental consequences of their excessive reliance on oil and coal, are also turning to natural gas. According to the Energy Department, gas consumption in China will grow by an estimated 7 percent per year between 2001 and 2025, five times the rate for the United States and the largest for any major industrial power; India and South Korea are also among the fastest-growing gas consumers. These projections help explain the aggressive steps being taken by these countries to secure additional supplies of gas.

The rising worldwide demand for gas is also influencing relations between the major consuming nations and their principal suppliers. A key factor in the geopolitics of natural gas is the heavy concentration of reserves in a relatively small number of producing countries. All told, the top ten gas producers harbor 76 percent of the world's proven reserves, while the top five—Russia, Iran, Qatar, Saudi Arabia and the United Arab Emirates—hold nearly 67 percent. This means, of course, that these countries are in a very strong position to control the global flow of gas and to influence market forces.

Russia, which owns 26.7 percent of the world's proven gas supplies (compared with 2.9 percent for the United States), will play a dominant role in the energy field for many decades to come. Although the United States and Russia produced similar amounts of gas in 2004–05 (543 billion and 589 billion cubic meters, respectively), America's output was about 10 percent of its total reserves while Russia's output was only 1 percent.

Russia already supplies a large share of Europe's natural gas, and when new pipelines are constructed, it will be capable of supplying vast amounts to China, Korea and Japan—even the United States, eventually. Until now, the Russians have been very careful to avoid giving the impression that they intend to exploit their dominant position in Europe for political advantage. Nevertheless, Moscow has been accused of engaging in such practices in the past: In December 2000, for example, it temporarily suspended gas deliveries to Georgia in a move perceived by many Georgians as punishment for the failure of its leaders, notably then-President Eduard Shevardnadze, to defer to Russia on key regional issues. The current blockage of gas to Ukraine can be seen as another instance of the same tactic.

Officials of the European Union are worried about the growing role of Gazprom in the delivery of natural gas to Europe. At present, Gazprom supplies approximately 40 percent of Europe's natural gas, and its share is likely to grow as gas fields in the North Sea are exhausted. Fearing that Moscow may someday exploit its role as Europe's major gas supplier to wring political concessions from its customers, EU officials have called for greater diversity in the procurement of energy—so far, to little avail.

Iran is also a major producer of natural gas. Under increasing diplomatic pressure from the Bush Administration to halt its suspected pursuit of nuclear weapons, Tehran has been eager to establish joint production and export projects with friendly nations in Europe and Asia. In the past two years alone, it has signed several multibillion-dollar deals with companies from France, Italy, Norway, Turkey, Japan and India for joint development of offshore gas fields in the Persian Gulf and the construction of new pipelines to Europe and Asia. Capping this drive was the signing in October 2004 of a $100 billion, twenty-five-year contract with the China National Petrochemical Corporation (Sinopec) for the joint production and export of liquefied natural gas (LNG), much of which will ultimately go to China. While all this makes perfect commercial sense, given Iran's need for foreign partners in the management of these ambitious projects, it is safe to assume Tehran is also seeking to increase the number of allies it can turn to in case of a showdown with the United States.

Qatar has tacked the opposite way, using its huge gas reserves to establish close ties with Washington and to insinuate itself beneath the US defense umbrella. Under a $10 billion, twenty-five-year agreement signed in 2003, ExxonMobil will build the world's largest LNG shipping facility in Qatar. Much of the resulting liquid will go to the United States to be converted back into gas. This will entail the construction of new LNG terminals at ports on the US Gulf Coast, a major undertaking.

Like Qatar's, many of the world's largest deposits of natural gas are located far from the areas where demand is greatest. The most efficient and economical way to transport gas to distant markets is by pipeline. As a result, vast natural gas pipeline networks have been built in North America, Europe and the former Soviet Union, and many more such conduits are under construction. These networks are easiest to construct on land or in relatively shallow, enclosed bodies of water like the Mediterranean and the Black Sea, both of which are now traversed by gas pipelines.

At present, however, it is impractical to build gas pipelines beneath a large ocean like the Atlantic or Pacific, so gas traveling from the Middle East or Africa to the United States or Japan must go by ship. Unlike crude petroleum, which can be pumped directly from the ground onto waiting ships, gas must first be converted to a liquid by cooling it to extremely low temperatures (around -160° centigrade, or -260° Fahrenheit), transported on mammoth refrigerated vessels and then converted back to a gas by raising its temperature, at giant regassification plants in the receiving country. This is very expensive and energy draining, making seaborne transport a far less attractive proposition than pipeline delivery. Still, in their hunger for ever-increasing supplies of energy, more and more countries are building LNG terminals in their harbors and negotiating with major gas suppliers like Iran, Qatar and Nigeria for long-term contracts.

Whether natural gas is transported by pipeline or ship, the growing commerce in it is likely to nurture new forms of international cooperation, like that between longtime rivals India and Pakistan, both desperate to boost their energy supplies in order to sustain strong economic growth. In June energy ministers from the two countries set up a joint working group to plan construction of a $4 billion, 1,700-mile gas pipeline from Iran, and ground breaking is projected for sometime later this year—unless, of course, the Bush Administration succeeds in arm-twisting one or the other into canceling the plan.

India is also looking eastward for additional supplies of natural gas. In January its officials met with their counterparts from Burma and Bangladesh to discuss the construction of a gas pipeline from Burma to India via Bangladesh. Such an arrangement would frustrate US efforts to isolate Burma for its egregious human rights behavior.

Increased cooperation in the transport of natural gas is developing too among Russia, China, Japan and the two Koreas. At the center of these efforts are the vast reservoirs of natural gas lying off Sakhalin Island in Russia's far east. To move this gas to international markets giant energy firms, including ExxonMobil and Royal Dutch/Shell, will build a huge LNG facility on Sakhalin's southern tip and at least one major pipeline. One pipeline is expected to extend from Sakhalin to northern China, while another might go to Japan; some visionaries have also proposed a branch line extending to South Korea via North Korea (a project that, if undertaken, would go a long way toward cementing the increasingly warm relations between the two). The LNG, meanwhile, will travel by ship to terminals in Japan and possibly the United States, if new LNG regassification plants are constructed along America's Pacific coast and/or in Baja California.

If the United States is to boost its imports of natural gas significantly, it will need many more LNG terminals in US harbors (there are only four now operating), and this prospect has already aroused considerable opposition from local authorities and environmentalists, who worry about the risk of explosions and other calamities. In a move little noticed by the American press or the public, Congress voted in July (as part of the new energy bill) to give the government the power to override local governments in the placement of future LNG terminals, a step that could lead to the construction of many more such facilities on the Atlantic and Pacific coasts and a sharp growth in US reliance on imported gas.

Although demand for natural gas has engendered cooperation between once-estranged nations, rival claims to oil and gas fields have frequently caused friction, even armed conflict. This has most often occurred in cases involving disputed offshore territories, notably in portions of the South China Sea, the East China Sea and the Strait of Korea. All these areas are believed to harbor substantial reserves of hydrocarbons in one form or another—oil and gas combined, gas alone or, as in the Korea Strait, gas hydrates (a crystal-like substance made up of methane and ice that can be converted into natural gas)—and all have been the site of violent or threatening confrontations between forces of the rival claimants involved. In each case, moreover, the United States is allied with one or more of the contending parties.

The most intense and prolonged of these conflicts has occurred in the South China Sea, a relatively shallow body of water believed to harbor substantial reserves of oil and gas. All of the countries with shorelines on the South China Sea—Brunei, China, Indonesia, Malaysia, the Philippines and Vietnam—have laid claim to a 200-mile offshore Exclusive Economic Zone in the area, many of them overlapping with one another, and all have laid claims to some or all of the small islands and reefs that dot the region. China, the dominant power in the area, claims all the islands and has been particularly aggressive in asserting its sovereignty over them—on several occasions using military force to drive away ships belonging to Vietnam and the Philippines. Several attempts have been made by the Association of Southeast Asian Nations to resolve the dispute peacefully, but China has not renounced its claim to the islands and continues to expand its small garrisons on some of the larger islets.

Japan is a party to two maritime boundary disputes in the region—the one with China discussed earlier and another with South Korea over a cluster of small islands in the Strait of Korea located roughly midway between the two nations. Here, too, the conflict revolves around the boundary between two overlapping Exclusive Economic Zones and the ownership of energy supplies that are thought to lie in the disputed territory—in this case, gas hydrates that could be mined and converted into natural gas. Efforts to resolve the conflict peacefully have so far come to naught, and warships and planes from both sides patrol the disputed area and occasionally approach each other in a threatening manner, risking an armed confrontation.

Whether the benefits of cooperation in procuring natural gas will come to be seen as more appealing than the rewards from unilateral action remains to be seen. One thing is certain: The world's growing demand for natural gas will play an ever more significant role in shaping the relations between major supplying and consuming nations. The need for energy will increasingly set the agenda of the major powers, and natural gas—long in the shadow of petroleum—is about to claim center stage.

Old King Coal Comes Back*

By Jeremy Main
Fortune, February 21, 2005

On a freezing, pristine day, with the Bighorn Mountains shining nearly 100 miles away across the Wyoming prairie, a huge dragline with an arm longer than a football field gulps 100 cubic yards of rock and soil by the mouthful to expose the underlying coal. Down below, near the face of an 80-foot-high coal seam, a massive shovel scoops up the black stuff and drops it into trucks capable of carrying up to 400 tons each. They rumble off to a nearby loading station where, night and day, mile-long trains snake around a double loop of tracks, slowing to load but never quite stopping, then set off across the country, hauling 15,000 tons of coal each. At 18 or more trains a day, that's more than a quarter-million tons of coal a day—out of a single mine.

This happens 365 days a year at Peabody Energy's North Antelope-Rochelle mine, the largest coal mine in the world. Last year the mine shipped 82 million tons of coal, or 8% of the coal used in the U.S. The mine lies in the heart of what miners like to call the Saudi Arabia of coal, the Powder River Basin in northeastern Wyoming and southern Montana. The U.S. has an estimated 268 billion tons of recoverable coal in existing mines, amounting to two to three times as much energy in coal as Saudi Arabia has in oil—enough to last a couple of centuries or more. Nearly half of that coal is right here in the Powder River Basin. Montana has 75 billion tons, which has hardly been touched, and Wyoming 42 billion tons. That's only the coal in existing mines. If you consider total recoverable reserves, the U.S. has nearly 500 billion tons, so on that basis Illinois can become a major new player too, with reserves of 105 billion tons.

Cheap, abundant, and safe from international crises—Old King Coal is coming back. Actually, it never went away. We just didn't notice it much, except as a polluter. During the last half of the last century other sources of energy caught our attention—nuclear power, imported oil—and in the 1990s, we became enthusiastic about cheap, clean natural gas. So we didn't see that coal had a future.

But it was there all the time, the largest single source of power generation in the U.S., providing just over half of our electricity. And our demand for electricity just keeps growing. Power production has increased steadily, by about 26% in the past ten years, and the Energy Information Administration predicts steady 1.8% growth annually to 2020.

This wealth of coal can't flow freely through the U.S. economy until some costly and difficult fixes are applied across the whole business of mining, transporting, and burning coal. Rail transport is tight. Compared to bituminous coal from Appalachia, which now dominates the U.S. coal-power scene, the Powder River Basin's sub-bituminous coal has less sulfur but also less energy. Many power plants will need costly renovations before they can use the Western coal.

Most important, the growth of coal plants in the U.S. and the even faster growth in China and India will add billions of tons of carbon to the atmosphere, overwhelming any possible gain from the Kyoto treaty. Assuming that the output of carbon dioxide and other pollutants from power plants proves to be the primary cause of global warming, as is increasingly evident, then burning coal could become our most serious environmental threat. However, new technologies offer the possibility of completely, or almost completely, emission-free burning. The government is spending $2 billion on clean-coal technology this decade. Corporate America is getting involved too. General Electric and Bechtel recently formed a partnership to build cleaner power plants.

The heads of two of the country's largest coal producers, Irl Engelhardt of Peabody Energy and Bret Clayton of Kennecott Energy, accept that coal needs to be cleaner. "We'll have to invest in technology to continue to make coal cleaner and cleaner," says Clayton. "The goal is near-zero emissions," says Engelhardt. They also urge the U.S. to try to keep a balanced mix of energy sources. But this will be difficult for now. Nobody is building new nuclear plants, and those built decades ago have started shutting down. Supplies of oil and gas are tightening, and prices have shot up.

Now the electric utilities are going back to coal. Natural gas costs three times what it did at the end of the 1990s, and instead of building gas-fired plants, as they did in the 1990s, utilities are planning coal-burning plants. Power industry consultant Robert McIlvaine counts about 100 new coal plants in the works in the U.S. Since most of these are still only projects, he believes many probably will never be built. Even so, dozens of new coal plants will go up in the next couple of decades. That's a lot of coal, a lot of electricity, and a lot of new pollutants.

The growth in coal production will have to come largely from the Powder River Basin. Eastern coal from Appalachia, which has powered American industry for more than two centuries, is starting to run short. The higher-quality Eastern coal has doubled in price in the past two years, from about $30 a ton to $60 or more. Meanwhile the price of Powder River Basin coal has remained remarkably steady for years at about $6 a ton, with only a small jog upward recently. It's not quite the bargain it seems, because the cost of transporting it a long way adds $30 or so a ton to the price, and it has about one-third less energy, so power companies have to buy more of it. Still, compared with any other source of energy except sunshine, wind, and falling water, Western coal is cheap.

At Peabody's North Antelope mine you can see where the huge coal bed came to the surface, for the rocks are burned red by coal ignited centuries ago in prairie fires set ablaze by Native Americans and by nature. The coal seams stretch miles to the West but slant deeper into the earth, so more and more "overburden" —the soil and sandstone and clay above the coal—has to be moved aside before miners can reach the coal. When the overburden gets to be 500 feet thick, the coal may no longer be worth mining. But right now the Peabody draglines are moving 210 feet of overburden to get at a rich seam 80 feet thick, stretching far out west. In Appalachia, miners have to go deep underground to get at a seam only six to eight feet thick.

In this form of surface mining, the first step is to loosen the overburden with explosives. Then the huge draglines, which cost $70 million each when new, move in to set the topsoil to one side and the rest of the overburden to another side. More explosives loosen the coal below. Then diesel shovels, with buckets big enough to fit two SUVs, pick up the loosened coal and drop it into those enormous trucks. The largest trucks cost $3.3 million apiece; each of their tires, over 12 feet tall, costs $30,000.

The trucks crawl like enormous beetles along wide dirt roads to loading stations, where they dump the coal into crushers. From the crushers it moves up conveyor belts into silos straddling the railway tracks. The double loop of tracks permits two trains to move through at a time if necessary. As each of the train's 100 or more cars moves under the silo, precisely 100 tons of coal drops into it. Once the train has its 15,000 tons, it rolls onward to a power plant hundreds or thousands of miles away.

At North Antelope and at Kennecott's nearby Cordero Rojo mine, which produces about half of North Antelope's 82 million tons a year, as well as at other mines in the basin, the same massive operation goes on all year round, 24 hours a day except when snow drifts block Route 59 north to Gillette, the "Energy Capital of America" (pop. 24,000). Fresh crews have to reach the mine every 12 hours.

In the final part of the operation, the dragline returns the overburden and topsoil to "approximately" the original contours of the prairie, as Wyoming law requires. Then the dragline waddles on huge pads to a new location at a speed of about six feet a minute. Wyoming's Department of Environmental Quality says that in the state as a whole, mining has torn up 110,580 acres of prairie, backfilled and graded 40,800 of those acres, and seeded 37,000 acres.

Environmentalists say that the coal companies sometimes skimp on buying the right prairie seeds and bushes, especially sagebrush. They also claim that the mining and the blasting spread dust and sometimes even poisonous fumes across the land. But on the whole they seem satisfied that the mines are relatively kind to the environment. "I think everyone will tell you they're doing a good job," says Harold Bergman, director of the Ruckelshaus Institute of the Environment and Natural Resources at the University of Wyoming. (Bergman will not say the same for another mining operation, the extraction of methane gas from some 12,000 small wells. Wyoming ranchers and environmentalists are incensed about the disruptions caused by drilling, traffic, power lines, and noisy equipment spread over 6,000 square miles.)

The strong demand for Powder River Basin coal is beginning to put strains on the coal supply chain. It takes three months to get one of those huge tires the dump trucks use. The railroads, which also are coping with growth in ship-container traffic, are stressed. Some utilities report getting coal deliveries in the nick of time or not at all.

In 2004 the recovery from the recent recession caught the railroads by surprise. Arch Coal, which owns the huge Black Thunder mine in the basin, wrote in its second-quarter report last year, "Rail difficulties resulted in missed shipments in both East and West, including some of the company's highest-margin Eastern business." The company said the rail delays cost it $8 million. The two railroads that serve the basin, Burlington Northern and Union Pacific, are beefing up. Union Pacific hired a record 5,000 workers to add to train crews last year, bought 700 locomotives, and ordered another 315.

Coal can also be transported, in a sense, along transmission lines. At some point it may even prove economical to build mine-mouth power plants in Wyoming and transmit the electricity long distances. Whether or not that happens, the national power grid needs strengthening. An invention by 3M, creator of Post-its and Scotch tape, may go a long way to doing just that: The company has come up with a transmission line that carries twice as much power as the wires used now, and in an emergency they can carry much more.

The new cable came about in the serendipitous way that things happen at 3M. The company was researching the use of ceramics in jet engines in the early 1990s and found that ceramic fibers and aluminum are compatible. Then Tracy Anderson, who now runs the power-line project, saw long transmission cables sagging across northern Minnesota lakes from one distant tower to another. Linking the research to the observation, 3M figured it could apply its jet-engine research to making a lighter high-performance cable. Conventional cable is made of aluminum wrapped around a steel cable. 3M's composite conductor, as it is dubbed, consists of heat-resistant zirconium-aluminum cable wrapped around a core of aluminum-oxide fibers. As conventional lines transmit electricity, they heat up and sag. If overloaded, they can sag into a tree or some other obstacle, which is what started the 2003 blackout that crippled the Northeast. The 3M cable withstands higher temperatures with less sagging and is stronger and lighter. While the average conductor may carry 800 to 1,000 amps, the 3M line handles 1,600 to 1,800 on average and has coped with five times as much as a conventional line.

The 3M cable has been tested successfully in short, one-mile segments, and now Excel Energy, a Twin Cities utility, is installing a ten-mile section through the suburbs on an existing right of way with the existing towers. A special advantage of the 3M product is that utilities don't need to battle for new rights of way, and they don't have to fight the NIMBY reaction or build new towers.

Despite its abundance, low price, and low sulfur, Powder River Basin coal creates problems for utilities that burn it. It contains chemicals that gum up boilers with lumps of black, rocklike slag. These lumps, which get up to the size of a VW Bug, reduce the efficiency of the plant. The slag may fall 60 to 80 feet from the upper reaches of the boiler and smash the floor of the furnace. More likely the slag will have to be attacked violently to remove it, sometimes even with small explosive charges or shotguns. The plant may be closed for days of cleaning.

Many existing plants can safely burn a mixture of 70% Western coal and 30% Eastern coal without getting slag problems, but if they go to 100% Western coal, which many are doing, then they will probably need new technology. Fuel-Tech N.V., a pollution-control company in Batavia, Ill., has developed a process to prevent slagging. The system squirts an atomized slurry of magnesium hydroxide and water into the boiler in exact doses, which changes the slag into a harmless, crumbly substance that can readily be removed.

Western Farmers' Electric Cooperative, an Oklahoma utility, was using 100% Western coal at its Hugo plant and as a result had to shut down twice a year for five or six days to attack the slag. The utility solved the problem two years ago by adopting Fuel-Tech's system, known as TIFI (for targeted in-furnace injection).

Robert Richard, vice president for fossil generation at DTE Energy, a major Michigan utility, is pleased with the Fuel-Tech process. DTE has converted two small stations and is adding two more. He regards the use of TIFI as a pilot, but results so far are good. The savings far exceed the cost of installing and running the system. New plants can be designed to handle Western coal without Fuel-Tech's help, but Fuel-Tech president Steven Argabright figures there are some 400 older boilers in the U.S. that need it. (The U.S. has roughly 1,000 coal-fired boilers at 411 plant sites.)

There are other new technologies in coal's future that will make it more efficient, cleaner, and more versatile. Some are already available, while others await pilot projects to prove their worth. Gasified coal can run cleaner plants, perhaps almost emission-free. Liquefied coal can run cars, as it has for years in South Africa.

Under the requirements of the 1970 Clean Air Act and its amendments, power plants have substantially reduced their emissions of particulates, sulfur, and nitrogen oxides. By installing scrubbers, they have cut sulfur-dioxide emissions, the main cause of acid rain, to half what they were in 1980.

But where do the plants stand with the big unknown—global warming? Carbon-dioxide emissions have been curbed only to the extent that the utilities have become more efficient and therefore burn less coal for the same output. Forget the Kyoto Accord. President Bush, whose Clear Skies Initiative calls for only voluntary constraints on carbon dioxide, brusquely rejected the treaty. And anyway, Kyoto aims for only a 5.2% reduction in carbon-dioxide emissions by 2010. So even if the U.S. had joined, CO2 emissions would still be going up rather than down. Developing countries are exempt from Kyoto, and the hundreds of plants that China and India plan to build—plus the plants the U.S. and others have in the works—will add billions of tons of carbon dioxide to the atmosphere.

Carbon dioxide can't be ignored, and coal is its primary producer. As Kennecott's Clayton says, "You can only address carbon by addressing coal." William Reilly, former EPA administrator and co-chairman of a bipartisan commission that issued an energy policy report last December, says, "Coal gasification, when combined with carbon sequestration, has the potential to revolutionize energy production."

He was referring to a technology called integrated gasification combined cycle, or IGCC. Today's natural-gas plants use a single cycle—after the natural gas burns, the resulting stream of hot exhaust turns a turbine that produces electricity. It's clean, but it's inefficient because all that hot gas then goes to waste. An IGCC plant captures the heat and uses it to create steam, which then produces more electricity—hence the name "combined cycle." Better still, IGCC plants can run on synthetic gas, or syngas, as it's called in the industry, which is made by partially oxidizing coal. Syngas burns cleaner than coal and makes it possible to remove the waste carbon dioxide. IGCC isn't economical yet on a vast scale. Nor does anyone really know what to do with all that "captured" carbon—billions of tons of it, once the plants are widespread. A possible solution is to bury it in old oil and coal fields, but that idea might run into the same opposition that nuclear waste has encountered.

Still, IGCC is coming. A sure sign that it has become a mainstream business became evident last year when General Electric bought ChevronTexaco's gasification operations and then went into partnership with Bechtel to commercialize IGCC technology. The partners had worked together on IGCC pilot plants, and now they are talking with Cinergy, a big Indiana utility, about building a 500- or 600-megawatt plant. But IGCC plants will not be ready before the end of the decade, and the technology that will make them carbon-free is still further off.

In the meantime, for the next ten or 20 years the world's growing power needs will be met by more coal-burning plants, certainly cleaner than the old ones, but not free of carbon emissions. Natural gas will generate a diminishing share of power. Other energy sources—hydrogen, fuel cells—may start to contribute, and nuclear power may well make a comeback. But coal will still be king for years to come.

It's Scary, It's Expensive, It Could Save the Earth*

By Charles Petit
National Geographic, April 2006

Nukes again? Maybe. The United States operates 103 nuclear power reactors—that's a quarter of the world's total—even if the most famous U.S. nuke isn't even real. That would be the Springfield plant, where doofus TV cartoon hero Homer Simpson is a safety inspector. "They're cash cows," says James Tulenko, a nuclear fuel specialist, University of Florida professor, and immediate past president of the American Nuclear Society. With hefty construction bills paid off at many plants, "you just deal with the operating costs. All those plants run flat out day and night," he says. And they deliver electricity more cheaply than gas or coal plants.

That's not the whole story, of course. The hopes of a burgeoning nuclear industry imploded 27 years ago after the partial meltdown at one of the Three Mile Island reactors in Pennsylvania, followed by the horror of Chernobyl seven years after that. Plus, decisions made by utility regulators in the 1970s and '80s left companies barely able to pay off billion-dollar nuclear construction bills. Now the U.S. produces half its electricity with cheaper coal-burning plants. The trouble with that is the two billion tons of climate-warming carbon dioxide spewing skyward every year. Industrializing nations, such as India and China, hungry for every megawatt of power they can produce, are also building new coal plants at a rapid clip.

Still, for nearly a decade, with no new plants, nukes' 20 percent share of U.S. electricity production has held steady, keeping pace as overall electricity output has risen 15 percent. In the 1970s and 80s unscheduled shutdowns for repairs or other problems limited U.S. plants to less than 65 percent of their potential output. Today, with experience and improved operating practices, output exceeds 90 percent.

So is it time to embrace the atom again? There's a "nuclear renaissance" buzz emitting from engineers who design and operate reactors, think-tank academics who worry about long-range energy and environmental strategies, utility company executives, top members of the Bush Administration, and members of Congress. Proponents say atomic energy is a proven technology for a 21st-century civilization desperate to swear off fossil fuels and not to go broke doing it. Nuclear fission emits none of the greenhouse gases that are warming the climate. The Nuclear Energy Institute estimates that without nuclear power playing its current role in the generation of electricity, the U.S. would spew 29 percent—190 million metric tons—more carbon than it does now.

Scratch a nuclear engineer these days, and you'll likely find, under the buttoned-down exterior, a raving green activist. Even among the ranks of environmentalists who a decade ago could barely tolerate the mention of nukes, the possibility is getting an occasional thumbs-up. Climate change, for many, trumps any fear of nuclear energy. Its overwhelming advantage is that it's atmospherically clean, writes Stewart Brand, founder of the 1970s Whole Earth Catalog.

Yet, Brand points out: "Nuclear certainly has problems—accidents, waste storage, high construction costs, and the possible use of nuclear fuel for weapons." Most experts agree that such problems are no small drawback to forging ahead with new nukes. So despite shifting attitudes, atomic allergy has eased only slightly if at all among the bulk of prominent environmental leaders. Analysts also point to other problems, such as unresolved waste questions and limited public input on the whole issue of nuclear power. The current strategy, predicts Gus Speth, co-founder of the Natural Resources Defense Council and Dean of Forestry and Environmental Studies at Yale University, will just replay the battles of the 1970s.

Other nations are watching the U.S., but not waiting. France gets 78 percent of its electricity from nuclear power and is considering replacing its older plants with new ones. And the industry is expected to burgeon in Asia in the next quarter century. China, on top of its headlong rush to build coal-burning plants, also has ambitious plans for new reactors: It can get 6,600 megawatts of power now from nine reactors. It's aiming for 40,000 megawatts.

India, a nation of 1.1 billion people—and one beset both by crushing poverty and a tumultuously expanding economy—has 15 nuclear power reactors already at work. Eight more are under construction, more than in any other nation. The Department of Atomic Energy lauds the greenhouse benefits of nukes, but the main impetus is sheer gigawatt lust. "Our energy policy is simple," says Baldev Raj, director of the Indira Gandhi Centre for Atomic Research near the Bay of Bengal city of Chennai. "If you have a way to make electricity, then we say, make as much as you can."

That would include building reactors such as those at Kaiga Generating Station in a clearing in the jungled Western Ghats mountains about 20 miles inland from southwest India's seacoast. Coming upon the two 220-megawatt, pressurized heavy-water reactors is like stumbling into a thumping big factory in the middle of Yellowstone National Park. The region gets more than 15 feet of rain yearly, and its forest is home to increasingly threatened species. "Tigers? Yes, they are near. Panthers and king cobra too," says Anwar Siddiqui, senior manager for the Nuclear Power Corporation of India.

A country with reactors in such places must really like them. Amid a jumble of construction cranes and heavy concrete walls, two similar reactors are rising next to the first two, and another pair, more than twice as powerful, will likely join them in coming years.

Back near the Indira Gandhi center a 500-megawatt breeder reactor is under construction and set to start up in 2010. Four more are to follow by 2020. They are very efficient at manufacturing plutonium fuel from their original uranium fuel load, which greatly increases the amount of energy they produce. But critics worry that the plutonium could possibly get in the wrong hands.

In part because of proliferation concerns, the U.S. has sworn off such breeder reactors for the time being. But outside powers have little leverage over India's nukes. With few exceptions they are entirely homegrown. India gave itself little choice about going it alone. In 1974, it set off an underground nuclear explosion using plutonium surreptitiously diverted from a test reactor that Canada helped it build in the 1950s.

India became a nuclear pariah. Other countries suspended technical assistance, and Canadian engineers walked off a job in Rajasthan. The Indians finished the plant themselves.

They are now enthusiastic masters of all things nuclear. The uranium fuel in Kaiga's reactors comes from mines west of Calcutta; workshops in the south provide the plant with gleaming, 65-foot-high, 110-ton steam generators that drive electric dynamos. Control systems, zircaloy fuel tubes, and 22-ton reactor components arrive from Hyderabad.

"We can't go back, we can only go forward," said Swapnesh Malhotra, a spokesman for India's atomic energy department. "Life depends on energy, and I ask, where do we get it? We will get it somewhere."

Meanwhile, the U.S. tiptoes ahead. In the nation that gave it birth, nuclear power may get its second wind in a mowed field outside the quiet town of Port Gibson, Mississippi. The field, close by a reactor that has been operating since 1985, is part of the Grand Gulf Nuclear Station, owned by a subsidiary of Entergy Corporation, the fourth largest electricity producer in the U.S.

Entergy hopes to fire up a new nuke here by 2015. First, General Electric (GE) and Westinghouse, the nation's only reactor makers, must finish detailed designs for machines they've been promoting as more foolproof and easier to operate than those they built decades ago. Formal license applications could be filed by 2008. Federal regulators might chew on them until 2010.

To expedite the process, Entergy organized a consortium in 2004 of nine utility companies plus GE and Westinghouse. The consortium, named NuStart, hopes to test new Nuclear Regulatory Commission procedures that will grant a combined construction and operating license to avoid the interminable hearings of the 1960s and '70s.

Only then, if GE, Westinghouse, or both, get approval, will Entergy and other NuStart members decide on actual orders. Construction would take four to five years.

That's if there's money. Congress last year passed an energy bill that guarantees loans made by investors and includes a subsidy of up to six billion dollars for running the first new plants. But the industry insists that it can't get private financing for construction of the plants without government loan guarantees. Environmentalists like Speth consider the nuclear industry mature enough to sink or swim without federal assistance—and with vigilant regulation.

Everyone in the business knows financial woes helped torpedo the first wave of atomic ambition four decades ago. Next to the vacant, waiting Grand Gulf field is an unfinished concrete silo that stares at the sky like an empty eye socket. It was to be the containment structure for a twin to the reactor there today. But just before Christmas 1979, staggered by construction costs, Entergy (then called Middle South Utilities) pulled the plug on the second silo.

Even so, the one reactor that was completed drained the company coffers. In 1984 it feared it wouldn't be able to make payroll. "We had the bankruptcy lawyers all lined up," says Randy Hutchinson, an Entergy senior vice president. American banks turned their backs. Only a high-interest loan from a consortium of European banks kept the company afloat.

In the long run, even nuclear advocates agree that the best hope for the future lies in new designs for reactors. In two or three decades the industry could see generation IV machines that run more efficiently at much higher temperatures, thus getting far more energy from their starting load of uranium. The intense nuclear reactions at such temperatures would leave waste that, compared to today's, is less toxic and lasts for a shorter period of time. Advanced reactors would have simpler safety features and require less sophisticated backup systems. They could cool themselves down in the event of an accident with little human intervention, making them less tempting targets for terrorists.

Last year's energy bill authorized 1.25 billion dollars for the Department of Energy's Idaho National Laboratory to build an experimental, high-temperature, helium-gas-cooled reactor specifically to learn how efficiently such a thing can produce both electricity and—no small extra—hydrogen gas, which could be used as vehicle fuel.

For now, however, the most ardent pro-nuke advocates can't argue with a worst-case scenario. A major release of radiation such as from Chernobyl in 1986; a terrorist attack that somehow penetrated elaborate security and steel-reinforced walls to purloin fuel or release a cloud of radiation; diversion of weapons-grade uranium or plutonium to rogue nations or criminal groups—all have visceral impact far beyond the pollution, coal-mine accidents, and climate-altering emissions of fossil fuel plants. In a speech at Grand Gulf, Gary Taylor, head of Entergy's nuclear division, stressed the hazard to both the public and the industry if a reactor should go seriously wrong. "We have 40 years in an industry that has proved itself to be safe—and I mean safe. Nukes haven't made news lately, but with just one major accident . . . " he snapped his fingers. "Everything we have worked for could die, just like that."

In the meantime, fields like the one at Grand Gulf lie untouched. Can a new nuclear era even get started? Nearby residents are eager to see action. National polls show a rising acceptance of nuclear energy, with some showing as high as 59 percent in favor. Port Gibson's mayor and board of aldermen endorse a new reactor for the boost its taxes would give local schools and other institutions.

Does anyone in town consider Grand Gulf's lone operating nuke a menace? Michael Herrin, pastor of Port Gibson's First Presbyterian Church, its tall spire topped by a golden hand pointing skyward, answers: "People from the plant speak at local meetings. We know the cloud of steam that comes from the cooling tower isn't radioactive. In this town, the dragon is unemployment. Entergy is the hero."

2

Good Bye to Gasoline? Ethanol and Biodiesel

Editor's Introduction

In the midst of all our energy woes, biofuels—particularly corn-based ethanol and biodiesel—have emerged as alternatives to conventional petroleum. Whether by themselves or mixed with gasoline, these substances are used principally as transport fuels, to power automobiles, and will hopefully help to alleviate our dependence on foreign oil and decrease our greenhouse gas emissions. However, just how effective these fuels may be, especially in reducing emissions, remains a matter of dispute. Corn ethanol especially has generated skepticism. Articles in this chapter, "Good-Bye to Gasoline? Ethanol and Biodiesel," describe these new fuels and consider their overall efficiency as well as their potential for widespread use.

An alcoholic substance derived from corn, sugarcane, and other crops, ethanol has taken a central role in efforts to combat climate change and otherwise ease our carbon footprint. While ethanol distilled from corn is the most prominent form of the fuel, many believe that ethanol produced from sugarcane and/or cellulosic material might be more effective in the long run. Moreover, there is no consensus as to what role ethanol should play in any future energy strategy. In "Is Ethanol the Answer," Marianne Lavelle and Bret Schulte provide a comprehensive overview of the complicated ethanol issue. They note that the ethanol boom has driven up the price of corn, which has in turn sent food prices soaring, while many doubt whether corn ethanol is any better for the environment than petroleum. The situation can best be summed up by the Sierra Club's Dan Becker, who states, according to Lavelle and Schulte, "I hate talking about ethanol . . . There are ways ethanol can be a boon to the environment, there are ways that it could be a disaster for the environment, and the devil's in the details."

David Rotman further analyzes the ethanol situation in the subsequent piece, "The Price of Biofuels." He reports that, "The irrational exuberance over ethanol that swept through the American corn belt over the last few years has given way to a dreary hangover."

With just a few alterations, a conventional diesel engine can be converted to run on biodiesel. Fuel can then be obtained from used cooking oil, for which fast-food restaurants serve as an ideal source. Frances Cerra Whittelsey explores the "do-it-yourself bio-diesel movement" as well as the blossoming biodiesel industry in "Fuel for Thought." Greg Pahl likewise examines the biodiesel sector in "Biodiesel: Homegrown Oil." In addition to describing the chemical reactions involved in the use of these fuels, he notes that many researchers believe that algae might prove an efficient source.

Is Ethanol the Answer?*

By Marianne Lavelle and Bret Schulte
U.S. News & World Report, February 12, 2007

This farming town of fewer than 400 people might be most memorable for what it doesn't have: a Wal-Mart, a high school, even a stoplight. But humble Galva [Iowa] and its environs have two things in abundance: corn and, by extension, hope.

"We feel we're on the cusp here as far as things happening," says Rita Frahm, an 18-year resident and president of the county's economic development corporation. That's because Galva is the lucky home of an ethanol plant.

Since opening in 2002, the plant has produced ever increasing dividends, to date putting more than $13 million into the hands of the 420 local farmers and investors who own it. That cash is slowly but markedly changing Galva's landscape. For the first time in 30 years, the town witnessed construction of three new homes at once, and a whole new street, Sixth Street, on which to place the houses. Those dwellings are now occupied by families "who saw an opportunity to stay rather than the community dying," Frahm says.

Heartwarming stories like Galva's—in a state that hosts the first presidential contest—help explain why Washington is so fired up over ethanol. In 2006, production skyrocketed, and Washington is poised to push it still higher. What's not to like? Every gallon theoretically means more money for the iconic American farmer and less cash lining the pockets of foreign sheiks. "There's almost a sense," says Iowa State University political scientist Steffen Schmidt, "that ethanol is morally better than oil."

Washington loves a "win-win," but there are plenty of doubts as to whether the love affair with ethanol qualifies. Even though the ethanol industry profited handsomely last year, it continued to benefit from billions of dollars in taxpayer subsidies. And as ethanol becomes a larger part of the energy mix, it is not clear that Washington is prepared for the fallout. Ethanol already consumes so much corn that signs of strain on the food supply and prices are rippling across the marketplace. Environmental impacts will multiply as more land and water are devoted to the prized yellow grain. And, even if these problems were overcome, ethanol's potential growth could be stunted by an energy system currently tailored to gasoline. Ethanol undoubtedly plays a role in the quest for energy independence and the desire to curb global warming. But some observers worry that ethanol development may take the place of more effective initiatives: forcing automakers to increase gas mileage, for instance, or mandating cuts in carbon dioxide emissions. "Some members of Congress are looking for quick fixes," says one economist who has studied the issue. "It's an easy bandwagon to jump on. But there's a lot of exaggeration about what ethanol is capable of doing."

BEGINNINGS

Ethanol is alcohol distilled from fermented, mashed grain. It took a century for it to make a big splash on the U.S. energy scene, even though Henry Ford built his first Model T in 1908 to run on either gasoline or ethanol. Over the decades, petroleum proved cheaper, and grain alcohol was relegated to college fraternity parties rather than gas tanks. No one looked seriously at ethanol as fuel until the oil price shocks of the 1970s, when Congress decided to subsidize a homegrown alternative—most significantly through a tax credit to oil companies for every gallon of the costly alternative they blended into gasoline. But when oil prices fell again in the late 1980s through the 1990s, the nation's dependence on petroleum imports mushroomed to 60 percent, and ethanol was reduced to a performance-boosting additive for some midwestern gasoline—a nice, subsidized side business for the dominant producer, Archer Daniels Midland.

Around 2000, ethanol started gaining traction when it emerged as the substitute to methyl tertiary butyl ether (MTBE), an oxygenate that reduced air pollution but leaked into drinking water at potentially dangerous levels. At the same time, upstart businesses like VeraSun of Brookings, S.D., were learning to produce ethanol more efficiently. Then came the Iraq war and high oil prices. Suddenly, the price ethanol refiners could fetch for their product from the big oil companies was far higher than the production cost. In places like Galva, where farmers had pooled their money to put up plants earlier, returns rolled in. It was a modern-day gold rush for grain farmers and investors. Today, 60 percent of ethanol production is in the hands of small companies.

POLITICS

The rush of new players strengthened the industry's clout. One of the largest stakes in the No. 2 producer, VeraSun, for instance, is owned by a midwestern venture capital firm, Bluestem, founded by Steve Kirby, former lieutenant governor of South Dakota and a big Republican donor. Among other big investors in small ethanol companies: Microsoft founder Bill Gates and the politically connected Carlyle Group private equity firm, where George H. W. Bush was once a director. The 10 largest ethanol producers and their trade groups have handed out $4.7 million in federal campaign contributions since 2000, says the Center for Responsive Politics. The Renewable Fuels Association has increased its lobbying spending 60 percent in the past seven years, and former Sens. Bob Dole of Kansas and Tom Daschle of South Dakota tout ethanol's national security benefits for a group of farm and energy interests called the 21st Century Agriculture Policy Project. Just as crucial, while far less tangible, has been Washington's veneration of the long-suffering small farmer, now turned ethanol entrepreneur.

It all paid off in 2005, when, with gasoline prices ratcheting higher, Congress wrote into its big energy bill a renewable fuel standard, an unprecedented mandate requiring refiners to double the amount of ethanol they blend into the nation's gasoline by 2012—a major coup for the industry. Congress's decision in that bill not to give the oil industry any protection from MTBE lawsuits made ethanol even hotter. Oil refiners immediately announced a switch to ethanol en masse, dramatically boosting demand.

Energy economist Philip Verleger is one of many who traced last summer's high gasoline prices to ethanol panic. As it turned out, the taxpayer paid twice. First, at the pump. Then, because of the long-standing ethanol tax breaks—now at 51 cents per gallon—the government sent $2.5 billion last year to the flush oil industry to blend ethanol it would have needed anyway.

In 2006, production exceeded Congress's renewable fuel standard mandate by 25 percent, reaching 5 billion gallons produced. Nearly half of the gasoline being sold in the United States now contains 10 percent ethanol. But that leaves half the market open to conquest. Some 76 ethanol refineries are now under construction, including in such unlikely states as New York and Oregon, adding to the 112 already squeezing fuel from corn. By some counts, 200 more have been proposed.

Of course, oil prices—generally falling since August—could rain on the parade. In fact, Wall Street is so worried that cheaper petroleum will cool ethanol profitability, as it has in the past, that the stock prices of companies that went public with fanfare last summer, VeraSun and Aventine, of Pekin, Ill., have slid 40 percent and 60 percent, respectively. Bill Gates would be $140 million richer if he had sold his stake in Pacific Ethanol of Fresno, Calif., when gas prices began to spike last spring. As it stands, he's doing a bit better than break-even because of the bounce his company took after President Bush made his pitch in the State of the Union address to increase renewable fuels—a universe now almost entirely made of ethanol—a staggering sevenfold by 2017. Congress is already on the case: All eyes are on the important farm bill being shepherded forward this year by Iowa Sen. Tom Harkin, chair of the Agriculture Committee, as the perfect vehicle to force increased ethanol demand on the market.

Indeed, ethanol has proved one of the few issues in Washington for which it's nearly impossible to find a sparring partner. Even Sen. John McCain, who gave up on Iowa in his 2000 presidential bid because of his opposition to ethanol subsidies, now says the fuel should be "carefully examined." Sen. Hillary Rodham Clinton, who once voted against the mandate, is calling for $1 billion in ethanol research.

CONSEQUENCES

A new ethanol surge could cause more problems than it solves. Last year's astounding growth in ethanol gobbled up 20 percent of the U.S. corn crop. That surpasses all the corn Americans consumed last year—whether in cereal, corn-syrup-sweetened soda, or on the cob. And the strain has become severe on the nation's primary use of corn—as feed for dairy and beef cattle, pigs, and chickens. Meat, dairy, and egg producers are reeling from corn prices that have doubled in one year—now trading above $4 a bushel for the first time in more than a decade.

The impact may really be felt when meat prices take off at the start of this summer's grilling season. "The American consumer is making a choice here," says Dick Bond, chief executive of Tyson Foods. "This is either corn for feed or corn for fuel." He indicated his company intends to be active in the farm bill debate on Capitol Hill, and some livestock groups recently wrote a letter to warn the secretary of agriculture of their concerns. Lester Brown of the Earth Policy Institute warns that ethanol is on track to consume half of the U.S. corn crop as early as 2008. He is calling for a moratorium on new refineries, similar to the one the world's No. 3 ethanol producer, China, announced in December. "We used to have a food economy and an energy economy," says Brown. "The two are merging. We need to . . . think through carefully what we're doing."

Ethanol's boosters are confident farmers will plant more acres and increase the yield of corn per acre, with the help of new seed and genetic engineering technology—easing the price pressure. But for now, the futures market shows corn prices climbing further. That's despite the fact that farmers are on track to plant 88 million acres of corn this year—up 10 million over 2006 and more than has been planted in the United States at any time since the 1940s, when crop yields were a fraction of today's.

The frenzy for the new yellow gold is not without environmental consequences, either. Plenty of greenhouse-gas emitting fossil fuels are used to produce ethanol—tractors in the field, trucks on the road, and nitrogen-based fertilizer born of natural gas. Some say that ethanol actually uses more energy than it returns. But only one oft-quoted study arrived at this conclusion by using apparently obsolete data. A Congressional Research Service analysis last year concluded that "most studies give corn-based ethanol a slightly positive energy balance." A tepid endorsement, at best. On climate issues, researchers are concerned with ethanol's reliance on natural gas or coal throughout the production process. "Overall benefits in terms of . . . greenhouse gases are limited," concludes CRS. That problem may get worse with the emergence of coal-fired ethanol plants, like one that opened last month in Richardton, N.D. Bob Dinneen of the Renewable Fuels Association points out relatively clean natural gas is the industry standard, and he believes more earth-friendly plants are the next wave, such as those that trap methane from cattle feedlots to fire their boilers. But without mandated emissions caps, refineries may have little incentive to invest in such costly technology.

Farmers most likely will grow their corn on acres they normally would have rotated to soybeans. But that zaps topsoil of nutrients while exacerbating pest problems and use of more fertilizers and insecticides, which can wind up in the water supply. Plus, some land currently held fallow in the Conservation Reserve Program is likely to be put back to work. The complex issues throw environmentalists into a briar patch. "I hate talking about ethanol," says Dan Becker, head of the Sierra Club's global warming program. "There are ways ethanol can be a boon to the environment, there are ways that it could be a disaster for the environment, and the devil's in the details."

LOGISTICS

Perhaps nothing illustrates the limits of an ethanol-fueled future better than the push for E-85—a mix that is 85 percent ethanol and 15 percent gasoline. It's available in only 1,000 of the nation's 180,000 gas stations, and Big Oil-branded stations haven't been quick to offer E-85. Ethanol boosters are hoping independent gas stations will step in, but it's costly. Trying to expand E-85's availability, the House is likely to pass a bill this year that will direct federal agencies to figure how to make the switchover more cheaply. Rep. Bart Gordon, chair of the House Science and Technology Committee, said such a move is necessary "if this country is serious about reducing our dependence on foreign oil."

Congress has been far more tentative in dealing with bigger delivery questions. No pipelines exist to move ethanol from the Midwest the way that gasoline is pumped out of the Gulf Coast; rail works well now to transport most ethanol, but 25 percent moves by truck (burning diesel petroleum along the way). As production increases, the transportation strain is sure to worsen.

And even if E-85 were widely available tomorrow, it could be pumped only into the 2.5 percent of the nation's cars that are flexible fuel vehicles. Automakers have pledged to churn out many more, but Congress created a perverse incentive allowing them to produce more gas guzzlers if they manufacture enough flex fuel cars. Carmakers earned enough of a break on their Corporate Average Fuel Economy Standards that the nation will burn 17 billion more gallons of gasoline from 2001 to 2008 as a result.

Thanks to such loopholes and foot dragging on improvement in CAFE standards, average new vehicle efficiency has dropped since 1988—a problem that comes home to roost with ethanol. Because of its lower energy content, it takes 1.5 gallons of ethanol to drive as far as 1 gallon of gasoline. Consumer Reports calculates E-85 ended up costing motorists about a dollar extra per gallon last year because of the need to buy more fuel. Renewable fuels lobbyist Dinneen points out that carmakers could solve the problem with improved engine technology. But with the fleet on U.S. roads now, and gasoline consumption continuing to creep upward, even today's incredible growth in ethanol production barely makes a dent in the nation's oil dependence. Ethanol now amounts to just 4.3 percent of gasoline sold by volume, and just 2.9 percent by energy content.

While corn-based ethanol production has room to grow, the industry acknowledges there's a ceiling—about 15 billion gallons yearly by most accounts, or three times the production in 2006. That's 20 billion gallons short of Bush's renewable fuels goal. Even with alternatives like natural gas vehicles, plug-in hybrids, or hydrogen cars, major advances in ethanol are necessary.

In the laboratory, so-called cellulosic ethanol can be wrung from fibrous materials like cornhusks and rice hulls, as well as fast-growing reedy crops that require little fertilizer or tending, like switch grass, and timber industry excess. This would ease reliance on edible grain and spread the economic benefits beyond corn communities. Another bonus: Biotech enzymes rather than heat energy would break down the cellulose to fuel, reducing greenhouse gases to a fraction of those produced by corn.

But it has never been tried commercially, and it's unlikely that the fuel will go from zero to 20 billion gallons in 10 years. Just to get to 1 billion gallons of ethanol production, the corn industry took 13 years. The government estimates the capital cost of cellulosic is very likely five times that of corn. The expense surely would be driven down if production scales up, but a "chicken and egg problem" exists, says Harkin. "Investors are not investing in cellulosic plants because there's no supply," he says. "And farmers are not planting switch grass or other energy crops because there's no market." He has pledged to "jump-start" both demand and supply with research money and loan guarantees in a new farm bill.

But it will take more than money for new cellulosic technology to substantially weaken the grip of the nation's oil addiction. Lee Lynd, Dartmouth College engineering professor and cellulosic pioneer, who founded Mascoma, a company that is building a pilot plant outside Rochester, N.Y., believes cellulosic will make "a much more limited contribution to energy supply" if behaviors don't change as well as technologies. Ethanol would make its greatest dent if Americans drove less and highly efficient cars were deployed widely, he says. Others agree. "Ethanol has a role to play in making the nation's energy situation more reliable," says economist Robert Wescott. "But it's not a panacea." That brings the debate back to the nitty-gritty fuel economy and conservation issues politicians have been mostly avoiding for years. They'd rather feel good, for the time being, about ethanol.

The Price of Biofuels*

By David Rotman
Technology Review, January/February 2008

The irrational exuberance over ethanol that swept through the American corn belt over the last few years has given way to a dreary hangover, especially among those who invested heavily in the sprawling production facilities now dotting the rural landscape. It's the Midwest's version of the tech bubble, and in some ways, it is remarkably familiar: overeager investors enamored of a technology's seemingly unlimited potential ignore what, at least in retrospect, are obvious economic realities.

More than a hundred biofuel factories, clustered largely in the corn-growing states of Iowa, Minnesota, Illinois, Indiana, South Dakota, and Nebraska, will produce 6.4 billion gallons of ethanol this year, and another 74 facilities are under construction. Just 18 months ago, they were cash cows, churning out high-priced ethanol from low-priced corn, raising hopes of "energy independence" among politicians, and capturing the attention—and money—of venture capitalists from both the East and West Coasts.

Now ethanol producers are struggling, and many are losing money. The price of a bushel of corn rose to record highs during the year, exceeding $4.00 last winter before falling back to around $3.50 in the summer, then rebounding this fall to near $4.00 again. At the same time, ethanol prices plummeted as the market for the alternative fuel, which is still used mainly as an additive to gasoline, became saturated. In the face of these two trends, profit margins vanished.

The doldrums of the ethanol market reflect the predictable boom-and-bust cycle of any commodity: high prices drive increased production, and soon the market is oversupplied, causing prices to crash. But the large-scale use of corn-derived ethanol as a transportation fuel has economic problems all its own. Even though crude oil is at near record prices, and companies that use ethanol in their gasoline receive a federal tax credit of 51 cents per gallon, ethanol struggles to compete economically. And with limited infrastructure in place to distribute and sell the biofuel, demand will remain uncertain for the foreseeable future.

More alarming, the boom in ethanol production is driving up the price of food. Of the record 93 million acres of corn planted in the United States in 2007, about 20 percent went to ethanol. Since most of the rest is used to feed animals, the prices of beef, milk, poultry, and pork are all affected by increases in the cost of corn. The international Organization for Economic Cooperation and Development (OECD) recently warned that the "rapid growth of the biofuels industry" could bring about fundamental shifts in agricultural markets worldwide and could even "cause food shortages."

All this comes at a time when the need for alternatives to petroleum-based transportation fuels is becoming urgent. At press time, the price of crude oil was near $90 a barrel. And worries about the impact of greenhouse-gas emissions from the roughly 142 billion gallons of gasoline used every year in the United States are deepening. Expanded use of biofuels is central to the federal government's long-term energy strategy. In his State of the Union speech on January 23, 2007, President Bush set the goal of producing 35 billion gallons of renewable and alternative fuels by 2017, citing the need for independence from foreign oil. The U.S. Department of Energy has set the similar goal of replacing 30 percent of gasoline use with biofuel use by 2030.

Hitting both targets, however, will require significant technological breakthroughs. In the United States, for now, ethanol means the corn-derived version. (Brazilian producers were expected to make 4.97 billion gallons of ethanol in 2007, mostly from sugarcane; but that semitropical crop is agriculturally viable in only a few parts of the United States.) Even proponents of corn ethanol say that its production levels cannot go much higher than around 15 billion gallons a year, which falls far short of Bush's goal.

While President Bush and other advocates of biofuels have often called for ethanol to be made from alternative feedstocks such as switchgrass—a plant native to the U.S. prairie states, where it grows widely—the required technology is, according to most estimates, at least four to five years from commercial viability, Meanwhile, advanced biological techniques for creating novel organisms that produce other biofuels, such as hydrocarbons, are still in the lab. So far, researchers are making quantities that wouldn't even fill the tank of a large SUV.

The economic woes and market limitations of corn ethanol are a painful reminder of the immense difficulties facing developers of new biofuels. "The bottom line is that you're going to have to make fuel cheap," says Frances Arnold, a professor of chemical engineering and biochemistry at Caltech. "We can all make a little bit of something. But you have got to make a lot of it, and you have got to make it cheaply. The problem is so huge that your technology has to scale up and do it at a price that is competitive. Everyone is going to be competing on price alone."

CORN BLIGHT

There may be no better place to get a realistic appraisal of biofuels than the Department of Applied Economics at the University of Minnesota. The large campus housing the department and the rest of the university's school of agriculture lies on a low hill in a quiet St. Paul neighborhood. Acres of fields where experiments are conducted spread out from the edge of the university. Nearby are the grounds of the Minnesota State Fair, a 12-day event that draws more than a million and a half visitors at the end of the summer.

The state is the fourth-largest producer of corn in the U.S., and much of its economy, even its culture, is intimately tied to the crop. The run-up of corn prices has been a boon for Minnesota's rural agricultural communities. And the governor and other state politicians have strongly pushed the use of ethanol as a transportation fuel. Still, you won't find much cheerleading for corn ethanol in the plain brick building that houses the department.

In his orderly office with its neat stacks of technical papers and farm reports, Vernon Eidman, an emeritus professor of agricultural economics, combines the authority of a scholar with the sternness of a Midwestern banker. "We could see this coming," he says, describing the current market plight of the ethanol producers. "It's not like [producers] didn't know it was coming. At least, they should have known it." In 2006 they "made profits like they never had before," Eidman says. "And that's a major factor that led to this tremendous buildup."

The numbers speak for themselves. Eidman's calculations show what it costs, given varying prices of corn, for a new, moderate-size facility to produce ethanol. At $4.00 a bushel of corn, ethanol production costs $1.70 a gallon; to gain a 12 percent return on equity, the producers need to sell ethanol at $1.83 a gallon. Then Eidman shows his figures for the prices that petroleum companies are paying when they buy ethanol to blend with their gasoline: this December, prices were about $1.90 a gallon, and bids for 2008 range between $1.75 and a $1.80 a gallon. In other words, the profit margins for ethanol producers are extremely tight. To make matters worse, Eidman says, production capacity, which was around 5.4 billion gallons at the beginning of 2007, is expected to reach 12.5 billion gallons by 2010.

While swelling ethanol production has led to worries about oversupply, the other side of the market equation is actually a cause for greater concern: the future demand for ethanol fuel is by no means certain. In a few parts of the country, particularly in the corn-belt states, drivers can buy fuel that's 85 percent ethanol. But for the most part, petroleum companies use ethanol at a concentration of 10 percent, to increase the oxygen content of their gasoline. Not only is such a market limited, but the 10-percent-ethanol blend delivers slightly reduced gas mileage, potentially damping consumer appetite for the fuel.

It is not just the short-term economics of ethanol that concern agricultural experts. They also warn that corn-derived ethanol is not the "green fuel" its advocates have described. That's because making ethanol takes a lot of energy, both to grow the corn and, even more important, to run the fermentation facilities that turn the sugar gleaned from the corn kernels into the alcohol that's used as fuel. Exactly how much energy it takes has been the subject of intense academic debate in various journals during the last few years.

According to calculations done by Minnesota researchers, 54 percent of the total energy represented by a gallon of ethanol is offset by the energy required to process the fuel; another 24 percent is offset by the energy required to grow the corn. While about 25 percent more energy is squeezed out of the biofuel than is used to produce it, other fuels yield much bigger gains, says Stephen Polasky, a professor of ecological and environmental economics at Minnesota. Making ethanol is "not a cheap process," he says. "From my perspective, the biggest problem [with corn ethanol] is just the straight-out economics and the costs. The energy input/output is not very good."

The high energy requirements of ethanol production mean that using ethanol as fuel isn't all that much better for the environment than using gasoline. One might think that burning the biofuel would release only the carbon dioxide that corn captures as it grows. But that simplified picture, which has often been conjured up to support the use of ethanol fuel, doesn't withstand closer scrutiny.

In fact, Polasky says, the fossil fuels needed to raise and harvest corn and produce ethanol are responsible for significant carbon emissions. Not only that, but the cultivation of corn also produces two other potent greenhouse gases: nitric oxide and methane. Polasky calculates that corn-derived ethanol is responsible for greenhouse-gas emissions about 15 to 20 percent below those associated with gasoline: "The bottom line is that you're getting a slight saving in terms of greenhouse gas emissions, but not much."

If corn-derived ethanol has had little impact on energy markets and greenhouse-gas emissions, however, its production could have repercussions throughout the agricultural markets. Not only are corn prices up, but so are soybean prices, because farmers planted fewer soybeans to make room for corn.

In the May/June 2007 issue of *Foreign Affairs*, C. Ford Runge, a professor of applied economics and law at Minnesota, cowrote an article titled "How Biofuels Could Starve the Poor," which argued that "the enormous volume of corn required by the ethanol industry is sending shock waves through the food system." Six months later, sitting in a large office from which he directs the university's Center for International Food and Agricultural Policy, Runge seems bemused by the criticism that his article received from local politicians and those in the ethanol business. But he is steadfast in his argument: "It is clearly the case that milk prices, bread prices, are all rising at three times the average rate of increase of the last 10 years. It's appreciable, and it is beginning to be appreciated."

The recent OECD report, released in early September, is just the latest confirmation of his warnings, says Runge. And because a larger percentage of their income goes to food, he says, "this is really going to hit poor people." Since the United States exports about 20 percent of its corn, the poor in the rest of the world are at particular risk. Runge cites the doubling in the price of tortillas in Mexico a year ago.

All these factors argue against the promise of corn ethanol as a solution to the energy problem. "My take," says Polasky, "is that [ethanol] is only going to be a bit player in terms of energy supplies." He calculates that even if all the corn planted in the United States were used for ethanol, the biofuel would still displace only 12 percent of gasoline consumption. "If I'm doing this for energy policy, I don't see the payback," he says. "If we're doing this as farm support policy, there may be more merit there. But we're going to have to go to the next generation of technology to have a significant impact on the energy markets."

SUPERBUGS

Since the oil crisis of the 1970s, when the price of a barrel of petroleum peaked, chemical and biological engineers have chased after ways to turn the nation's vast reserves of "cellulosic" material such as wood, agricultural residues, and perennial grasses into ethanol and other biofuels. Last year, citing another of President Bush's goals—reducing U.S. gasoline consumption by 20 percent in 10 years—the U.S. Department of Energy (DOE) announced up to $385 million in funding for six "biorefinery" projects that will use various technologies to produce ethanol from biomass ranging from wood chips to switchgrass.

According to a 2005 report by the DOE and the U.S. Department of Agriculture, the country has enough available forest and agricultural land to produce 1.3 billion tons of biomass that could go toward biofuels. Beyond providing a vast supply of cheap feedstock, cellulosic biomass could greatly increase the energy and environmental benefits of biofuels. It takes far less energy to grow cellulosic materials than to grow corn, and portions of the biomass can be used to help power the production process. (The sugarcane-based ethanol produced in Brazil also offers improvements over corn-based ethanol, thanks to the crop's large yields and high sugar content.)

But despite years of research and recent investment in scaling up production processes, no commercial facility yet makes cellulosic ethanol. The economic explanation is simple: it costs far too much to build such a facility. Cellulose, a long-chain polysaccharide that makes up much of the mass of woody plants and crop residues such as cornstalks, is difficult—and thus expensive—to break down.

Several technologies for producing cellulosic ethanol do exist. The cellulose can be heated at high pressure in the presence of oxygen to form synthesis gas, a mixture of carbon monoxide and hydrogen that is readily turned into ethanol and other fuels. Alternatively, industrial enzymes can break the cellulose down into sugars. The sugars then feed fermentation reactors in which microörganisms produce ethanol. But all these processes are still far too expensive to use commercially.

Even advocates of cellulosic ethanol put the capital costs of constructing a manufacturing plant at more than twice those for a corn-based facility, and other estimates range from three times the cost to five. "You can make cellulosic ethanol today, but at a price that is far from perfect," says Christopher Somerville, a plant biologist at the University of California, Berkeley, who studies how cellulose is formed and used in the cell walls of plants.

"Cellulose has physical and chemical properties that make it difficult to access and difficult to break down," explains Caltech's Arnold, who has worked on and off on the biological approach to producing cellulosic ethanol since the 1970s. For one thing, cellulose fibers are held together by a substance called lignin, which is "a bit like asphalt," Arnold says. Once the lignin is removed, the cellulose can be broken down by enzymes, but they are expensive, and existing enzymes are not ideal for the task.

Many researchers believe that the most promising way to make cellulosic biofuels economically competitive involves the creation—or the discovery—of "superbugs," microorganisms that can break down cellulose to sugars and then ferment those sugars into ethanol. The idea is to take what is now a multistep process requiring the addition of costly enzymes and turn it into a simple, one-step process, referred to in the industry as consolidated bioprocessing. According to Lee Lynd, a professor of engineering at Dartmouth College and cofounder of Mascoma, a company based in Cambridge, MA, that is commercializing a version of the technology, the consolidated approach could eventually produce ethanol at 70 cents a gallon. "It would be a transformational breakthrough," he says. "There's no doubt it would be attractive."

But finding superbugs has proved difficult. For decades, scientists have known of bacteria that can degrade cellulose and also produce some ethanol. Yet none can do the job quickly and efficiently enough to be useful for large-scale manufacturing.

Nature, Arnold explains, offers little help. "There are some organisms that break down cellulose," she says, "but the problem is that they don't make fuels, so that doesn't do you much good." An alternative, she says, is to genetically modify E. coli and yeast so that they secrete enzymes that degrade cellulose. But while many different kinds of enzymes could do the job, "most them don't like to be inserted into E. coli and yeast."

Arnold, however, is optimistic that the right organism will be discovered. "You never know what will happen tomorrow," she says, "whether it's done using synthetic biology or someone just scrapes one off the bottom of their shoe."

She didn't quite scrape it off her shoe, but Susan Leschine, a microbiologist at the University of Massachusetts, Amherst, believes she just might have stumbled on a bug that will do the job. She found it in a soil sample collected more than a decade ago from the woods surrounding the Quabbin Reservoir, about 15 miles from her lab. The Quabbin sample was just one of many from around the world that Leschine was studying, so it was several years before she finished analyzing it. But when she did, she realized that one of its bacteria, Clostridium phytofermentans, had extraordinary properties. "It decomposes nearly all the components of the plant, and it forms ethanol as the main product," she says. "It produces prodigious amounts of ethanol."

Leschine founded a company in Amherst, Sun Ethanol, that will attempt to scale up ethanol production using the bacterium. There's "a long way to go," she acknowledges, but she adds that "what we have is very different, and that gives us a leg up. We already have a microbe and have demonstrated it on real feedstocks." Leschine says that other useful microbes are probably waiting to be discovered: a single soil sample, after all, contains hundred of thousands of varieties. "In this zoo of microbes," she says, "we can think that there are others with similar properties out there."

BLOOMING PRAIRIES

Whether ethanol made from cellulosic biomass is good or bad for the environment, however, depends on what kind of biomass it is and how it is grown.

In his office in St. Paul, David Tilman, a professor of ecology at the University of Minnesota, pulls out a large aerial photo of a field sectioned into a neat grid. Even from the camera's vantage point far above the ground, the land looks poor. In one plot are thin rows of grasses, the sandy soil visible beneath. Tilman says the land was so infertile that agricultural use of it had been abandoned. Then he and his colleagues scraped off any remaining topsoil. "No farmer has land this bad," he says.

In a series of tests, Tilman grew a mixture of native prairie grasses (including switchgrass) in some of the field's plots and single species in others. The results show that a diverse mix of grasses, even grown in extremely infertile soil, "could be a valuable source of biofuels," he says. "You could make more ethanol from an acre [of the mixed grasses] than you could from an acre of corn." Better yet, in a paper published in *Science*, Tilman showed that the prairie grasses could be used to make ethanol that is "carbon negative": the grasses might consume and store more carbon dioxide than is released by producing and burning the fuel made from them.

The findings are striking because they suggest an environmentally beneficial way to produce massive amounts of biofuels without competing with food crops. By 2050, according to Tilman, the world will need a billion hectares more land for food. "That's the land mass of the entire United States just to feed the world," he says. "If you did a lot of biofuels on [arable] land—it is very easy to envision a billion hectares for biofuels—you will have no nature left and no reserve of land after 50 years." Instead, Tilman argues, it makes sense to grow biomass for fuels on relatively infertile land no longer used for agriculture.

But down the hill from Tilman's office, his colleagues in the applied-economics department worry about the practical issues involved in using large amounts of biomass to make fuel. For one thing, they point out, the technology and infrastructure that could efficiently handle and transport the bulky biomass still need to be developed. And since the plant material will be expensive to move around, biofuel production facilities will have to be built close to the sources of feedstock—probably within 50 miles.

The amount of biomass needed to feed even one medium-size ethanol facility is daunting. Eidman calculates that a facility producing 50 million gallons per year would require a truck loaded with biomass to arrive every six minutes around the clock. What's more, he says, the feedstock is "not free": it will cost around $60 to $70 a ton, or about 75 cents per gallon of ethanol. "That's where a lot of people get fooled," he adds.

Since no commercial cellulosic facility has been built, says Eidman, it is difficult to analyze the specific costs of various technologies. Overall, he suggests, the economics look "interesting"—but cellulosic ethanol will have to compete with corn-derived biofuels and get down to something like $1.50 a gallon. Eidman believes it will be at least 2015 before biofuels made from cellulose "are much of a factor" in the market.

EXILED

While chemical engineers, microbiologists, agronomists, and others struggle to find ways of making cellulosic ethanol commercially competitive, a few synthetic biologists and metabolic engineers are focusing on an entirely different strategy. More than fifteen hunched miles away from the Midwest's corn belt, several California-based, venture-backed startups founded by pioneers in the fledgling field of synthetic biology are creating new microorganisms designed to make biofuels other than ethanol.

Ethanol, after all, is hardly an ideal fuel. A two-carbon molecule, it has only two-thirds the energy content of gasoline, which is a mix of long-chain hydrocarbons. Put another way, it would take about a gallon and a half of ethanol to yield the same mileage as a gallon of gasoline. And because ethanol mixes with water, a costly distillation step is required at the end of the fermentation process. What's more, because ethanol is more easily contaminated with water than hydrocarbons are, it can't be shipped in the petroleum pipelines used to cheaply distribute gasoline throughout the United States. Ethanol must be shipped in specialized rail cars (trucks, with their relatively small payloads, are usually far too expensive), adding to the cost of the fuel.

So instead of ethanol, the California startups are planning to produce novel hydrocarbons. Like ethanol, the new compounds are fermented from sugars, but they are designed to more closely resemble gasoline, diesel, and even jet fuel. "We took a look at ethanol," says Neil Renninger, senior vice president of development and cofounder of Amyris Biotechnologies in Emeryville, CA, "and realized the limitations and the desire to make something that looked more like conventional fuels. Essentially, we wanted to make hydrocarbons. Hydrocarbons are what are currently in fuels, and hydrocarbons make the best fuels because we have designed our engines to work with them." If the researchers can genetically engineer microbes that produce such compounds, it will completely change the economics of biofuels.

The problem is that nature offers no known examples of microorganisms that can ferment sugars into the types of hydrocarbons useful for fuel. So synthetic biologists have to start from scratch. They identify promising metabolic reactions in other organisms and insert the corresponding genes into E. coli or yeast, recombining metabolic pathways until they yield the desired products.

At LS9 in San Carlos, CA, researchers are turning E. coli into a hydrocarbon producer by reëngineering its fatty-acid metabolism (see "Better Biofuels," *Forward*, July/August 2007). Stephen del Cardayré, LS9's vice president of research and development, says the company decided to focus on fatty acids because organisms naturally produce them in abundance, as a way of storing energy. "We wanted to take advantage of a pathway that [naturally] makes a lot of stuff," del Cardayré says. "Just grab your middle." Del Cardayré and his coworkers use many of the existing pathways in E. coli's fatty-acid metabolism but divert them near the end of the metabolic cycle. Since fatty acids consist of a hydrocarbon chain with a carboxyl group, it is relatively straightforward to make the hydrocarbon fuels. "Think of it as a highway," says del Cardayré. "Near the end of the highway, we add a detour, a pathway we designed and stuck there, so the fatty acids have a better place to go. We pull them off and chemically change them, using this new synthetic pathway that takes them to products that we want."

Amyris, too, is taking the synthetic-biology approach, but instead of tweaking fatty-acid metabolism, it is working on pathways that produce isoprenoids, a large class of natural compounds. So far, however, both LS9 and Amyris are making their biofuels a few liters at a time. And while the companies have ambitious schedules for commercializing their technologies—both claim that their processes will be ready by 2010—improving the yield and the speed of their reactions remains a critical challenge. "It's where most of the biological work is going on," says Renninger. "We still have a little way to go, and that little way is very important."

If eventually commercialized, the hydrocarbon biofuels made by LS9 and Amyris could overcome many of the economic disadvantages of ethanol. Unlike ethanol, hydrocarbons separate from water during the production process, so no energy-intensive distillation step is necessary. And hydrocarbon biofuels could be shipped in existing petroleum pipelines. "It's all about cost," says Robert Walsh, president of LS9. But a critical factor will be the price of feedstock, he says. "We want dirt-cheap sugars."

Indeed, the synthetic-biology startups face the same problem that established ethanol producers do: corn is not an inexpensive source of biofuels. "The next generation [of feedstock] will be cellulosic," says John Melo, CEO of Amyris. "But we are not sure which cellulosic technology will emerge as the winner." Whichever technology prevails, Melo says, Amyris expects to be able to "bolt it" onto its fermentation process, giving the company the advantages of both cheap cellulosic feedstocks and practical hydrocarbon fuels.

For now, though, the lack of an alternative to corn is driving Amyris right out of the country. The company, which plans to retrofit existing ethanol plants so that they can make hydrocarbons, will initially work with Brazilian biofuel facilities that are using sugarcane as a feedstock. Given the price of corn and the amount of energy needed to produce it, Melo says, Brazilian cane offers the most "viable, sustainable" way to make biofuels today.

NO CHOICE

Even in a Silicon Valley culture that reveres successful venture capitalists, Vinod Khosla has a special place of honor. A cofounder of Sun Microsystems in the early 1980s, Khosla later joined the venture capital firm Kleiner Perkins Caufield and Byers, where in the late 1990s and early 2000s he gained a reputation for ignoring the dotcom excitement in favor of a series of esoteric startups in the far less glamorous field of optical networking. When several of the startups sold for billions of dollars to large companies gearing up their infrastructure for the Internet boom, Khosla became, in the words of one overheated headline of the time, "The No. 1 VC on the Planet."

These days Khosla, who is now among the world's richest people (the Forbes 400 lists him at 317, with a net worth of $1.5 billion), is putting most of his investments in alternative energies. He counts among his portfolio companies more than a dozen biofuel startups—synthetic-biology companies LS9 and Amyris, cellulosic companies like Mascoma, and corn ethanol companies like Cilion, based in Goshen, CA. But to call Khosla simply an investor in biofuels would greatly understate his involvement. In the last several years, he has emerged as one of the world's leading advocates of the technology, promoting its virtues and freely debating any detractors (see *Q&A*, March/April 2007).

Khosla seems exasperated by the biofuels naysayers. Climate change, he says, is "by far the biggest issue" driving his interest in biofuels. If we want to head off climate change and decrease consumption of gasoline, "there are no alternatives" to using cellulosic biofuels for transportation. "Biomass is the only feedstock in sufficient quantities to cost-effectively replace oil," he says. "Nothing else exists." Hybrid and electric vehicles, he adds, are "just toys."

In particular, argues Khosla, any transportation technology needs to compete in China and India, the fastest growing automotive markets in the world. "It's no big deal to sell a million plug-in electrics in a place like California," he says. The difficulty is selling a $20,000 hybrid vehicle in India. "No friggin' chance. And any technology not adoptable by China and India is irrelevant to climate change," he says. "Environmentalists don't focus on scalability. If you can't scale it up, it is just a toy. Hence the need for biofuels. Hence biofuels from biomass."

In a number of opinion papers posted on the website of Khosla Ventures, a firm he started in 2004 that has invested heavily in biofuels and other environmental technologies, Khosla envisions biofuel production rapidly increasing over the next 20 years. According to his numbers, production of corn ethanol will level off at 15 billion gallons a year by 2014, but cellulosic ethanol will increase steadily, reaching 140 billion gallons by 2030. At that point, he predicts, biofuels will be cheap and abundant enough to replace gasoline for almost all purposes.

While Khosla readily acknowledges the limitations of corn-derived ethanol, he says it has been an important "stepping-stone": the market for corn ethanol has created an infrastructure and market for biofuels in general, removing many of the business risks of investing in cellulosic ethanol. "The reason that I like [corn ethanol] is that its trajectory leads to cellulosic ethanol," he says. "Without corn ethanol, no one would be investing in cellulosics."

But back in the Midwest, there is a "show me" attitude toward such blue-sky projections, and there are lingering questions about just how the nation's vast agricultural infrastructure will switch over to biomass. If Khosla's projections prove out, "then wonderful," says the University of Minnesota's Runge. "Meanwhile, we're stuck in reality." Perhaps the main point of contention, Runge suggests, is whether corn ethanol will in fact lead to new technologies—or stand in their way. "It is my opinion that corn ethanol is a barrier to converting to cellulosics," he says, pointing to the inertia caused by political and business interests heavily invested in corn ethanol and its infrastructure.

Runge is not alone in his skepticism. "Unless the cost is reduced significantly, cellulosic ethanol is going nowhere," says Wally Tyner, a professor of agricultural economics at Purdue University. Making cellulosic ethanol viable will require either a "policy mechanism" to encourage investment in new technologies or a "phenomenal breakthrough"—and "the likelihood of that is not too high," Tyner says. Farmers and ethanol producers currently have no incentive to take on the risks of changing technologies, he adds. There is "no policy bridge" to help make the transition. "The status quo won't do it."

Despite the sharp differences of opinion, there's still some common ground between people like Khosla, whose unbridled faith in innovation has been nurtured by the successes of Silicon Valley, and the Midwesterners whose pragmatism was forged by the competitive economics of agriculture. In particular, most observers agree that annual production of corn-derived ethanol will level off within a few years. After that, any growth in biofuel production will need to come from new technologies.

But if cellulosic biofuels are to begin replacing gasoline within five to ten years, facilities will need to start construction soon. This fall, Range Fuels, a company based in Broomfield, CO, announced that it had begun work in Georgia on what it claims is the country's first commercial-scale cellulosic-ethanol plant. The Range facility, which will use thermochemical technology to make ethanol from wood chips, is scheduled to reach a capacity of 20 million gallons in 2008 and eventually increase to 100 million gallons a year. Meanwhile, Mascoma has announced several demonstration units, including a facility in Tennessee that will be the first cellulosic-ethanol plant built to use switchgrass. But these production plants are federally subsidized or are a result of partnerships with state development organizations; attracting private investment for commercial-scale production will be another matter.

Indeed, ramping up the capacity of cellulosic-ethanol production will be a huge and risky challenge, says Colin South, president of Mascoma. "When people talk about cellulosic ethanol as if it is an industry, it is an unfair portrayal," he says. "There are a number of pilot plants, but none of them have gotten out of the pilot scale. We still need to show we can actually run these in the form of an operating chemical plant." South says that Mascoma hopes to begin construction of a commercial plant in 2009 and have it up and running by early 2011. But he adds that the company will only proceed when "the numbers are good enough."

Perhaps the most crucial number, however, will be the price of crude oil. If it stays high, cellulosic-ethanol production could become economically competitive much sooner. But few people, least of all the investors who would risk hundred of millions of dollars on new plants, are willing to take that bet. Many remember the late 1970s, when the federal government earmarked roughly a billion dollars to fund biomass-related research, only to abandon it when crude-oil prices fell in the early 1980s. And while the price of a barrel of crude hovered in the mid-$90s this fall, and wholesale gas prices reached $2.50 a gallon, biofuel experts say they cannot count on such high prices. Many producers of next-generation biofuels say they want to be competitive with crude oil at around $45 a barrel to ensure long-term viability in the market.

Indeed, announcements about new cellulosic-ethanol plants tend to obscure the fact that the technology is still not economically viable. Gregory Stephanopoulos, a professor of chemical engineering at MIT, describes himself as "very optimistic" about the future of biofuels. But even he is quick to add that it will take another 10 years to optimize production processes for cellulosic biofuels. Among myriad other problems, he says, is the need for more robust and versatile microbes to make them.

In a small conference room outside his office, Stephanopoulos takes out a pencil and paper and begins to draw a series of circles. You can imagine, he says, a biorefinery surrounded by sources of different types of biomass. He connects the circles at a central point, making lines like spokes on a wheel. You could, he goes on, imagine pipelines from these sources. What if the biomass were treated and piped to the biorefinery as a slurry? Stephanopoulos would be the first to acknowledge that such an ambitious infrastructure would take years to put in place, and that the idea raises numerous technical and engineering questions. But for the rest of the interview, the drawing sits patiently on the table—a simple target.

Fuel for Thought*

By Frances Cerra Whittelsey
Smithsonian, September 2005

Every few weeks, [illegible] to a Chinese restaurant and fills a couple of five-gallon pails with [illegible] Back in her garage, the 59-year-old philanthropist and grandmo[illegible]ough a cloth filter and then pours it into a custom-made second [illegible]003 Volkswagen Jetta diesel station wagon. Once the car is warme[illegible]fuel toggle on the dashboard to switch to the vegetable oil. Wher[illegible]he's trailed by the appetizing odor of egg rolls.

Sean Parks of Davis, [illegible]cts his cooking oil from a fish-and-chips restaurant and a corn-dog shop. He purifies it chemically in a 40-gallon reactor that he built himself for about $200. The processed oil can be used even when his car's engine is cold, at a cost of about 70 cents a gallon. Parks, 30, a geographer for the U.S. Forest Service, makes enough processed oil to fuel his family's two cars.

Kantor and Parks are willing to go the extra mile to reduce their dependence on petroleum and cut down on pollution. But these days environmentalists are not the only ones banking on biodiesel, as diesel-engine fuel made from vegetable oil is known. Entrepreneurs and soybean farmers are creating a new biodiesel industry, with some 300 retail biodiesel pumps nationwide so far. Commercial production of biodiesel grew 25 percent in 2004, making it the fastest-growing alternative fuel in the United States. Even the singer Willie Nelson recently started a company to market the fuel at truck stops.

The greening of the diesel engine is a return to its roots. Rudolf Diesel, the German engineer who in 1892 invented the engine that bears his name, boasted that it ran on peanut and castor oil. "Motive power can be produced by the agricultural transformation of the heat of the sun," he said. The inventor foresaw a future of virtually unlimited renewable energy from plants, but the idea slipped into obscurity because petroleum was so much cheaper than vegetable oil.

A century later, customers for commercial biodiesel include the U.S. Postal Service, the U.S. Army, the Forest Service, the city of Denver and numerous private truck fleets. Almost all use blends of 2 to 20 percent biodiesel mixed with standard petroleum diesel. The mixture helps federal and state agencies comply with a 2000 executive order by President Clinton mandating less petroleum consumption. Minnesota recently became the first state to require that all diesel fuel sold there be 2 percent biodiesel. Daimler-Chrysler's 2005 diesel Jeep Liberty comes off the production line with its tank filled with a 5 percent biodiesel mixture.

The major obstacle to wider use is price. Pure biodiesel sells for $2.50 to $3 a gallon, about 50 cents to $1 more than petrodiesel. To spur biodiesel's use, some European nations levy no taxes on it, and in October 2004, President Bush signed into law a 50 cent to $1 credit to fuel manufacturers for every gallon of biodiesel blended into petrodiesel.

Diesel engines differ from gasoline engines in their use of high pressure rather than a spark plug to ignite the fuel and drive the pistons. Diesel engines can run on fuel that is heavier than gasoline, making it possible to substitute filtered waste grease for petrodiesel. Both used and virgin vegetable oil contain glycerin—a syrupy liquid used in hand lotions. It burns well in a hot engine, as in Etta Kantor's retrofitted diesel, but clogs a cold one. Removing the glycerin yields biodiesel, which is suitable for even a cold engine.

Skeptics have questioned whether it takes more fossil fuel to produce biodiesel—to fertilize crops, transport them and press them for their oil—than the resulting biodiesel replaces. But Jim Duffield, an agricultural economist with the U.S. Department of Agriculture (USDA), says the "few lone voices" who still make that point have not kept up with improvements in agriculture and biodiesel technology. Indeed, a study by the U.S. Departments of Agriculture and Energy in 1998 and another in 2002 for the French government show that soybeans and canola oil yield three to four times more energy than is needed to make the fuel. (Similar skepticism has also dogged ethanol, a corn-based fuel mixed with gasoline to create gasohol. But USDA and other studies show that today's ethanol provides up to 30 percent more energy than it takes to make it.)

Another benefit of burning biodiesel is cleaner air. Compared with fossil fuels, it emits less carbon monoxide and hydrocarbons, as well as sulfur compounds related to acid rain. Pure biodiesel also substantially reduces overall emission of carbon dioxide, a major contributor to climate change, because the plants from which the oil was extracted absorbed atmospheric carbon dioxide while they were growing. A bus running on pure biodiesel would emit 32 percent less particulate matter, which has been implicated in the dramatic increase in asthma cases in cities. The only air pollution downside of pure biodiesel, according to the 1998 U.S. study, is a slight increase of smog-inducing nitrogen oxides.

The inspiration for the do-it-yourself biodiesel movement came from Joshua Tickell, 29, of Baton Rouge. While studying in Germany in 1996, he was astonished to see a farmer using canola oil to run his tractor. Back in the States, Tickell used his last student loan check to help buy a 1986 diesel Winnebago. He painted sunflowers on his "Veggie Van" and, for two years beginning in 1997, toured the country, towing a simple reactor that turned restaurant oil into biodiesel. In 2000, he coauthored what would become the biodiesel bible, *From the Fryer to the Fuel Tank*. "My goal is very simply to make OPEC obsolete," he says.

Vegetable power also appeals to 50-year-old Marty Borruso, a chemist and partner in Environmental Alternatives in New York City, who insists he's no "environmental crazy."' He produces biodiesel for a generator that makes electricity and hot water for an 87-family apartment house. He also sells the fuel to a tow truck fleet and anyone who comes to a pump he operates next to his production facility in Staten Island. In a 7,000-gallon reactor, Borruso processes out-of-date virgin vegetable oils, which he buys at a steep discount, and free grease from a fried chicken emporium. But he spurns grease from a seafood restaurant. "It smells like calamari," he says. "I love calamari, but I don't know if I want to drive it."

On average, fast-food restaurants in any major U.S. city generate about 22 pounds of waste grease each year per city resident, according to a 1998 study by the National Renewable Energy Laboratory (NREL). The National Biodiesel Board, a trade group in Jefferson City, Missouri, estimates that more than 2.5 billion pounds of waste cooking grease are available annually—enough to make 100 million gallons of biodiesel.

Of course, America's appetite for petroleum is huge: 2004 consumption was nearly 315 billion gallons, including 139 billion in gasoline and 41 billion diesel. Robert McCormick, a fuels engineer at NREL, says that biodiesel could displace 5 percent of the petrodiesel used in the United States within ten years. To replace more will require growing vegetable crops specifically for fuel—and America's soybean farmers are standing by. Some proponents envision growing aquatic algae—richer in oil than any other plant—in pools next to electric power stations. In an ecological two-for-one, the smokestack carbon dioxide would feed the algae, which would churn out biodiesel.

Grass-roots fans aren't waiting. Kantor, who paid $1,400 to outfit her VW diesel with a second fuel tank, says she gets nearly 200 miles per petrodiesel gallon. "This is not about money," says Kantor, who speaks at schools about protecting the environment. "I'm doing this to set an example."

Biodiesel*

Homegrown Oil

By Greg Pahl

The Mother Earth News, February/March 2006

Imagine a renewable, clean-burning fuel that can be produced from local crops and could power a large number of existing vehicles—starting now. That fuel is biodiesel, which is made primarily of vegetable oil and alcohol and can be used in any modern diesel engine.

In the last few years, many farmers, environmentalists and other renewable energy advocates have begun promoting biodiesel as an alternative fuel that could replace at least a portion of the world's petroleum-based diesel fuel market. Using biodiesel is an idea with widespread appeal because it pollutes far less than petroleum-based diesel and could help reduce our need for foreign oil.

In fact, biodiesel already is widely used in Europe, where tax policies are structured to support its use. In Germany—where diesel engines power close to 40 percent of passenger cars—more than 1,800 filling stations offer biodiesel at a price competitive with that of petroleum-based diesel fuel.

In the United States, the public is just becoming aware of the potential of biodiesel, but the development of a biodiesel industry is already well underway. Many Midwestern soybean farmers have joined forces with other entrepreneurs to build biodiesel production capacity and infrastructure. At the same time, federal and state agencies and independent organizations have been testing biodiesel performance and setting production standards. With that firm foundation, the commercial biodiesel industry is growing rapidly, and biodiesel is becoming more accessible to drivers eager to fill their cars with this eco-friendly fuel. However, biodiesel can be used for more than fueling diesel-powered cars or trucks. In fact, the majority of the world's heavy-transportation is diesel-powered, and all of these vehicles could be powered by biodiesel: buses, trucks, tractors, heavy machinery, boats and even trains. Biodiesel also can be used in any diesel-powered electrical generator, as well as in oil-fired furnaces and boilers (see "Heat Your Home with

Biodiesel," December/ January 2004, or at www.MotherEarthNews.com).

LIQUID SOLAR ENERGY

Although "diesel" is part of its name, pure biodiesel does not contain any petroleum-based diesel, also called "petrodiesel." Instead, biodiesel is created from organic matter. It can be made from virtually any vegetable oil, including soy, corn, rapeseed (canola), peanut or sunflower—as well as from recycled cooking oil, animal fats or even algae.

Biodiesel has been called "liquid solar energy" because its energy content is derived from plants that capture solar energy during photosynthesis. The plants grown to produce biodiesel consume carbon dioxide (CO_2), so they naturally balance most of the CO_2 released when the fuel is combusted, offsetting a major contributing factor to global warming.

Using vegetable oil for fuel is not a new idea. When Rudolf Diesel invented the original diesel engine in the 1890s, he designed it to run on a wide range of fuels—including vegetable oils. But beginning in the early 1900s, diesel engines were adapted to burn mainly petrodiesel, a cheaper fuel. During the energy crisis of the 1970s, researchers began to reconsider vegetable oil fuels and found a simple method for turning vegetable oil into a usable diesel fuel. This process, called "transesterification," was developed in the late 1970s and early 1980s. It involves blending vegetable oil with alcohol, and adding a catalyst that will initiate the reaction that forms biodiesel.

MAKING BIODIESEL

Because the process for making biodiesel is relatively simple and can be extremely low-tech, it has attracted a global community of "home brewers." Although industrial-sized biodiesel facilities use high-tech equipment, the process is basically the same for a small-scale facility located in a garage or backyard shed.

Here's how the process works. Carefully measured amounts of alcohol and vegetable oil are mixed with the catalyst. The alcohol can be either ethanol or methanol. For making biodiesel, methanol is usually preferred over ethanol because it's less expensive and produces a more predictable reaction.

You can use one of two catalysts: sodium hydroxide or potassium hydroxide. Sodium hydroxide, which is commonly referred to as lye or caustic soda, is the same chemical used to unclog kitchen or bathroom drains. Potassium hydroxide can be used instead, but a larger quantity is required. These chemicals are dangerous and must be handled carefully.

Here's a basic example of how you would brew biodiesel, using methanol as the alcohol and sodium hydroxide (lye) as the catalyst. Methanol and lye are mixed to create sodium methoxide, which is then mixed with the vegetable oil and stirred or agitated—and sometimes heated. The catalyst causes the oil to react with the alcohol and form two byproducts: methyl esters (biodiesel) and glycerin. The biodiesel rises to the top of the tank while the glycerin and the catalyst settle at the bottom.

After about eight hours, the glycerin and catalyst are drawn off the bottom, leaving biodiesel in the tank. In most cases the biodiesel needs to be "washed" with water to remove any remaining traces of alcohol, glycerin and the catalyst. In this procedure, water is mixed with the biodiesel, allowed to separate from the oil for several days and then removed.

Home brewers sometimes skip the wash process, but most commercial producers must use it to meet industry standards. If used cooking oil is the feedstock, the process is essentially the same, but may require more lye and filtration.

FEEDING DEMAND

One advantage of biodiesel is that a variety of crops from around the world will produce essentially the same biodiesel fuel. Hundreds of oil-producing crops can be used to create biodiesel, but some produce more vegetable oil than others. Soybeans are the primary biodiesel feedstock in the United States. Although they are a relatively low-yielding oil crop, one advantage of using soybeans is that they require less nitrogen fertilizer than many other oil crops.

Worldwide, rapeseed (canola) is the primary biodiesel feedstock (84 percent of production), followed by sunflowers (13 percent).

Currently, total global output of biodiesel is between 425 and 570 million gallons annually, with about two-thirds of that capacity generated in Western Europe. In 2004, the United States produced about 30 million gallons of biodiesel. That doesn't go far toward meeting our need for oil: Every year, the United States consumes about 58 billion gallons of the petroleum fuels that biodiesel could potentially replace.

Just how much of that demand we could meet by expanding biodiesel production is the subject of much debate. One concern is that production of crops for biodiesel will always be limited by the amount of land needed to produce food. However, the United States has many resources that could be tapped immediately for biodiesel production.

We currently generate about 3 billion gallons of used frying oil every year. Assuming that half of this oil could be converted to biodiesel, that would represent about 2.5 percent of the current petrodiesel market. If half of the 11 billion pounds of animal fats produced in the United States could be processed into biodiesel, they would yield about 750 million gallons of biodiesel, or 1.25 percent of the petrodiesel market.

The 60 million acres of fallow U.S. cropland are another good resource for producing vegetable oil. If all this acreage were planted with rapeseed and yielded 100 gallons of oil per acre, that would produce another 6 billion gallons, or about 10 percent of the current petrodiesel marker.

The total estimated production from all of these sources comes to 8.25 billion gallons, or about 14 percent of the U.S. petrodiesel market. In Europe, biodiesel has the potential to replace somewhere between 10 percent and 15 percent of the current petrodiesel market.

However, this projection does not take into account potential biodiesel production from algae, a promising new oil crop. Pond algae may seem like a bizarre source of diesel fuel, but most of the world's petroleum resources were formed from vast amounts of algae that were transformed by heat and pressure over millions of years.

Today, algae can be grown in ponds in just a few days, and oil can be extracted directly from the harvested algae. Some experts predict that one acre of algae could yield an enormous amount of oil—3,654 gallons per year or more. Research on algae is still in the beginning stages, and any large-scale use of algae for biodiesel would require massive investments in production facilities. That would take many years and large amounts of money to develop, but it might be possible if the United States were willing to commit the resources to developing this renewable fuel.

BUYING INTO BIODIESEL

In May 2001, the first commercial biodiesel pump opened in Sparks, Nev., followed less than 24 hours later by another in San Francisco. Since then, biodiesel fuel stations and wholesale retailers have been increasing in numbers nationwide; there are now more than 600 retail fuel outlets in the United States. To find a retailer near you, visit www.biodiesel.org/buyingbiodiesel/guide.

The price of pure biodiesel has been significantly higher than diesel fuel. However, biodiesel can be mixed with petrodiesel in any percentage, which makes it possible to produce blends that are less expensive than 100 percent biodiesel. Biodiesel often is sold as B20 (20 percent biodiesel and 80 percent petrodiesel), a concentration that has demonstrated significant environmental benefits over petrodiesel, with only a small increase in cost to consumers.

For example, according to the most recent report from the U.S. Department of Energy, the average nationwide price of pure biodiesel was $3.40 per gallon in September 2005. In comparison, petrodiesel averaged $2.81 per gallon, and B20 cost just 10 cents more at $2.91 per gallon.

Biodiesel is catching on in many niche markets, largely because it is a cleaner-burning fuel. Biodiesel is free of lead, contains virtually no sulfur and produces lower quantities of cancer-causing particulate emissions than petrodiesel. In particular, using biodiesel in school buses makes a lot of sense. Young children are more susceptible than adults to the toxic and potentially cancer-causing emissions from petrodiesel. This fact has led more than 50 school boards across the nation to require that their buses use biodiesel fuel.

This cleaner-burning fuel also is an attractive option in recreation areas. Yellowstone National Park was the first national park to test biodiesel as a fuel, and the project was such a success that the National Park Service has introduced biodiesel to another 20 parks across the country. Biodiesel also is being used as vehicle fuel by numerous cities including Columbia, Mo.; Breckenridge, Colo.; and Missoula, Mont.; as well as by many universities, including Harvard and Purdue.

Europe has been the main focus of biodiesel activity for many years, but countries around the world are developing active biodiesel programs, including India, Brazil and Canada. It will take an enormous cooperative effort from the entire global community to wean ourselves from our present addiction to petroleum. Biodiesel is not the single solution to all our energy problems, but it can be part of the transition from our current near-total dependency on fossil fuels to the use of a wide range of renewable energy resources. At the same time, it would create jobs, assist farmers, reduce pollution and promote greater energy security.

3

The Sun and the Wind: Renewable Twins?

Editor's Introduction

Of all the alternative energy sources, the sun and the wind are perhaps the most intriguing. As naturally occurring phenomena, they are both clean and renewable. Moreover, wind power has been widely used for centuries. Yet, despite these traits, their contribution to global energy generation remains minor. A number of factors bear responsibility for this. In particular, many contend that the technology has not advanced far enough for wind and solar power to be cost-effective, especially when compared to fossil fuels. Nevertheless, researchers believe that wind and solar will soon emerge as vital assets in the effort to counteract global climate change and build a sustainable future. The articles in this chapter, "The Sun and the Wind: Renewable Twins," explore these energy sources, their shortcomings, and their vast potential.

Jim Motavalli offers an expansive analysis of wind energy in "Catching the Wind," the first piece in this section. Of particular interest is an almost allegorical dispute over a proposed wind farm off the coast of Cape Cod, in Massachusetts. Proponents claim the project would reduce greenhouse gas emissions in the region by one million tons per year. On the other hand, opponents believe such figures are exaggerated and object to the construction of towering windmills amid the natural beauty of Nantucket Sound

For those seeking to reduce their individual contribution to greenhouse gas emissions and save money on energy bills, small-scale wind power is becoming an ever more affordable option, as Greg Pahl demonstrates in "New and Improved Wind Power." While wind turbines are both large and expensive, if energy prices continue to rise and the federal government opts to provide tax subsidies to those who purchase them, they may become increasingly common.

Given the central role the sun plays in life on his planet, solar energy has long been regarded as a potential solution to all our energy woes. Yet, despite decades of hope, anticipation, and scientific effort, solar power plays a very minor role in worldwide energy production. Despite this apparent lack of progress, Steve Heckeroth believes solar energy is due for an upswing, as he explains in "Solar Is the Solution." Indeed, he claims a "solar-electric economy is well within our reach."

Aimee Cunningham examines several projects aimed at improving solar-cell technology in "Reaching for Rays: Scientists Work Toward a Solar-Based Energy System." She observes that silicon-based solar cells, of which most solar panels in use today are made, are unlikely to challenge the dominance of fossil fuels. However, researchers are more hopeful about the potential for cells made from organic sources and/or nanomaterials.

Catching the Wind*

By Jim Motavalli
E: The Environmental Magazine, January/February 2005

At the base of the Sagamore Bridge, the gateway to Cape Cod, is a nostalgia-inducing fake windmill that looks like it belongs with tulips and wooden shoes in an image of Holland's colorful past. In fact, it's advertising for a Christmas tree store, but its mere presence is an irony as the Cape is convulsed in an epic battle over some very real wind turbines. Cape Wind plans to build the first offshore wind park in the U.S. in Nantucket Sound, just five miles off the coast of some of the most exclusive real estate in America. If the project is built, it will at least temporarily set a record as the largest wind farm in the world, its 130 turbines producing 420 megawatts of electricity. If it is defeated by a well-funded opposition group with some highly placed political allies, it will be a resounding defeat for wind power in the U.S., but possibly just a minor setback for a worldwide renewable energy movement that is filling its sails with the inexhaustible power of the wind.

THE GROWING POWER OF WIND

Even as the world experiences ever-more-severe storms and sets new temperature records that are being linked to global warming, we're also setting new records for installed wind energy. The two phenomena might appear to be unrelated, but actually they're closely tied together. Wind energy is zero-emissions energy, a renewable resource that is one of our last, best hopes for staving off devastating climate change. Wind energy has grown 28 percent annually over the last five years, and the so-called "installed capacity" (the generating power of working wind turbines) doubles every three years: It is the fastest-growing energy source in the world. Some 6,000 megawatts of wind capacity—enough to power 1.5 million homes—are added annually.

The old-fashioned windmills that once pumped water for local farmers have been replaced with high-technology, high-efficiency industrial-grade turbines. The General Electric turbines scheduled to be installed by Cape Wind (resulting from GE's purchase of Enron's wind assets at fire-sale prices) offer a whopping 3.6 megawatts each, are 40 stories tall on thin towers, and boast three prop-like blades the length of two jumbo jets.

As *Business 2.0* reports, "Since 1985, the electric generating capacity of a typical windmill has gone from about 100 kilowatts of constant power to 1.5 megawatts, with a corresponding reduction in cost from 12 cents per kilowatt-hour to less than five cents." Because of federal tax credits (recently renewed until the end of 2005), the real cost of wind power is getting close to such perennials as nuclear, coal and natural gas, which explains the interest of big profit-oriented companies like GE. In 2001, 6,500 megawatts of new wind-generating capacity were installed worldwide, and by 2003 the world had 39,000 megawatts of installed wind power.

FASCINATING HISTORY

Wind technology has increased steadily since the first windmills for pumping water and grinding grain were developed in ancient Persia around 500 to 900 A.D. More than six million small windmills were installed in the U.S. between 1850 and 1970. They were small units producing the equivalent of one horsepower or less and their primary duties were supplying water for animals and human needs. Rural electrification in the 1930s made most of them obsolete, but many remained in place to serve as evocative backgrounds in Hollywood westerns.

Poul La Cour, a Danish inventor, built a practical four-blade windmill in 1891, and by 1917 windmills producing 25 kilowatts were in common use in Denmark (still a wind energy pioneer today). The first utility-scale wind generator was the 100-kilowatt Balaclava windmill, built on the shores of the Caspian Sea in 1931. Experimentation on large wind machines continued in the U.S., France, Germany, Great Britain and Denmark.

The U.S. government developed a newfound interest in wind power after the oil embargoes of the 1970s left the country feeling vulnerable about energy supplies. The U.S. Federal Wind Energy Program was created at that time, and California became a showplace for large-scale wind farms. Some 17,000 machines of 20 to 350 kilowatts (producing 1,700 megawatts in total) were installed between 1981 and 1990. A 15 percent federal energy credit helped, as did a 50 percent California energy credit (both were gone by the mid-1980s).

Unfortunately, many of the California windmills suffered from insufficient development time and operating difficulties, including the well-known Transpower wind farm in the Tehachapi Mountains. Compounding the difficulties, the tax credits were issued on the basis of "installed generator capacity" rather than the actual output of the wind turbines.

After many rushed American designs failed to deliver on their promises, the much healthier Danish wind business had captured 50 percent of the U.S. market by 1986. U.S. companies, including U.S. Windpower, Zond Systems (since acquired by Enron, then by General Electric, a powerhouse today), Southwest Wind Power and Bergey Windpower, gradually began a comeback in the 1990s.

A BRIGHT FUTURE . . . WITH CLOUDS

The U.S. (6,374 megawatts at the end of 2003) and Europe dominate the development and installation of wind power. Large-scale wind farms, both on- and off-shore, can now be found from Denmark to New Zealand. Europe has more than 28,000 installed megawatts of wind power (70 percent of world capacity). World wind leaders include Germany, the U.S., Spain, Denmark and India, each with more than 2,000 megawatts. Germany is in the lead, with 14,609 megawatts installed by the end of 2003. The wind energy industry in Germany employs 35,000 people and supplies 3.5 percent of the nation's electricity. Denmark has the world's highest proportion of electricity generated by wind, more than 20 percent. The Danish Wind Energy Association would like to see that ratcheted up to 35 percent wind power by 2015.

In the U.S. (which gets less than one percent of its energy from wind) the industry rebounded somewhat in the late 1990s. There are now clusters of wind turbines in Texas and Colorado, as well as newly updated sites in California. According to the American Wind Energy Association (AWEA), there are now wind energy products in almost every state west of the Mississippi, and in many Northeastern states. California leads with more than 2,042 megawatts of installed wind energy, followed by Texas, which experienced 500 percent wind growth in 2001 and now has 1,293 megawatts. AWEA explains that one megawatt of wind capacity is enough to supply 240 to 300 average American homes, and California's wind power alone can save the energy equivalent of 4.8 million barrels of oil per year.

AWEA says the U.S. wind industry will install up to 3,000 megawatts of new capacity by 2009. If that proves true, the U.S. will have nearly 10,000 megawatts of wind power, enough to power three million homes. The economics of wind are looking increasingly good. The cost of generating a kilowatt-hour of electricity from wind power has dropped from $1 in 1978 to five cents in 1998, and is expected to drop even further, to 2.5 cents. Wind turbines themselves have dropped in installed cost to $800 per kilowatt. Although, according to the *Financial Times*, wind power is still twice as expensive as generation from a modern oil-fired plant, federal subsidies and tax benefits available in many countries level the playing field.

One of the biggest hindrances to even greater wind installation in the U.S. is the on-again, off-again nature of the federal wind energy production tax credit (PTC). Introduced as part of the Energy Policy Act of 1992, PTC granted 1.5 cents per kilowatt-hour (since adjusted for inflation) for the first 10 years of operation to wind plants brought on line before the end of June 1999. A succession of short-term renewals and expirations of PTC led to three boom-and-bust cycles (the most recent a boom in 2003 and a bust in 2004) in wind power installation. Its current extension to the end of 2005 may see some wind projects struggling to meet the PTC requirements before the credit expires once again.

The U.S. could go further, and states with big wind resources would reap major rewards. If Congress were to establish a 20 percent national renewable energy standard by 2020 (requiring utilities to sell a fifth of their energy from sustainable sources), the Union of Concerned Scientists reports, wind-rich North Dakota could gain $1.4 billion in new investment from wind and other renewables. North Dakota consumers would save $363 million in lower electricity bills annually if the standard were combined with improvements in energy efficiency. The environment would also benefit with a 28 percent reduction in carbon dioxide emissions from the plains states. A watered-down version of this "renewables portfolio standard" (RPS) was included in the 2002 and 2003 versions of the failed federal energy bill, but failed to make the final cut.

Just such an RPS, on the state level, was enacted when George W. Bush was governor of Texas, and led that state to its pre-eminent status as the number two wind generator in the U.S. Governor George Pataki recently issued an executive order establishing such an RPS for New York State: 20 percent renewables by 2010. New York currently gets 17 percent of its electricity from renewable sources, principally hydro power. The 2004 elections may have been terrible news for the environment, but one bright spot was the passage of a Colorado RPS that will require the state to buy 10 percent of its energy from renewable sources by 2015. Seventeen states have now enacted RPS rules.

AWEA thinks that, with a favorable political climate, the U.S. could have 100,000 megawatts of installed wind power by 2013, with a full potential of 600,000 megawatts. The group points out that wind power could offset a projected three to four billion cubic feet per day natural gas supply shortage in the U.S.

Even in the absence of a lucrative production tax credit, wind projects are moving forward. Current projects include construction of the world's third-largest wind farm, with 136 turbines and 204 megawatts capacity, in New Mexico as part of the utility-run New Mexico Wind Energy Center. FPL Energy is also installing 162 megawatts of 1.8-megawatt Danish-made Vestas turbines in Solano County, California for the High Winds project. New England can boast of Green Mountain Power's project in Searsburg, Vermont, which was completed in 1997 and features 11 turbines generating six megawatts.

Other projects are underway in Oklahoma and South Dakota, on the Rosebud Sioux reservation. Tex Hall of the National Congress of American Indians observes that "tribes here [in the Great Plains] have many thousands of megawatts of potential wind power blowing across our reservation lands. . . . Tribes need access to the federal grid to bring our value-added electricity to market throughout our region and beyond."

OFFSHORE WIND AND LOCAL OPPOSITION

Many of the largest wind farms today are being built offshore, with varying amounts of controversy. Despite its proximity to Jones Beach, one of the largest summer recreational destinations in the New York area (with six million annual visitors), the proposed Long Island Offshore Wind Initiative (with between 25 and 50 turbines, producing up to four megawatts each) has not generated significant opposition, although it could develop as plans move forward. The Long Island wind farm "will be pollution-free, boundless and blow a gust of clean air into the future of energy production," says Ashok Gupta of the Natural Resources Defense Council.

With peak energy demand on Long Island soaring (up 10 percent just between 2001 and 2002), there is clearly a need for new and cleaner sources of electricity. On the western end of the South Shore, the utility-owned wind farm would be two to five miles offshore and provide electricity for 30,000 homes when completed in 2007. Long Island's suffering air would benefit from the annual reduction of 834 tons of sulfur dioxide, 332 tons of nitrogen oxide and 227,000 tons of climate-altering carbon dioxide.

Taken as a whole, Long Island has incredible potential wind resources along its south shore extending past Montauk Point. According to one study, a string of wind farms in that region could produce 5,200 megawatts of power, or enough to meet 77 percent of Long Island's ever-expanding needs.

Germany is a world leader in offshore wind, and recently finalized an agreement to build a 350-megawatt project (with 70 five-megawatt turbines) off the island of Rügen. Britain's Crown Estate, which owns the UK's territorial seabed, has granted approval for 13 offshore wind farms, and British utility Powergen has plans to develop a giant 500-megawatt offshore farm in the Thames estuary near London. The Irish government has approved a 520-megawatt wind farm offshore southeast of Dublin. China is building a 400-megawatt facility 60 miles from Beijing, and says confidently it will be generating 12 percent of its energy from renewables by 2020.

None of these projects have met with the kind of opposition that stalks the Cape Wind project, a planned $700 million development that would cover 26 square miles off Cape Cod. That wind farm, with General Electric turbines up to 40 stories tall, would surpass Denmark's Horns Reef as the world's largest.

The proposal has split the environmental community, drawing opposition from such powerful environmental allies as Robert Kennedy, Jr. "I'm a strong advocate of wind farms on the oceans and high seas," says Kennedy. "But there are appropriate places for everything. We wouldn't put one of these in Yosemite, and I think environmentalists are falling into a trap if they think the only wilderness areas worth preserving are in the Rocky Mountains or American West. The most important are the ones close to our cities, where the public has access to them. And Nantucket Sound is a wilderness, which people need to experience. I always get nervous when people talk about privatizing the commons. In this case, the benefits of the power extracted from Nantucket Sound are far outweighed by the other values that our communities derive from it."

Writer Bill McKibben, however, argues in *Orion* that the criticisms amount to "small truths." The bigger point is that Nantucket's air contains 370 parts of carbon dioxide, up from 275 parts per million before the Industrial Revolution. "And if we keep burning coal and gas and oil, the scientific consensus is that by the latter part of the century the planet's temperature will have risen five degrees Fahrenheit to a level higher than we've seen for 50 million years." The choice, he writes, "is not between windmills and untouched nature, it's between windmills and the destruction of the planet's biology on a scale we can barely begin to imagine."

SEETHING PASSIONS

The Cape seemed deceptively tranquil on a recent visit. Seething passions were just below the surface. The latest attempt to scuttle the project had just been made public: an amendment to the Defense Authorization Act introduced by Senator John Warner (R-VA), which would have required Congressional approval for any offshore wind project in the U.S. If it had been adopted (it was, instead, withdrawn the next day), it would have forced Cape Wind back to the beginning of what had already been a three-year regulatory process.

The permitting process has been a long, hard slog for Cape Wind Associates, which has spent an estimated $15 million trying to get its offshore farm built. With Warner's amendment lifted (reportedly because of the objections of House Republicans), the next step was the U.S. Army Corps of Engineers' draft Environmental Impact Statement (EIS), a staggering 3,800 pages released November 9. The EIS had been expected in September, but it sat for several months, some say for political reasons, on the desk of one Raymond DuBois, an undersecretary of defense in the Pentagon for military installations and environmental programs.

As had been expected, the draft EIS is largely favorable to Cape Wind. "This report is a big step towards greater energy independence," said a jubilant Jim Gordon, Cape Wind's president. But opponents, led by the Alliance to Protect Nantucket Sound, were subdued. "This is a flawed report, written and paid for largely by Cape Wind," said Alliance Assistant Director Audra Parker.

For the record, Warner's family has property whose view would be affected by the Cape Wind Project. So does Senator Ted Kennedy (D-MA), whose famous "compound" is in Hyannis, near Ground Zero. Everybody on the Cape has an opinion about the project, though it's not generally expressed with the usual bumper stickers and lawn signs. Instead, there are intense activist groups on both sides of the fence, and public opinion polls that indicate a population that is dramatically split on the project.

The tide has been turning somewhat against the project after a concerted media campaign by the Alliance to Protect Nantucket Sound. The Alliance has some environmental trappings, but its founder, Doug Yearley, is chairperson emeritus of mining giant Phelps Dodge Corporation and a board member of Marathon Oil (a winner of the Toxic Action Center's "Dirty Dozen Award"). To be fair, he's also a member of the World Wildlife Fund's National Council. The Alliance raised $1.8 million in 2003 through donations from such high-profile Cape residents as Paul Fireman of Reebok, but it spent even more, $2.4 million, on what the *Boston Herald* called "a small army of hired lawyers, lobbyists and publicists."

Even with the draft EIS released, there will still be a long slog. There will be public hearings, the issuance of a final EIS (expected in mid 2005), more comments, then a permitting decision by the Army Corps. The state has a role also in the form of the Office of Coastal Zone Management. Even if a permit is issued (it can be approved with conditions or denied outright), there's a good chance the Alliance would then file a lawsuit.

There are articulate voices on both sides. "This project in this place is inappropriate for any number of reasons," says the passionately persuasive Audra Parker. "We're supportive of renewable energy, but this is risky technology—the first offshore wind project in the U.S.—and do we really want to turn our priceless Nantucket Sound into a scientific experiment?"

The Alliance raises the specter of Cape Wind as a stalking horse for at least three more large-scale wind farms in Nantucket Sound. It says the five million people who visit the Cape and the islands (Nantucket and Martha's Vineyard) every year will be "confronted by 130 huge towers in the Sound," each 100 feet higher than the famous Bourne and Sagamore bridges. In fliers, the group warns about "a risky new technology and a developer who has never built a wind plant."

Supporters say that Cape Wind can replace 113 million gallons of oil per year, that it will reduce regional greenhouse gas emissions by one million tons per year (the equivalent of taking 162,000 cars off the road) and reduce New England's wholesale electric prices by $25 million per year. They also say its construction will create 1,000 new jobs.

Bill Eddy, a local Episcopal priest, has been a vocal supporter and founder of the 3,500-member Clean Power Now, which supports the project as strongly as the Alliance opposes it. "The wind farm could contribute 75 percent of our electrical needs and have a noticeable and positive impact on our electricity costs for the life of the project," says the gray-haired Eddy in a booming, pulpit-friendly voice. He also thinks the wind project will improve Cape Cod's surprisingly bad air quality (it's 50 percent worse than Boston's, Eddy says).

Eddy built his own first wind generator in 1976, to celebrate the national Bicentennial. A wind farm on Nantucket Sound, he says, "represents a compelling vision for our future." He quotes King Solomon from the Bible's Book of Proverbs, "Where there is no vision, the people perish." Eddy feels betrayed by America's national leaders, who talk about the need for energy independence, but then refuse to take a stand in supporting key projects. "Sometimes I think they'd rather see Arlington National Cemetery expanded with a thousand new markers for young men who died fighting to protect our oil supply than to have to endure the sight of wind turbines producing clean energy off Cape Cod," he says.

When *E* visited, the unassuming Mark Rodgers, a spokesperson for Cape Wind, was combative about the well-organized opposition. "The Alliance approach has created a lot of unnecessary fears," he says. "They've dramatically outspent us with incessant fear-mongering." The Alliance's spending has produced results, Rodgers admits. In 2002, 55 percent of Cape residents supported the project, but after two years of Alliance undermining the situation has reversed, and a *Cape Cod Times* poll shows 55 percent oppose the wind farm. (Rodgers points out, however, that the *Times* has vehemently opposed Cape Wind, and that its reporting on the poll failed to disclose the 20 percent who simply refused to answer the newspaper's question.)

Rodgers says that alarmist wind opponents can point to grandiose proposals by the New York-based Winergy to construct as many as 2,000 turbines off the coasts of New England, Delaware, Maryland and Virginia, ruining the view for millions. "They've gone up and down the coast and announced plans for wind farms everywhere," Rodgers says. "It's easy to send out press releases, but much harder to actually do the hard work of licensing wind farms. Their approach has created a lot of unnecessary concern." Dennis Quaranta, whose experience comes from developing a fish farm in Long Island Sound's Gardner Bay, says that Winergy doesn't plan to operate wind farms, but will bring in management teams after it obtains the necessary permits. But it's unclear if any of the company's projects have moved very far.

Rodgers believes the release of the Cape Wind EIS will pave the way for the wind farm to begin construction in 2007. "The document, put together by the Army Corps with input from other agencies, shows that there are compelling public interest benefits from this clean energy project," he says. But a lot of wind will be blown before then. Both supporters and opponents of Cape Wind make comparisons to the Horns Reef wind farm off Denmark's west coast. There are indeed many similarities. The projects are of comparable size (though Cape Wind will be larger), and both are in parts of the country heavily used by recreational visitors. But two years after Denmark's turbines started generating power, the controversy has died down. Despite the Alliance's determined efforts to make Horns Reef appear to be a disaster, it has been woven into the fabric of a nation firmly committed to wind power.

DENMARK: RUNNING WITH THE WIND

On a fast train ride across Denmark from east to west, passengers get used to the sight of rows of tall white Vestas wind turbines turning slowly in the ever-present breeze. The Danes pioneered wind energy development dating back to the pioneer and inventor Poul la Cour in the 1890s. A Danish engineer, Johannes Juul, was the first to connect a wind turbine with an AC generator to the electrical grid. Denmark-based companies also helped spark the modern wind movement in the 1970s. In 2003, Danish manufacturers had nearly 40 percent of the world turbine market, which grows at the astounding rate of 20 percent per year. Ninety percent of the turbines manufactured in the country go for export. Wind is the third-largest contributor to the Danish economy, after pharmaceuticals and Lego blocks, and provides 20,000 jobs in all of its dimensions. Denmark itself has 3,100 megawatts of installed wind power, but that figure will undoubtedly be outmoded by the time this article goes to press.

Denmark is a small country, with just 5.4 million people, but it is a mighty force in the wind industry. Just one industrial giant, Vestas (which recently merged with its largest competitor, NEG Micron) has 35 percent of the international market and employs 8,500 people. Its turbines are being installed all over Europe (including largest customer Germany, as well as Spain, Great Britain, Portugal and Greece), Canada, Australia and many other countries. When tax incentives are in place, the U.S. is also a large-scale Vestas customer.

Blavand is a beachside resort town at Denmark's western tip, a summer mecca for hordes of German tourists who rent the colorful thatched-roof summer houses that line the dunes. On a blustery but sunny afternoon in October, they thronged the town's main shopping street and made pilgrimages to the top of its 100-year-old lighthouse.

The 120-foot lighthouse, with its 170 worn wooden steps, is a great vantage point for birders who come to see grebes, gannets, skuas and the occasional shearwater or storm petrel on their migratory route through Scandinavia. But it's also the best place to see one of the world's largest offshore wind farms, Horns Reef.

Unfortunately, on cloudy days there's not much to see: The wind farm includes 80 two-megawatt turbines, located 8.5 to 12 miles out in the North Sea, and from a beach littered with German World War II military bunkers it's an indistinct cluster of what appear to be toothpicks sticking out of the water. As Bill Eddy (who accompanied a Cape Cod delegation to Blavand) has observed, it "occupies only a small portion of the horizon, perhaps 20 degrees. . . . Horns Reef is smaller than I thought."

Jan Toftdal of the Danish Tourist Board, who escorts visiting journalists around his picturesque region, admits that the wind farm was controversial when first proposed. The project went forward without much local input, he says, and there was some concern it would wreck the tourist-dependent economy.

"But now people are very accepting," says Toftdal, who has visited Cape Cod as a guest of Cape Wind supporters. "We have not seen one single tourist saying anything negative about it. There was recently a survey of people on the beach, and the most common response was 'What wind farm?' They just don't even see it."

The Cape-based Alliance has tried to spin this in another direction, touting the views of "economic expert" Chresten Andersen, who told Massachusetts audiences that it is "widely known" in Denmark that wind farms are undesirable neighbors. But that would appear to be contradicted by the facts on the ground in Blavand, where the tourist economy is booming and housing prices are rising.

In her office in downtown Copenhagen, decorated by a scale model of a Vestas turbine, Hanne Jersild of the Danish Wind Energy Association shakes her head when asked about declining property values. "There is simply no analysis to show an impact," she says. "When Horns Reef was built two years ago, there was talk about it, but the opposition has melted away." Now, she says, Horns Reef will be considerably expanded with another 200 megawatts of wind power within two years. Thanks in part to a "depowering" scheme that makes it advantageous to replace older, less-productive turbines with more efficient models, Denmark is likely to increase its wind capacity so that it can meet 25 percent of the country's energy needs by 2008. The Wind Energy Association's goal is 35 percent of national needs by 2015.

In place of fear, there is now mostly optimism about this expanding industry, particularly in an environmentally conscious country where 20 percent of all travel is by bicycle. "The development of the wind industry here has been very rapid in the last 15 years," says Jersild. "China is a big potential market for us, and we have large markets already in Germany, Spain and Great Britain." Denmark is becoming something of a specialist in offshore wind development. "The marine environment is challenging, because of greater construction costs for the foundations, and wear and tear on the equipment, but offshore wind turbines are more productive," Jersild says. Thanks to more persistent wind, "an offshore turbine typically produces some 30 to 40 percent more energy per kilowatt than an onshore turbine."

Peter Helmer Steen is associate director of Energistyrelsen, the Danish energy ministry, and he says the government has encouraged investment in wind research since the 1970s. The idea from the beginning, he says, was that local ownership of wind turbines should be encouraged, "so that you don't have windmills in Jutland owned by investors in Copenhagen. We recognized that people who are part-owners would be more willing to accept the noise and changes to the landscape." More than 100,000 Danish families are members of wind energy cooperatives, which have installed 86 percent of the country's turbines.

Denmark is an energy exporter, with the capacity to produce 170 percent of its domestic needs. It sells North Sea oil on the world market, surplus electricity to the Scandinavian countries (as much as 50 percent of production, says Steen) and natural gas to Sweden. Many of Denmark's existing power plants are coal-fired (with coal imported principally from South Africa), but the approximately 35 percent of the grid dependent on coal is offset by 27 percent from renewables (largely wind power, but also including biomass and electricity from organic waste).

In addition to wind power, there are plants creating electricity from biomass and straw, and an efficient cogeneration system that distributes waste heat from power generation and incinerators to warm more than 300,000 homes in Copenhagen alone. Denmark hopes to reduce its greenhouse gas footprint 21 percent, in part through a carbon dioxide emissions trading system that begins this year. "Perhaps Denmark could be a model for the rest of the world in meeting the Kyoto climate goals," says Steen.

Can Denmark really meet 35 percent of its energy needs with wind by 2015?

"It depends on how rapidly we develop commercial offshore wind farms," says Steen. "We want to see more competition for the contract to deliver large-scale, 250-megawatt wind farms. Production costs are decreasing rapidly [a 75 percent reduction between 1973 and 2003], so it may be feasible."

For his part, Vestas CEO Svend Sigaard says that for the last dozen years wind power has been surpassing the annual 20 percent growth rate internationally, achieving nearly 35 percent growth. He admits the U.S. market has been "quite low" because of the absence of tax credits, and that most current North American Vestas projects are in Canada. "The U.S. market over the last six years has been very on and off," Sigaard says, "and it's difficult to plan for the fluctuations in the regulations. But 2005 will be a better year for us in the U.S."

Vestas has had some setbacks at Horns Reef, due to manufacturing errors in transformers and other equipment (not built by Vestas) that have needed on-land repairs. "We've learned quite a lot from the experience," says Sigaard, who is cautiously optimistic about the 35-percent-by-2015 figure. "It's certainly possible, considering the ongoing replacement of our smaller turbines and the 1,000 megawatts in offshore projects that are under development," he says.

Not all of Denmark's offshore wind farms (it has eight) are in remote locations. The Middelgrunden project, capable of producing 100,000 megawatt-hours of electricity per year, is located just outside Copenhagen harbor, and consists of 20 two-megawatt turbines arrayed in a two-mile arc. Far from a visual blight, it's actually hard to see at all unless you find a rare high vantage point in this low-rise city. But when you finally do get a look at it, the white towers topped by gently spinning propeller-like blades present a visual picture of environmental progress.

OBJECTING TO WIND

Like public transit, which is plagued by self-appointed "experts" who try and stop every proposed project, wind power has opponents like Glenn Schleede, a former senior vice president of the National Coal Association. His mantra: Wind power equals huge machines producing very little electricity. Wind advocates, he says, greatly underestimate "the true cost of wind energy, as well as the adverse environmental, ecological, scenic and property value impacts."

But the American Wind Energy Association answers him point by point. "The cost of electricity from new wind plants is competitive with the cost of new conventional power plants, when the federal wind energy production tax credit is taken into account," the association says. "It is true that few wind plants would be built without this incentive. But it is also true that the traditional energy industries [including nuclear and coal] are generously subsidized in a variety of ways."

Do wind farms affect property values? Not according to a 2003 study by the Renewable Energy Policy Project (REPP). The group gathered a large database and examined more than 25,000 property transactions. "If there were any systematic harm to property values from wind power projects, it would have shown up in the data," says REPP Research Director George Sterzinger. In the majority of transactions, property values actually rose in the period studied.

The libertarian Cato Institute complains that wind power is "not cheap and not green." It charges that renewable energy is, on average, twice as expensive as "the most economical fossil-fuel alternative," meaning dirty coal. But such estimates fail to take into account the cost of health effects caused by polluted air and global warming.

Another charge is that wind power is intermittent, and therefore not as dependable as fossil-fuel energy. In California, says Cato, wind power operated at only 23 percent of its average capacity factor. Cato compares that to nuclear power, with a 75 percent average capacity factor. But to make wind energy appear inefficient it's necessary, again, to ignore the external costs of nuclear power production—including storing nuclear waste and protecting nuclear plants from 9/11-style attacks. Pacific Gas and Electric forecast in the early 1990s that wind could ultimately become the least-expensive electricity generation source. The cost of wind energy is also dropping faster than the cost of conventional generation, AWEA says, about 15 percent with each doubling of installed capacity worldwide.

Wind opponents, when they're not creating facsimiles of how bad offshore wind projects will look, point to the fact that birds collide with wind turbines. This is indeed tragic, but cell towers and other obstacles are a large part of the problem. A Western EcoSystems Technology report points out that as many as a billion birds are killed by collisions with manmade structures annually in the U.S. alone.

Although as many as 40,000 birds die annually after hitting windmills, and that's a significant number, some 60 to 80 million die from colliding with vehicles, and as many as 980 million from hitting buildings and windows. Communications towers take out four to 50 million birds a year, and power lines kill many thousands more. The Exxon Valdez oil spill killed an estimated 375,000 to 500,000 birds. Further, newer, slow-moving turbines "are designed to provide little perching and no nesting structure," the report says, reducing bird proximity.

The Center for Biological Diversity says that wind turbines at the Altamont Pass Wind Resource Area (APWRA) in California, which is located on a major bird migratory route with high raptor density, "kill more birds of prey than any other wind facility in North America." Estimates range from 800 to 1,300 raptor deaths annually. But even the litigation-prone Center isn't proposing to shut Altamont down. Instead, it proposes that "turbine owners take reasonable measures to reduce bird kills and adequately compensate for impacts to imperiled bird populations."

Altamont was installed in the early 1980s, and wind developers have since become considerably more bird-friendly, designing less-lethal turbines using repellant devices and colors, and placing them away from migratory routes.

Also of concern is the issue of bat collisions with wind turbines, a phenomenon that has not received sufficient study. A 2003 report based on observations at the Buffalo Ridge Wind Resource Area in Minnesota (354 turbines operated by Xcel Energy) concluded that 849 bats were killed in 2001 and 364 in 2002, for an average of 2.16 per turbine per year.

WIND-GENERATED HYDROGEN?

Can zero-emission wind power be used to produce hydrogen for fuel cells as part of a completely clean energy loop? There's some evidence that it can.

According to the Nuclear Information and Resource Service, the Bush administration's plans to use nuclear power to generate hydrogen are off base, and wind power presents a better option. "Electricity from wind is currently four cents per kilowatt-hour," the group says. "This is a verifiable, experienced cost. Wind energy and photovoltaic systems coupled to electrolyzers used for hydrogen separation are perhaps the most versatile of the approaches and are likely to be the major hydrogen producers of the future." Princeton researcher Joan Ogden, a booster of solar and wind-based hydrogen, adds that nuclear hydrogen is dependent on "difficult technology that is much further from commercialization than many other hydrogen-production options."

There are, however, certainly realistic obstacles to overcome before wind-based hydrogen can become a reality. A report by Science for Democratic Action concluded that "there are no real cost advantages to integrating fuel cells into the electricity system on a large scale." Bill Leighty, director of the Leighty Foundation in Juneau, Alaska, has some sobering second thoughts on the idea of transmitting large amounts of wind-generated electricity via a hydrogen pipeline from North Dakota, for example, to Chicago, a possibility examined in a study underwritten by his foundation.

"Hydrogen transmission does not appear to offer an economically attractive alternative to gigawatt-scale transmission of Great Plains wind energy via high-voltage [electric lines] because of the extra costs of conversion from electric to hydrogen energy at the Great Plains source," said a key sentence in Leighty's paper. "Capital, operations and maintenance, and energy conversion loss costs are significant, though energy storage as compressed hydrogen gas in the pipeline is a valuable benefit."

Leighty says wind-generated hydrogen is dependent on what the *Hydrogen and Fuel Cell Letter* describes as "the emergence of a large market for pure hydrogen . . . for [fuel-cell-based] transportation and for distributed generation."

But what if that market does develop? Claus Moller of the Danish Wind Energy Association says that the concept of hydrogen from wind is being actively pursued in Denmark, with small-scale demonstration projects and long-term feasibility studies underway in research institutes. If economics of scale come into play to dramatically reduce the cost of wind-powered hydrogen electrolyzers, reports a paper by Harry Braun of the Hydrogen Political Action Committee posted on EV World, then electricity could be generated at a cost of one cent per kilowatt-hour, resulting in liquid hydrogen produced for the same cost as gasoline at $1.95 a gallon.

Braun calls for 12 million wind systems to be mass-produced and installed within 24 months and coupled to an interstate hydrogen pipeline. "It is possible for the U.S. to be energy independent, with a pollution-free and inexhaustible energy resource within five to 10 years," he says.

The Earth Policy Institute's Lester Brown offers a plausible scenario for wind-based hydrogen. "Surplus wind power can be stored as hydrogen and used in fuel cells or gas turbines to generate electricity, leveling supply when winds are variable," says Brown. "Wind, once seen as a cornerstone of the new energy economy, may turn out to be its foundation. The wind meteorologist who analyzes wind regimes and identifies the best sites for wind farms will play a role in the new energy economy comparable to that of the petroleum geologist in the old energy economy.

"With the advancing technologies for harnessing wind and powering motor vehicles with hydrogen, we can now see a future where farmers and ranchers can supply not only much of the country's electricity, but much of the hydrogen to fuel its fleet of automobiles as well. For the first time, the United States has the technology and resources to divorce itself from Middle Eastern oil."

AN UNLIMITED FUTURE

As the fastest-growing source of energy in the world, with the fewest long-term drawbacks, wind power would seem to have an unlimited future. Lester Brown describes wind power as "the missing link in the Bush energy plan." Bush has called for the addition of 393,000 megawatts of electric generating capacity by 2020, and he's proposed financial aid to businesses that construct new nuclear power plants, as well as streamlined plant licensing. But no nuclear plant has been ordered in 30 years, and mammoth financial incentives may not be enough to offset the huge waste and liability questions.

But Bush's generating goals could be reached with wind power alone. Just three Great Plains states—North Dakota, Kansas and Texas—have enough wind potential to meet America's entire energy needs. Farmers and ranchers support wind projects because of the financial boon that comes with leasing their land. Wind projects completed just in 2003 will generate $5 million annually in payments.

Wind energy designers are starting to think big. A project called Rolling Thunder, in South Dakota near the Iowa border, would generate 3,000 megawatts when it comes online in 2006, making it five times larger than any previous wind farm and one of the largest energy developments in the world today. At the same time, the federal Bonneville Power Administration (BPA) says it will buy 830 megawatts of wind power from seven plants—five to be built in Washington and two in Oregon. Already the nation's biggest supplier of hydroelectric power, BPA will be the largest wind energy supplier.

The pieces are in place for a massive expansion of wind resources worldwide at a time when concern about oil supply and location is proving to be massively troubling. All the signs are positive, but will wind power achieve its true potential? The answer, of course, is blowing in the wind.

New and Improved Wind Power*

By Greg Pahl
The Mother Earth News, June/July 2007

For many, home energy costs recently have increased by 50 percent (or more), motivating a growing number of people to look for alternatives. The proliferation of net metering laws, in about 40 states, as well as a growing number of state residential wind incentive programs, has given a strong boost to the small-scale wind turbine industry.

What's more, recent technical developments have reduced blade noise and improved both turbine efficiency and longevity. There now are a number of new home-stale wind turbines with advanced technology, and there's the promise of more to come in the near future.

For many years, residential wind turbines have been most popular in rural locations where zoning laws tend to be less restrictive and neighbors less likely to object to them (mainly on aesthetic grounds). That may be about to change. Many in the small-scale wind turbine industry think residential wind power is about to enter suburbia with simpler, less expensive systems that perform more like household appliances than complicated renewable energy systems. And the potential is enormous; it's estimated there are at least 15 million homes with the resources necessary to make a wind installation cost effective.

But does it really make sense to install a wind turbine in your back yard? Maybe, maybe not. A wind power system that works well in one location may not work in another. There are many variables to consider: the size of your lot, zoning restrictions, wind speeds in your area, the cost and amount of electricity you use, whether your utility offers net metering, and the availability of state rebates and incentives.

* Excerpted from *Mother Earth News* magazine. Read the full story at www.MotherEarthNews.com or call (800) 234-3368 to subscribe.

WIND POWER PICKS UP SPEED

Harvesting the wind to generate electricity is not a new idea. In 1888, Charles F. Brush of Cleveland created a wind turbine for this purpose. Early turbines could supply enough energy for a house or two. Today, large commercial-scale turbines can produce about 3 megawatts or more, enough to power about 750 U.S. homes. The recent growth of this industry in the United States has been dramatic. Wind power capacity increased by 27 percent in 2006 and is expected to increase an additional 26 percent this year, according to the American Wind Energy Association. Enthusiasm for small-scale wind also is on the rise, with sales for residential systems at $17 million in 2005, up 62 percent from 2004, according to the association.

Residential wind turbines were first commercialized in the United States in the 1920s and were fairly popular until the Rural Electrification Administration extended electric fines to many remote areas in the 1930s and '40s. The oil crises of the 1970s spurred a flurry of renewed interest in residential wind power until the tax credits and other government incentives that supported the industry ended in the 1980s.

But now, interest in residential wind power is on the rebound. Mike Bergey, president of Bergey Windpower Co., attributes the company's recent growth to robust state and utility rebate programs and growing interest in clean energy technology. (Visit the Database of State Incentives for Renewable & Efficiency at www.dsireusa.org to see if incentives are available in your state.)

Net metering laws, which simplify the connection of residential renewable energy systems to the electric grid, also have made wind more attractive to those looking for a way to reduce their energy bills. Robert Preus, the founder of Abundant Renewable Energy (ARE), agrees and points to the impact of grid interconnection on the solar-electric market as instructive. "In the past, the vast majority of solar was battery-connected off-grid: now it's just the opposite," he says. Grid-interconnection allows the homeowner to reduce their grid-based energy use, while not requiring them to rely solely on wind for their needs.

Many others in the industry point to the increasing number of financial incentive programs that help reduce the high initial cost of wind systems. But according to Andy Kruse, co-founder of Southwest Windpower, people also are choosing wind simply because it's the right thing to do. "Another key factor is unquestionably the environment," he says. "People are looking for ways to make a difference."

These days there are high hopes in the residential wind industry for the passing of legislation that would establish a federal tax credit for those who purchase wind turbines. According to Bergey, a federal credit would not only be an immediate benefit to taxpayers, but would also drive turbine prices down through increased manufacturing. (For help contacting Congress to voice your support, visit www.windenergy.com/takeaction.htm.)

THE BASIC TECHNOLOGY

Residential wind power has come a long way from the 1920s, but in some respects the basic technology hasn't changed much. Turbine subsystems include a rotor (the blades) that convert the wind's energy into rotational shaft energy; a nacelle (enclosure) containing a drive train and a generator; the tower to support the turbine; and electronic controls, electrical cables and grid interconnection equipment. Off-grid turbines do not have interconnection equipment, but normally have banks of batteries to store electricity for use during windless periods. Grid-connected turbines, on the other hand, essentially use the grid as their storage battery.

Because the rotor is what actually captures the wind, its size is extremely important. In general, the larger the rotor the better, as long as it's matched to an appropriately sized generator.

Improved airfoil designs have boosted efficiency by as much as 35 percent at the average wind speeds typical of many residential locations. Wooden blades have been replaced by reinforced fiberglass, which reduces blade maintenance (although routine turbine and tower upkeep is still extremely important). The blades also have been redesigned to reduce the amount of noise they produce. Bergey Windpower, for example, used the new airfoil design in its 10-kilowatt BWC Excel model to improve efficiency in wind speeds as low as 9 miles per hour. In addition, new direct-drive permanent magnet alternators have been paired with sophisticated controls and inverters designed specifically for small wind turbines. Alternator efficiency on some models has been improved by about 25 percent. "We introduced the Excel back in 1983," Bergey says. "But the one you buy today has vastly improved rotor blades and power electronics."

Some of these advances owe at least partial credit to research and development conducted by the National Renewable Energy Laboratory's Wind Technology Center in Golden, Colo. Bergey Windpower and several others have benefited from collaboration with the laboratory. The team-up helped Abundant Renewable Energy design two new residential, grid-connected turbines that are especially well-suited for harsh environments. In January 2006, the company shipped its first 2.5-kilowatt unit (the ARE 110), followed later that year by the 10-kilowatt model (the ARE 442). Both turbines are designed to operate quietly and produce more electricity in lower wind speed locations.

Southwest Windpower, which also collaborates with the laboratory, has been producing battery-charging wind turbines since 1987. Recently Southwest released a grid-connected turbine, the Skystream 3.7, that is paired with a monopole tower as short as 33 feet to make it easier to install in residential settings where zoning regulations often limit taller structures. Among a number of improvements, the new 1.8-kilowatt turbine has an extremely low "cogging torque" (resistance to start up), making it easier to start in low winds. The Skystream is a smaller unit with a lower price tag than industry averages.

PLUG AND PLAY

One thing that sets the Skystream apart from the competition is its "plug and play" design. All of the sophisticated electronic components that would normally be located in separate boxes at or near the base of the tower have been incorporated into the turbine itself, making the connection to your home's electrical system (and the grid) a relatively simple matter. Another characteristic that sets the Skystream apart is its use of the generator to control the rotor speed. Most other small wind turbines use a "furling" strategy, which turns or tilts the turbine and blades out of the wind to protect them from overspeeding in high winds, which can destroy the generator. The Skystream, on the other hand, uses what amounts to dynamic braking by the generator to limit rotor speed.

Jim Green, senior project leader at the Wind Technology Center, explains the advantages and disadvantages of these two strategies: "The furling method is passive and relatively fail-safe because when the wind forces become sufficiently high the turbine will furl," he says. "The alternative approach used by Skystream hopefully will be a reliable strategy, but it does require some active control in the machine. They address that by having redundant systems and fairly fail-safe power designs." If the power goes off in a grid failure, for example, there is a switch that stops the turbine.

"One of the reasons I think the Skystream approach is going to be attractive is that the rotor speed is truly limited," Green says. "Furling wind turbines, on the other hand, tend to let the rotor accelerate to generate the high thrust that causes the furling to take place. So, there are some higher speeds and higher forces involved that the whole machine has to deal with in that approach—but with proper design that's OK."

However, when it comes to tower height, residential wind expert Mick Sagrillo and others in the industry stress that the 33-foot tower that's often part of the Skystream package is simply not tall enough to avoid wind turbulence; most in the industry recommend an 80-foot tower minimum.

"The site always determines the height of the tower," Sagrillo says. The three most common mistakes that people make with small wind installations, according to Sagrillo, are: 1. Too short a tower; 2. Too short a tower; and 3. Too short a tower. Bergey also emphasizes this point by comparing a turbine on a short tower to a solar power collector in the shade.

Kruse argues that a general rule of thumb is to ensure the rotor extends at least 20 to 30 feet above any surrounding object within 500 feet of the tower. He agrees that a site should be thoroughly assessed; while the 33-foot monopole tower may perform well in the Texas panhandle, a taller tower might be required in areas such as upstate New York or Vermont.

At least one new Skystream feature impresses virtually all observers—the turbine's wireless communication system. It enables the homeowner to track the turbine's output and other operational statistics on their home computer and also allows for real-time troubleshooting if a problem should develop. Software patches and other system upgrades can be uploaded to the turbine via the same system, eliminating the need to lower the turbine to the ground for these procedures.

REAL-WORLD PERFORMANCE

So, how do residential wind turbines actually perform? If they are properly installed and maintained, the record is good. Bergey Windpower, with installations in all 50 states and more than 90 countries, has a long track record of success. Abundant Renewable Energy has only a small number of its new ARE 110 turbines installed so far, but early feedback has been positive.

"We did have an initial problem with a turbine component," says Tom Carter, director of operations at Crossroads for Youth, a residential school for at risk children in Oxford, Mich. "But after it was repaired, the system has operated flawlessly. We're very pleased with it."

Southwest Windpower's Skystream 3.7 turbine is new to the market, but one prototype has been in successful operation at the Wind Technology Center for more than two years. An additional 20 Skystreams have been in a beta testing program for more than six months in various residential locations around the country. The tests have gone well overall, and except for the usual minor glitches for any new product, no major system failures have been reported. Paul Westbrook of Fairview, Texas, had his beta Skystream installed in September 2006.

"Overall it's running fine," he says. Westbrook reports there have been no noise complaints from the neighbors. "In fact, I've been getting inquiries from them about how it works, how much it costs and how much power it's producing," he says. "There's been a lot of interest."

Westbrook does acknowledge the 33-foot tower was not a good match for his site, because part of his property is heavily wooded. "I put the turbine on a clear hill near the street in a corridor that I thought would have pretty good winds, but I have been stunned by how much reduction in wind has resulted from turbulence caused by the trees. Consequently, my power output is running at about one-eighth what it should be." Westbrook plans to install a taller tower to get the turbine well above the trees.

Westbrook had another problem—getting his system connected to the grid. He's served by an electric cooperative that had no net metering provisions and no interest in establishing any. It took five months of persistent negotiation to get the connection. Installation experiences like these highlight how crucial it is to study all the issues involved with a site before you proceed. With proper siting, residential wind may be a great way to reduce your energy costs and make a positive difference for the environment.

With growing consumer interest, there's a good deal of optimism in the small wind sector. "We're in a very dynamic, emerging market right now with all these state incentives in place," Green says. "But a lot still depends on the future of energy prices." Kruse agrees. "I'm very optimistic about it," he says. "Provided that the cost of utility energy keeps on going up, and we keep the cost of renewable energy down with innovative technologies, it's going to be very exciting."

Solar Is the Solution*

By Steve Heckeroth

The Mother Earth News, December 2007/January 2008

We know that relying on coal, oil and natural gas threatens our future with toxic pollution, global climate change and social unrest caused by diminishing fuel supplies. Instead of relying on unsustainable fossil fuels, we must transform our economy and learn to thrive on the planet's abundant supply of renewable energy.

I have been studying our energy options for more than 30 years, and I am absolutely convinced that our best and easiest option is solar energy, which is virtually inexhaustable. Most importantly, if we choose solar we don't have to wait for a new technology to save us. We already have the technology and energy resources we need to build a sustainable, solar-electric economy that can cure our addiction to oil, stabilize the climate and maintain our standard of living, all at the same time. It is well past time to start seriously harnessing solar energy.

FOSSIL-FUELED PROBLEMS

[. . .] Coal is burned mainly to produce electricity, and coal-fired power plants produce more than half the electricity used in the United States. But burning coal has serious drawbacks. One is that it releases carbon dioxide, which contributes to global warming. It also releases heavy metals, such as mercury and sulfur. These toxins that were locked in the Earth's crust over billions of years are suddenly spewed into the atmosphere and thus degrade our air, water and soil. The exhaust from burning coal contains more pollutants and global warming emissions per unit of energy produced than *any other fossil fuel.* In addition, the methods used to mine coal are destructive to the land and dangerous for the miners.

Now consider that coal is enormously inefficient from a total energy perspective. It took billions of years of solar energy to form the coal we have today. And while coal is the most abundant fossil resource, the total amount of energy pro-

* Excerpted from *Mother Earth News* magazine. Read the full story at www.MotherEarthNews.com or call (800) 234-3368 to subscribe.

duced by burning all the coal on the planet would only be equivalent to the solar energy that strikes the Earth every *six days*.

Natural gas supplies more than half the fuel used to heat buildings and about 15 percent of the electricity in the United States. Natural-gas-fired power plants only emit about half the pollutants produced by coal plants, as long as the fuel is extracted close to where it is burned. However, U.S. natural gas extraction can no longer keep up with demand, so expensive and hazardous methods to liquefy and ship foreign natural gas are being devised. In the future, natural gas for the United States would have to be imported from countries such as Russia, Kazakhstan, Qatar and Iran, which together have 60 percent of the world's reserves. When all the externalities, such as the cost and pollution caused by liquefying and transporting this fuel, are included, liquefied natural gas (LNG) is much more expensive than coal, and almost as dirty.

Natural gas is the second most abundant fossil fuel, but its total potential energy is equivalent to only about *1½ days* of sunshine striking the Earth.

Nuclear power plants fueled by radioactive isotopes of uranium produce 20 percent of the electricity used in the United States. When radioactive materials were sequestered and dispersed deep under the Earth's surface, they presented very little threat to life. But we've made those materials far more dangerous by mining and concentrating them, and the byproducts left over after a nuclear reaction are even more dangerous than the original isotopes. Nuclear power plants create hundreds of thousands of tons of radioactive waste that will continue to be a threat to life for longer than humans will walk the Earth.

Even if the problem of radioactive waste could be solved, the recoverable world reserve of fissionable uranium is equivalent to less than 1½ days of the energy striking the Earth from the nuclear reaction of the sun.

Oil-fired power plants have all but disappeared in the United States, but oil (mostly diesel fuel and gasoline) powers nearly all our transportation. More than 60 percent of the oil consumed in the United States is now imported. Demand for petroleum will soon exceed world production capacity and at that point the price of fuel will start to rise dramatically. We should be asking ourselves how we will cope with gas prices as they rise from $2.50 to $5 to $10 per gallon and keep rising. It's hard to imagine the hardship that will be faced by countries that remain addicted to oil, and even harder to imagine the suffering in countries that have oil, but do not have the strength to protect their resources or themselves.

Now consider that the entire recoverable world oil reserve is equivalent to the solar energy that strikes the Earth in *one* day.

BIOFUELS AND HYDROGEN

Before we explore the solar-electric future let's discuss biofuels and hydrogen as other possible alternatives. Although both have received a lot of good press, I believe neither are viable solutions for our future energy needs.

Waste oil and biomass can make good transition fuels but unless human population growth slows, we will need all existing agricultural land to grow food. There are already many examples of food crop land that is being used to create ethanol to power SUVs and other flex-fuel vehicles. The cost of tortillas has quadrupled in Mexico in the last year because of rising demand for corn to make ethanol. If we let demand for biofuels increase, the impact on the world's poor will be much more severe.

According to some studies, it takes 1,000 gallons of water and more than a gallon equivalent of fossil fuel to produce 1 gallon of corn ethanol. Finally, consider that biofuels just aren't very efficient. When you do the math, the overall efficiency of biomass used as transportation fuel, from sun to wheel, is about 0.01 percent to 0.05 percent. In contrast, the overall efficiency of using solar panels to charge electric vehicles from sun to wheel is 3 percent to 20 percent. This means that solar-charged electric vehicles are from *60 to 2,000 times more efficient* than vehicles burning ethanol or biodiesel. Which solution makes more sense?

Hydrogen fuel cell vehicles are no more efficient than biofuels. Hydrogen is much lighter than air, and it must be contained in order to keep it from escaping the Earth's atmosphere, unless it is bound up in water or hydrocarbon molecules. The strong bonds that hold these molecules together take a significant amount of energy to break apart to extract hydrogen. Once the hydrogen is extracted, more energy is needed to compress it into a container that is small enough to store on a vehicle. In order for a fuel cell vehicle to go 200 or 300 miles on a tank, the hydrogen must be stored in metal hydrates or at 10,000 psi in heavy containers.

Even after more than 20 years of development, fuel cell vehicles still cost more than a million dollars each and don't last very long or go very far. Finally, it takes about four times more renewable energy to drive a fuel cell vehicle than it does to charge the batteries in an electric vehicle to go the same distance. *This is like the difference in fuel economy between a Hummer and a Prius.* If you are wondering why hydrogen fuel cell vehicles continue to receive billions of dollars in funding given all these barriers, the fact that 96 percent of all hydrogen is currently extracted from fossil fuels may have something to do with it. There are powerful vested interests controlling our energy policy. Only informed citizens acting together can steer the best course.

A BRIGHT, SOLAR-ELECTRIC FUTURE

A solar-electric economy is well within our reach. We're already generating solar electricity at the utility scale using powerful concentrating solar power technology. We're also generating electricity through wind energy, which many experts consider an indirect form of solar energy because it's driven by temperature differences.

But also consider that simply incorporating passive solar design strategies, energy efficiency, conservation and other active solar heating strategies in the construction of buildings can save up to 95 percent of the energy used in conventional buildings. With the addition of building-integrated photovoltaics, buildings can be turned into net energy producers. Energy from the sun can be used to power our vehicles, and that includes not only our cars, but also heavy vehicles such as tractors.

Electric Vehicles & Plug-in Hybrids. Electric vehicle drivetrains are inherently five to 10 times more efficient than internal combustion engines and they produce no greenhouse gases at the tailpipe. Even if powered by fossil-fuel electricity, emissions at the power plant are much lower per mile traveled than with internal combustion engines. In addition, electric vehicles can be charged directly from renewable sources, thereby eliminating emissions altogether.

One of the main excuses the auto industry offers for the lack of electric vehicles is that "the batteries are not developed yet." But consider how quickly cell phone batteries developed, transforming mobile phones from heavy, bulky, short-lived nuisances to amazingly light, small and long-lasting necessities. The oil companies are doing a good job of protecting the American consumer from "dangerous" batteries, but in parts of the world where oil companies have less control, large format battery development is progressing at rapid speeds.

Electric Tractors and. Agriculture. Experts have estimated that it takes eight to 10 units of fossil energy to put one unit of food energy on American tables, and that it takes the equivalent of 10 barrels of oil to feed each person in the country. Hearing those figures, it's frightening to imagine what will happen as oil prices rise. To begin with, how would we fuel our farm machinery?

The good news is that not only can tractors run on electricity, they run even better on electricity than passenger vehicles do because of their greater weight and slower speeds. An electric tractor can quietly accomplish all the tasks necessary to maintain productivity on a small farm.

Dealing with the rising cost of mobility and energy are huge challenges, and the biggest challenge facing humanity may be maintaining an affordable and nourishing food supply. But we can have fresher and more nourishing food without fossil fuels. What it will take is public support for a switch to local food production on small organic farms using solar irrigation pumps and solar-charged electric tractors.

WE HAVE THE POWER

It's easy to feel confused, cynical and even hopeless about the state of the planet these days. But I am excited and optimistic because I *know* we have the technology now that will allow us to wean ourselves from fossil fuels and move to a renewable solar-electric energy system.

Yes, I know—solar panels are still too expensive for many of us. But 10 years ago, nobody gave hybrid cars a chance of succeeding. Today, the Toyota Prius is the hottest thing going. Plug-in hybrids and all-electric options should be available soon. If we all work together and demand that our government set a wise energy policy and use taxes to support the right renewable energy options, I predict we can put the brakes on climate change and enjoy clean, true-green energy.

Reaching for Rays*

Scientists Work Toward a Solar-Based Energy System

By Aimee Cunningham
Science News, May 26, 2007

In the bright blue skies that he enjoys from his academic perch in southern California, Nathan S. Lewis sees the answer to the world's energy needs. "The sun is the champion of all energy sources," says Lewis, a chemist at the California Institute of Technology in Pasadena. "More energy from the sun hits the Earth in 1 hour than all of the energy consumed by humans in an entire year."

Lewis and other scientists consider the sun's rays the optimal means of satisfying the planet's substantial—and ever-growing—energy habit. In 2001, the world consumed energy at an average rate of more than 13 trillion watts (terawatts, TW), according to the Department of Energy. Taking into account population increases, worldwide economic growth, and conservation and energy-efficiency measures, some researchers predict that the global energy-consumption rate will double by 2050 and triple by the end of the century.

Of that 2001 energy consumption, 86 percent derived from coal, oil, and natural gas. However, evidence tying global warming to the carbon dioxide that these fossil fuels pump into the atmosphere continues to grow (*SN*: 2/10/07, p. 83). "As we go hunting around for how to replace fossil fuels, solar is the one place where we can see a truly abundant and renewable resource," says A. Paul Alivisatos, a materials scientist at Lawrence Berkeley (Calif.) National Laboratory and the University of California, Berkeley.

Among non-fossil fuel choices, the sun offers by far the deepest energy reserves. To achieve energy generation of 10 TW through nuclear power, a 1-gigawatt electric-power plant fueled by nuclear fission would need to be built every one and a half days for the next 45 years, says Lewis. The remaining exploitable hydroelectric resources around the world could contribute less than 0.5 TW, according to the United Nations. And the Intergovernmental Panel on Climate Change estimates that the total amount of extractable wind power available worldwide is 2 to 4 TW.

The sun, however, showers Earth with energy at a rate of 120,000 TW, notes Lewis. Added together, the other energy sources "aren't even close to the amount of energy the sun gives," he says.

But the planet is taking advantage of only a tiny slice of the sun's largesse. Less than 0.1 percent of the world's electricity came from the sun in 2001, according to the Department of Energy. A major issue is cost. For current silicon-based solar cells, the price of electricity must be around 30 cents per kilowatt-hour to make up for the cost of the installed system, notes Lewis. This can't compete with fossil fuel-derived electricity, which now costs less than 4 cents per kilowatt-hour, he says.

Moreover, "the sun has this nasty habit of going out locally every night," Lewis continues. "Unless you can find a way to cost-effectively store massive amounts of energy, then the sun could only be a peak supplement on a sunny day."

A completely solar-based system would not only create electricity for immediate use but also turn some of the sun's energy into fuel that would power homes or vehicles when the sun isn't shining. Realizing this vision will require breakthroughs in chemistry, physics, materials science, and engineering, scientists say. Some researchers are focusing on solar capture and its conversion to electricity. Others are examining strategies to store that energy in the chemical bonds of hydrogen gas that can later generate electricity in a fuel cell.

If the work succeeds, rolls of electricity-producing solar cells—processed like newsprint—could span rooftops and deserts, while other solar devices churn out hydrogen gas. "Every roof looks at the heavens," says Stephen R. Forrest, an electrical engineer at the University of Michigan in Ann Arbor. "So why can't it be generating energy?"

CREATING A BUZZ

Solar cells already adorn some rooftops. The majority of these panels are made of silicon doped with two materials that create an electric field in the cell. When light strikes the cell, its energy frees electrons within the silicon. Driven by the electric field, the electrons travel to an electrode and thence into an electrical circuit. These cells convert 10 to 20 percent of the solar energy striking them into electricity.

Although the cost of purifying silicon has decreased over the years, scientists don't expect traditional silicon-based solar cells to become competitive with fossil fuels for electricity production.

So, researchers are looking for new solar cell technologies that combine high performance with low cost. "To really impact the [energy] problem, we have to come up with something that scales to big areas," Alivisatos says.

Some groups believe that the answer lies in solar cells composed of organic materials, nanomaterials, or both. Researchers have been developing organic solar cells in the laboratory for the past 20 years. Some of the earliest prototypes have been improved during this time, leading to devices that can convert up to 5 percent of light to electricity. Groups also continue to introduce new models in the quest for the right combination of materials, efficiency, and cost.

A common organic-based approach combines two materials in a film, explains Sean E. Shaheen, a physicist at the National Renewable Energy Laboratory in Golden, Colo. When light hits the cell, the sun's energy creates an exciton—an electron paired with its positively charged counterpart, a hole—in one of the materials, called the donor. But to become electricity, the electron needs to separate from the hole. This split occurs when the electron moves from the donor into the other material, called the acceptor. Freed electrons travel through the acceptor to one electrode, while holes travel to another electrode. Those electrodes act as the poles of a battery do and can power an electric circuit.

Excitons can travel about 5 or 6 nanometers before they decay, so a donor-acceptor boundary should be available every 10 nm, says Shaheen. At the same time, the donor-acceptor mixture must have clear pathways to the electrodes, so that charges don't become trapped in islands of material.

Some of the recent research in organic solar cell technology focuses on ways to introduce a more orderly structure into the system. Forrest and his group make solar cells in which buckyballs—nanoscale cages of carbon—act as the acceptor and an organic material called copper phthalocyanine is the donor. In their latest version of these cells, the researchers formed the two materials into a crystallike network, which improved the mobility of the charges, they reported in March at the American Physical Society meeting in Denver.

A new approach, reported by Alivisatos and his colleagues in the February *Nano Letters*, combines hyperbranched nanocrystals of cadmium selenide with a polymer. The nanocrystals have diameters of 100 to 200 nm, says team member Neil A. Fromer. This matches the thickness of the composite film. Therefore, an electron released in the nanocrystal has a clear path to its electrode at the film's surface, says Fromer.

The structure of these composites is largely determined by the shapes and sizes of the nanocrystals, which the researchers can control. That makes the devices tolerant of slight variations that occur during mixing, which leads to better reproducibility for solar cells of this type, notes Fromer.

While this is an "exciting time" in solar cell research, says Alivisatos, he cautions that the latest technology remains very much laboratory based. "Nobody yet has achieved the kind of performance that's ultimately needed," he says.

"Our efficiency is too low," agrees Shaheen. Before organic solar cells can be ready for large-scale development, they'll need to demonstrate efficiencies of 10 percent or more, scientists say.

But the potential for low-cost manufacturing will also determine the future of this technology. That's "the promise of the organics," Shaheen says. It may be possible for an assembly process to print hundreds to thousands of square meters of these solar cells per day onto sheets of plastic. "Then, ideally, you have this big roll of solar cells," Shaheen says. "You unroll it, anchor it, plug it in, and you're ready to go."

HOLDING ON TO HELIOS

To bask in the sun's energy at night or on a cloudy day requires storage. Current methods to store energy, such as batteries, aren't yet capable of storing the amounts necessary, says Daniel G. Nocera, a chemist at the Massachusetts Institute of Technology (MIT). "You don't want big, heavy batteries that are 10 times the weight of your car," he says.

Another solution—one that offers a much higher energy density, says Nocera—relies on chemical bonds. Plants store the sun's energy this way. A crucial step in photosynthesis is the splitting of water into hydrogen and oxygen. Plants release the oxygen and ultimately store the hydrogen in sugars.

Nocera and other chemists are working to better understand how nature splits water so that they can "build something artificial outside of the leaf," he says. By developing hydrogen- and oxygen-producing catalysts, chemists could use the sun's energy to break the bonds in water.

Engineers have already developed fuel cells that combine hydrogen and oxygen to create electricity. "What we are really interested in doing is making a fuel cell that runs in the reverse direction," says Christopher C. Cummins, an inorganic chemist at MIT.

Among the challenges is that water is a very stable molecule. Chemists know a great deal about reactions that, thermodynamically speaking, move downhill, releasing heat or some other form of energy as they proceed, says Cummins. But splitting water consumes energy. There is a dearth of chemical know-how about such uphill reactions, he notes.

To establish principles critical to water-splitting, Nocera's group has been working with a complex molecule incorporating ruthenium. This compound catalyzes the production of oxygen from water. With the mechanism in place, chemists could try making catalysts with more-abundant metals, such as iron or manganese, Nocera says.

Cummins' team has begun work on oxygen-producing catalysts that contain manganese or cobalt. The researchers are designing a new type of architecture in their catalysts to foster the formation of oxygen-oxygen bonds.

To complete the splitting of water, however, a second catalyst must jump-start a reaction that forms hydrogen gas. Jonas C. Peters of the California Institute of Technology and his colleagues will soon publish results on a hydrogen-producing catalyst that contains cobalt.

Ultimately, researchers would like to pour their newfound knowledge of water splitting into a device. Although this stage of the project would require some engineering and materials science expertise, the basics are as follows. The device would have two catalyst-containing segments—one to produce oxygen, the other to produce hydrogen. A barrier between the two would capture sunlight, much as a solar cell does, to power the reaction.

Working out the science behind artificial photosynthesis "is a hard problem—we shouldn't expect to be running a car on this soon," says Peters. But the good news, he adds, is that "we already know it's chemically doable, because plants do it."

SOLAR SUPPORT

As researchers learn to better tap into the sun's rays, solar energy stands to become an important resource for the planet. Whether sunlight becomes the sole source of sustainable energy or works in concert with wind and other renewables, scientists are optimistic that the planet can break its dependence on fossil fuels.

"The research community really wants to work on this problem," says Alivisatos. "If you talk to young students about this, their eyes light up."

Some researchers point out, however, that the funding doesn't match the urgency of the energy situation. "It's incredible how slow we've been as a nation to actually start pumping the kinds of resources toward this problem that are commensurate with the problem," says Peters.

"We should treat energy in research like we treat health," says Lewis. "It's as great a challenge as curing cancer, except that in 20 years, if we don't cure cancer, the world will be the same. If we don't develop ways to provide people with clean, cheap energy, we absolutely know that we will have emitted so much carbon dioxide that the world isn't going to be the same."

4

The Hydrogen Revolution: Is It Feasible?

Editor's Introduction

Hydrogen has been heralded as a potential panacea for all our energy problems, theoretically capable of curing the world of its fossil-fuel addiction. If properly harnessed, hydrogen could transform the automotive sector: Cars powered by hydrogen fuel cells would eliminate our dependence on foreign oil and, performance-wise, compare favorably to traditional gas-powered vehicles. President George W. Bush has been a vocal proponent of the technology, sponsoring various initiatives to support research and development. However, hydrogen technology is still in its infancy and researchers will need to surmount a host of obstacles if the envisioned hydrogen economy is to become a reality. Questions of generation, storage, and infrastructure currently present no easy solutions, though researchers are hard at work at devising them. The entries in this section, "The Hydrogen Revolution: Is It Feasible?," consider hydrogen's viability as an alternative fuel, taking into account the various impediments to its emergence as a primary power source.

Joan Ogden and Daniel Sperling present the case for and against hydrogen fuel cells in "The Hope for Hydrogen." For background they chart the history of alternative transportation fuels, all of which—from methanol to propane—failed for two reasons: "They provided no private benefits, and claims of large public benefits regarding pollution and energy security proved to be overstated." However, Ogden and Sperling believe that hydrogen is unlikely to suffer from the same shortcomings as its predecessors. Nevertheless, the authors believe that a number of challenges will need to be overcome if hydrogen is to become the fuel of the future.

In the next piece, "Fueling U.S. Transportation: The Hydrogen Economy and Its Alternatives," Michael K. Heiman and Barry D. Solomon further explore hydrogen's potential as a fuel source. They compare hydrogen with other alternative fuels, such as ethanol, and sound the alarm on the threat posed by our reliance on petroleum, noting that transportation accounts for a quarter of global greenhouse gas emissions. In addition, they discuss the various private initiatives currently underway to develop hydrogen technology, noting the myriad obstacles that have impeded progress, while also voicing skepticism about the rosy scenarios put forward by those involved in the projects.

In the final piece of this section, "Beyond Batteries: Portable Hydrogen Fuel

Cells," Carol Potera documents private initiatives that seek to lay the groundwork for the hydrogen economy. Specifically, she discusses efforts by Jadoo Power Systems, a company based in India, to mass produce portable hydrogen fuel cells.

The Hope for Hydrogen*

By Joan Ogden and Daniel Sperling

Issues in Science and Technology, Spring 2004

The history of alternative transportation fuels is largely a history of failures. Methanol never progressed beyond its use in test fleets, despite support from President George H. W. Bush. Compressed natural gas remains a niche fuel. And nearly every major automotive company in the world has abandoned battery-electric vehicles. Only ethanol made from corn is gaining market share in the United States, largely because of federal and state subsidies and a federal mandate. Some alternatives have succeeded elsewhere for limited times, but always because of substantial subsidies and/or government protection.

Is hydrogen different? Why do senior executives of Shell, BP, General Motors, Toyota, Daimler-Chrysler, Ford, and Honda tout hydrogen, and why do Presidents George Bush and Romano Prodi of the European Union and California Governor Arnold Schwarzenegger all advocate major hydrogen initiatives? Might hydrogen succeed on a grand scale, where other alternative fuels have not?

Hydrogen clearly provides the potential for huge energy and environmental improvements. But skeptics abound, for many good reasons. Academics question near-term environmental benefits, and activists and environmental groups question the social, environmental, and political implications of what they call "black" hydrogen (because it would be produced from coal and nuclear power). Others say we are picking the wrong horse. Paul MacCready argues in the forthcoming book of essays *The Hydrogen Energy Transition* that improved battery technology will trump hydrogen and fuel cell vehicles. And many, including John DeCicco of Environmental Defense, also in *The Hydrogen Energy Transition*, argue that the hydrogen transition is premature at best. A February 2004 report on hydrogen by the National Academies' National Academy of Engineering and National Research Council agrees, asserting that there are many questions to answer and many barriers to overcome before hydrogen's potential can be realized.

What is remarkable in the early stages of the debate is the source of public opposition: It is not coming from car or oil companies but primarily from those most concerned about environmental and energy threats. The core concern, as Joseph J. Romm argues so well [. . .], is that, "a major effort to introduce hydrogen cars before 2030 would actually undermine efforts to reduce emissions of heat-trapping greenhouse gases such as CO_2."

In fact, the hydrogen debate is being sucked into the larger debate over President Bush's environmental record. The environmental community fears that the promise of hydrogen is being used to camouflage eviscerated and stalled regulations and that it will crowd out R&D for deserving near-term energy efficiency and renewable energy opportunities. What the administration and others portray as a progressive long-term strategy, others see as bait and switch. Indeed, a backlash is building against what many see as hydrogen hype.

Perhaps this skepticism is correct. Perhaps it is true that without a hydrogen initiative, government leaders would pursue more aggressive fuel economy standards and larger investments in renewable energy. We remain skeptical. And even if true, what about the larger question of the size of the public R&D energy pie? If energy efficiency and climate change are important public issues, then quibbling over tens of millions of dollars in the U.S. Department of Energy budget is missing the point. It should not be seen as a zero sum game. If energy efficiency and climate change are compelling initiatives, then shouldn't the debate really be over the size of the budget?

In any case, we believe there is a different story to tell. First, hydrogen must be pursued as part of a long-term strategy. (Indeed, any coherent energy strategy should have a long-term component.) Second, hydrogen policy must complement and build on near-term policies aimed at energy efficiency, greenhouse gas reduction, and enhanced renewable energy investments. Hydrogen vehicles will not happen without those policies in place. In fact, hybrid vehicles are an essential step in the technological transition to fuel cells and hydrogen. And third, if not hydrogen, then what? No other long-term option approaches the breadth and magnitude of hydrogen's public benefits.

THE LESSONS OF HISTORY

All previous alternative transportation fuels ultimately failed, largely for two reasons: They provided no private benefits, and claims of large public benefits regarding pollution and energy security proved to be overstated. The private benefits from compressed natural gas, ethanol, methanol, propane, and early battery-electric vehicles were nil. When compared to petroleum-fueled vehicles, all have shorter distances between refueling and different safety and performance attributes, often perceived as inferior. The only clear benefits are emissions and energy security, but few consumers purchase a vehicle for public-good reasons.

Overstated claims for new fuels were not intentionally deceptive. Rather they reflected a poor understanding of energy and environmental innovation and policy. Two errors stand out: understated forecasts of oil supply and gasoline quality and overstated environmental and economic benefits of alternative fuels. Oil turned out to be cheap and abundant, thanks to improved technologies for finding and extracting oil; gasoline and diesel fuel were reformulated to be cleaner; and internal combustion engines continued to improve and now emit nearly no harmful air pollutants.

What do these lessons imply for hydrogen? First, hydrogen is unlikely to succeed on the basis of environmental and energy advantages alone, at least in the near to medium term. Hydrogen will find it difficult to compete with the century-long investment in petroleum fuels and the internal combustion engine. Hybrid electric vehicles, cleaner combustion engines, and cleaner fuels will provide almost as much energy and environmental benefit on a per-vehicle basis for some time. During the next decade or so, advanced gasoline and diesel vehicles will be more widespread and deliver more benefits sooner than hydrogen and fuel cells ever could. Hydrogen is neither the easiest nor the cheapest way to gain large near- and medium-term air pollution, greenhouse gas, or oil reduction benefits.

What about the long term? Although incremental enhancements are far from exhausted, there is almost no hope that oil or carbon dioxide (CO_2) reduction improvements in vehicles could even offset increases in vehicle usage, never mind achieve the radical decarbonization and petroleum reductions likely needed later this century.

THE CASE FOR HYDROGEN

The case for hydrogen is threefold. First, hydrogen fuel cell vehicles appear to be a superior consumer product desired by the automotive industry. Second, as indicated by the National Academies' study, the potential exists for dramatic reductions in the cost of hydrogen production, distribution, and use. And third, hydrogen provides the potential for zero tailpipe pollution, near-zero well-to-wheels emissions of greenhouse gases, and the elimination of oil imports, simultaneously addressing the most vexing challenges facing the fuels sector, well beyond what could be achieved with hybrid vehicles and energy efficiency.

The future of hydrogen is linked to the automotive industry's embrace of fuel cells. The industry, or at least an important slice of it, sees fuel cells as its inevitable and desired future. This was not true for any previous alternative fuel. The National Academies' report highlights the attractions of fuel cell vehicles. It notes that not only are fuel cells superior environmentally, but they also provide extra value to customers. They have the potential to provide most of the benefits of battery-electric vehicles without the short range and long recharge time. They offer quiet operation, rapid acceleration from a standstill because of the torque characteristics of electric motors, and potentially low maintenance requirements.

They can provide remote electrical power—for construction sites and recreational uses, for example—and even act as distributed electricity generators when parked at homes and offices. Importantly, they also have additional attractions for automakers. By eliminating most mechanical and hydraulic subsystems, they provide greater design flexibility and the potential for using fewer vehicle platforms, which allow more efficient manufacturing approaches. Fuel cells are a logical extension of the technological pathway automakers are already following and would allow a superior consumer product—if fuel cell costs become competitive and if hydrogen fuel can be made widely available at a reasonable cost.

Those two "ifs" remain unresolved and are central to the hydrogen debate. Fuel cell costs are on a steep downward slope and are now perhaps a factor of 10 to 20 too high. Huge amounts of engineering are still needed to improve manufacturability, ensure long life and reliability, and enable operation at extreme temperatures. Although some engineers believe that entirely new fuel cell architectures are needed to achieve the last 10-fold cost reduction, a handful of automotive companies seem convinced that they are on track to achieve those necessary cost reductions and performance enhancements. Indeed, massive R&D investments are taking place at most of the major automakers.

The second "if" is hydrogen availability, which is perhaps the greatest challenge of all. The problem is not production cost or sufficient resources. Hydrogen is already produced from natural gas and petroleum at costs similar to those of gasoline (adjusting for fuel cells' higher efficiency). With continuing R&D investment, the cost of providing hydrogen from a variety of abundant fossil and renewable sources should prove to be not much greater than that of providing gasoline, according to the National Academies' study.

The key supply challenges are as follows. First is the need for flexibility. There are many possible paths for making and delivering hydrogen, and it is difficult at this time to know which will prevail. Second, because private investment will naturally gravitate toward conventional fossil energy sources, currently the lowest-cost way to make hydrogen, government needs to accelerate R&D of zero-emission hydrogen production methods. Renewable hydrogen production is a key area for focused R&D. CO_2 sequestration—a prerequisite if abundant coal in the United States, China, and elsewhere is to be used—is another possible path to very-low-emission hydrogen. Although the cost of capturing carbon from large fossil fuel plants and sequestering it is not prohibitive in a large range of locations and situations, CO_2 sequestration faces uncertain public acceptance. Will CO_2 be perceived in the same light as nuclear waste, leading to permitting delays and extra costs?

The third supply-related challenge is logistical in nature. How can hydrogen be provided at local refueling sites, offering both convenience and acceptable cost to consumers during a transition? Today's natural gas and petroleum distribution systems are not necessarily good models for future hydrogen distribution, especially in the early stages of hydrogen use when consumption is small and dispersed. If future hydrogen systems attempt to simply mimic today's energy systems from the beginning, distribution costs could be untenably large, and the hydrogen economy will be stillborn. Unlike liquid transportation fuels, hydrogen storage, delivery, and refueling are major cost contributors. Astoundingly, delivering hydrogen from large plants to dispersed small hydrogen users is now roughly five times more expensive than producing the hydrogen. Even for major fossil fuel-based hydrogen production facilities under study, distribution and delivery costs are estimated to be equal to production costs.

Clearly, a creative, evolutionary approach is needed, eventually leading to a system that serves both stationary and mobile users, relies on small as well as large hydrogen production facilities, accesses a wide variety of energy feedstocks, incorporates CO_2 capture and sequestration, and is geographically diverse. In the very early stages of a transition, hydrogen might be delivered by truck from a central plant serving chemical uses as well as vehicles or be produced at refueling sites from natural gas or electricity. Distributed generation will be a key part of the solution, with production near or at the end-use site. The National Academies' report argues that the hydrogen economy will initially and perhaps for a very long time be based on distributed generation of hydrogen. (Honda and General Motors propose placing small hydrogen refueling appliances at residences.) Other innovative solutions would be needed, especially during the early phases. In cities with dense populations, pipelines would probably become the lowest-cost delivery option, once a sizeable fraction of vehicles run on hydrogen. The transportation fuel and electricity and chemical industries might become more closely coupled, because the economics can sometimes be improved by coproduction of electricity, hydrogen, and chemical products. Transitions would proceed in different ways, depending on regional resources and geographic factors.

NO NATURAL ENEMIES

Although the challenges are daunting, perhaps the most important factor is the absence of natural political or economic enemies. For starters, hydrogen is highly inclusive, capable of being made from virtually any energy feedstock, including coal, nuclear, natural gas, biomass, wind, and solar.

The oil industry is key. It effectively opposed battery-electric vehicles, because companies saw no business case for themselves. Hydrogen is different. Oil companies are in actuality massive energy companies. They are prepared to supply any liquid or gaseous fuel consumers might desire, although of course they prefer a slow transition that allows them to protect their current investments. Most, for instance, prefer that initial fuel cell vehicles carry reformers to convert gasoline into hydrogen. They have been disappointed that all major car companies are now focused strictly on delivered hydrogen.

Oil companies will not allow the hydrogen economy to develop without them. Indeed, some have played key roles in promoting hydrogen, and many are active participants in hydrogen-refueling demonstration projects around the world. But oil companies would not realize a rapid payoff from being the first to market. Rather, they anticipate large financial losses that would be stanched only when hydrogen use became widespread. Without government support during the low-volume transition stage, oil companies are unlikely to be early investors in the construction of hydrogen fuel stations. They are best characterized as watchful, strategically positioning themselves to play a large role if and when hydrogen takes off.

Automakers see a different business reality. They see benefits from being first to market. They see hydrogen fuel cells as the desirable next step in the technological evolution of vehicles. Hydrogen's future appears to be tightly linked to automaker commitments to move fuel cells from the lab to the marketplace. The key question is whether and when they will ratchet up current investments of perhaps $150 million per year (in the case of the more aggressive automakers) to the much larger sums needed to tool factories and launch commercial products. Without automaker leadership, the transition will be slow, building on small entrepreneurial investments in niche opportunities, such as fuel cells in off-road industrial equipment, hydrogen blends in natural gas buses, innovative low-cost delivery of hydrogen to small users, and small energy stations simultaneously powering remote buildings and vehicle fleets.

IF NOT HYDROGEN, THEN WHAT?

What are the alternatives to hydrogen? The only other serious long-term alternatives for fueling the transport sector are grid-supplied electricity and biomass. Electricity is quite appealing on environmental and energy grounds. It allows for many of the same benefits as hydrogen: accessing renewable and other feedstocks and zero vehicular emissions. But every major automaker has abandoned its battery-electric vehicle program, except for Daimler-Chrysler's small factory in North Dakota producing the GEM neighborhood vehicle. For battery-electric vehicles to be viable, several-fold improvements in batteries or other electricity storage devices would be required, or massive investments would be needed in "third rail" electricity infrastructure that would require substantial added cost for vehicles. These massive improvements are unlikely. Continued battery improvements are likely, but after a century of intense research, there still remains no compelling proposal that might reduce material costs sufficiently to render batteries competitive with internal combustion engines. The same is not true of fuel cells.

The other long-term proposal is biomass. Cellulosic materials, including trees and grasses, would be grown on the vast land areas of the United States and converted into ethanol or methanol fuel for use in combustion engines. Although this energy option is renewable, the environmental effects of intensive farming are not trivial, and the land areas involved are massive. Moreover, there are few other regions in the world available for extensive energy farming.

Other options include fossil-based synthetic fuels, in which shale oil, oil sands, coal, and other abundant materials are converted into petroleum-like fuels and then burned in combustion engines or converted into hydrogen at fuel stations or on board vehicles for use in fuel cells. But with all these options, carbon capture at the site is more difficult than with coal-to-hydrogen options, CO_2 volumes would be massive, and the overall energy efficiency would be far inferior.

We conclude that hydrogen merits strong support, if only because of the absence of a more compelling long-term option.

HYDROGEN'S PRECARIOUS FUTURE

The transition to a hydrogen economy will be neither easy nor straightforward. Like all previous alternatives, it faces daunting challenges. But hydrogen is different. It accesses a broad array of energy resources, potentially provides broader and deeper societal benefits than any other option, potentially provides large private benefits, has no natural political or economic enemies, and has a strong industrial proponent in the automotive industry.

In the end, though, the hydrogen situation is precarious. Beyond a few car companies and a scattering of entrepreneurs, academics, and environmental advocates, support for hydrogen is thin. Although many rail against the hydrogen hype, the greater concern perhaps should be the fragile support for hydrogen. Politics aside, we applaud the United States, California, and others for starting down a path toward a sustainable future. Although we do not know when or even if the hydrogen economy will eventually dominate, we do believe that starting down this path is good strategy.

The key is enhanced science and technology investments, both public and private, and a policy environment that encourages those investments. Fuel cells and hydrogen provide a good marker to use in formulating policy and gaining public support. Of course, policy should remain focused on near-term opportunities. But good near-term policy, such as improving fuel economy, is also good long-term policy. It sends signals to businesses and customers that guide them toward investments and market decisions that are beneficial to society. It appears to us that hydrogen is a highly promising option that we should nurture as part of a broader science, technology, and policy initiative. The question is how, not if.

Fueling U.S. Transportation*

The Hydrogen Economy and Its Alternatives

By Michael K. Heiman and Barry D. Solomon
Environment, October 2007

Transportation is responsible for one-fourth of global greenhouse gas emissions and consumes 75 percent of world oil production. The U.S. transportation sector alone accounts for almost 10 percent of global energy-related greenhouse gas emissions.[1] Insofar as it is a carrier and a storage medium for energy (unlike electricity, the other main energy carrier), hydrogen has been promoted as ideal for future transportation, and interest in it has been increasing in the last decade.[2] Before a costly and potentially irreversible commitment to a hydrogen energy system is made, it will be critical to first consider criteria for a sustainable transport sector and then determine how hydrogen might measure up and over what time frame. Society's limited time and resources may make it unfeasible to fully pursue all available options for addressing the problems of climate change and oil dependence, such as energy conservation; diesel, hybrid, and electric vehicles; and biomass fuels. Therefore, a careful comparison of options may be necessary.

Interest in alternative-fueled vehicles can be attributed to rising concern over global climate change, peak world oil production, and growing dependence on insecure oil imports by the United States, Europe, and Japan. Hydrogen energy and hydrogen fuel cell vehicles (HFCVs), while not the only alternative for the

* From *Environment*, vol. 49, no. 8, pp10–25, October 2007. Reprinted with permission of the Helen Dwight Reid Educational Foundation. Published by Heldref Publications, 1319 Eighteenth St., NW, Washington, DC 20036-1802.

1 J. Ogden, R. Williams, and E. Larson, "Societal Lifecycle Costs of Cars with Alternative Fuels/Engines," *Energy Policy* 32, no. 1 (2004): 7–27; J. Ogden, "High Hopes for Hydrogen," *Scientific American* 295, no. 3 (2006): 94–101; and U.S. Environmental Protection Agency (EPA), *A Wedge Analysis of the U.S. Transportation Sector*, EPA 420–R–07–007 (Washington, DC: EPA, April 2007).

2 J. J. Romm, *The Hype about Hydrogen: Fact and Fiction in the Race to Save the Climate* (Washington, DC: Island Press, 2004); J. Riflkn, *The Hydrogen Economy* (New York: Tarcher, 2003); S. Dunn, "The Hydrogen Experiment," *Worldwatch* 13, no. 6 (November/December 2000): 14–25; B. D. Solomon and A. Banerjee, "A Global Survey of Hydrogen Energy Research, Development and Policy," *Energy Policy* 34, no. 7 (2006): 781–92; U.S. Department of Energy (DOE), *National Hydrogen Energy Roadmap* (Washington, DC: DOE, 2002); Japan Hydrogen and Fuel Cell Demonstration Project, http://www.jhfc.jp/e/index.htrmi (accessed 15 September 2006); and European Commission (EC), EC High Level Working Group on Hydrogen and Fuel Cells, *Hydrogen Energy and Fuel Cells: A Vision of Our Future: Final Report* (Brussels: EC, 2003), http://ec.europa.eulresearchienergy/pdf/hydrogenreport–en.pdf (accessed 26 June 2007).

transportation sector, have received considerable attention from government officials, automakers, and the media.

Although the United States failed to ratify the 1997 Kyoto Protocol, the treaty was implemented by U.S. trading partners, and took effect in February 2005. California's ambitious carbon-emissions reduction program, announced in 2006, will be linked to it.[3] Much of the world seems to be searching for viable (and preferably sustainable) alternatives to petroleum-based transportation to combat climate change. Consequently, a potentially emissions-free, locally available fuel such as hydrogen would be hard to resist, presuming consumer acceptance and cost-effective technologies. However, hydrogen as an energy carrier is only as green as its energy source. If that source is renewable, are there more appropriate uses for the input energy, and more attractive alternatives to power transportation, particularly if energy efficiency and reduced greenhouse gas emissions are primary goals?

As envisioned by Jules Verne in his 1874 book *L'Ile Mystérieuse*,[4] the "hydrogen economy" recently called for by world leaders would not have to start from scratch.[5] Hydrogen, one of the most abundant elements on Earth and lightest gas, has been a crucial raw material for many decades. About 85 percent of hydrogen consumed globally is used to produce ammonia for fertilizers or to remove sulfur from gasoline, heating oil, and diesel fuels.[6] In addition, the National Aeronautics and Space Administration has been a major user of liquid hydrogen for rocket fuel since 1958.[7] Roughly 90 billion normal cubic meters (cubic meters of a gas at standard temperature and pressure, Nm^3) of hydrogen are produced annually in the United States and 500 billion Nm^3 worldwide—a figure growing by 10 percent per year.[8] Economics dictates that 95 percent of current U.S. hydrogen is produced by steam-methane reforming of non-renewable natural gas, so production in this manner is unsustainable. This method also results in more than 10 tons of carbon dioxide (CO_2) emissions for each ton of hydrogen produced.[9]

Fortunately there are many other ways to make hydrogen, such as electrolysis of water (just 2 percent of current U.S. production), petroleum refining (30 percent of world production but negligible in the United States), and gasification of biomass or coal. While electrolysis is potentially the cleanest option, it is usually

3 United Nations Kyoto Protocol to the Framework Convention on Climate Change, http://unfccc.int/resource/docs/convkp/kpeng.html (accessed 28 June 2007); and Office of the Governor (California), "California, New York Agree to Explore Linking Greenhouse Gas Emission Credit Trading Markets," press release (Sacramento: 16 October 2006).

4 J. Verse, *L'ile Mysterieuse* (Paris: Hetzel, 1874).

5 President George W. Bush and former European Commission (EC) President Romano Prodi are strong supporters of increased research and development to develop hydrogen as a transportation fuel substitute. For example, see G. W. Bush, "State of the Union Address," 28 January 2003, Washington, DC: The White House, Office of the Press Secretary; and R. Prodi, "European Hydrogen and Fuel Cell Technology Platform General Assembly," speech before the European Hydrogen and Fuel Cell Technology General Assembly, Brussels, 20 January 2004, http://europa.eu.int/rapid/pressReleasesAction.do?reference=SPEECH/ 04/26&format=HTML&aged=0&language=EN&guiLanguage=en (accessed 26 June 2007).

6 DOE, Office of Power Delivery, Office of Power Technologies, Energy Efficiency and Renewable Energy, *A Multiyear Plan for the Hydrogen R&D Program*, Rationale, Structure and Technology Roadmaps (Washington, DC: DOE, 1999).

7 P. Hoffmann, *The Forever Fuel—The Story of Hydrogen* (Boulder, CO: Westview Press, 1981).

8 Ronim, note 2 above, pages 71–72; C. J. Winter, "Into the Hydrogen Economy–Milestones" (editorial), International Journal of Hydrogen Energy 30, no. 7 (2005): 681–85; and A. B. Lovins, *Twenty Hydrogen Myths* (Snowmass, CO: Rocky Mountain Institute #E–03–05, 2003), http://www.rmi.org/images/other/Energy/E03–05_20HydrogenMyths.pdf (accessed 26 June 2007).

9 N. Z. Muradov and T. N. Veziroglu, "From Hydrocarbon to Hydrogen-Carbon to Hydrogen Economy," *International Journal of Hydrogen Research* 30, no. 3 (2005): 225.

prohibitively expensive when compared to the cost of using the electricity directly as a primary energy carrier instead of as a hydrogen producer.[10] Moreover, electrolysis currently costs 3–4 times as much to generate hydrogen compared to steam reforming of natural gas, while its associated CO_2 emissions depend on the fuel source that produces the electricity.[11] Reformation of hydrogen from coal (an abundant fossil fuel in the United States) with resulting CO_2 sequestration has received much attention from the current Bush administration, with the U.S. Department of Energy (DOE) sponsoring pilot projects. However, while promising, this technology is as yet unproven geologically, economically, or thermodynamically on a scale large enough to support commercial production.

ENERGY FOR TRANSPORTATION IN THE UNITED STATES

The United States used 20.6 million barrels of non-renewable petroleum a day in 2006, almost a quarter of the total daily global demand of 84.5 million barrels. About 56 percent of this petroleum demand is used for motor gasoline and on-highway diesel in autos, sport utility vehicles, vans, trucks, buses, and motorcycles. Another 8 percent is used for jet fuel, with smaller amounts for ship fuel, petrochemicals, plastics, and myriad other products made or derived from petroleum. Crude oil and petroleum product imports have been growing and currently account for 66 percent of U.S. oil use. It is difficult to envision this demand changing much in the next decade. As a result, the transport sector is highly dependent on oil, which accounts for 97.8 percent of total transport energy use in the nation.[12]

Underscoring the importance of the addiction to unsustainable oil use in the United States is recent concern with "peak oil." While 1970 was the peak year for domestic oil production, substantial debate has occurred over when world oil output will similarly peak. Most of the discussion has centered on the applicability of the model of the visionary geophysicist Marion King Hubbert, who accurately applied statistical physical methods to correctly predict the peak in crude oil production of the United States 14 years beforehand.[13] For various reasons, application of his techniques to the world oil situation has been much more vexing, and debate over the ultimate peak date has increased in the last decade. Some analysts claim that world production already peaked in 2005, while others have argued for a date after 2030. More important than the exact date is the immutable geophysical fact that the supply will eventually peak and decline soon thereafter.[14]

10 B. E. Logan, "Extracting Hydrogen and Electricity from Renewable Resources," *Environmental Science & Technology* 38, no. 9 (May 2004): 162A-63A.

11 T. E. Lipman, *What Will Power the Hydrogen Economy? Present and Future Sources of Hydrogen Energy*, report prepared for the Natural Resources Defense Council (Davis, CA: Institute of Transportation Studies, University of California, 2004).

12 Energy Information Administration, DOE, *Annual Energy Review* 2006, http://www.eia.doe.gov/emeu/aer/contents.html (accessed 29 June 2007); Energy Information Administration, DOE, *International Energy Annual* 2004, http://www.eia.doe.gov/iea/contents.html (accessed 26 June 2007).

13 R. Heinberg, *The Party's Over: Oil, War and the Fate of Industrial Societies*, revised edition (Gabriola Island, BC, Canada: New Society Publishers, 2005), 95-136.

14 R. K. Kaufmann and L. D. Shiers, "The Effect of Resource Uncertainty on the Peak in Global Oil Production and the Production of Alternatives," submitted to the *Proceedings of the National Academy of Sciences*, 2007.

The reality is that while the world will not be running out of oil anytime soon, it will be facing increasingly tight market conditions in the next decade as we run out of economically and politically affordable oil. Unless global oil demand tapers off, petroleum products will face continuous upward price pressures. Higher prices encourage oil companies to explore for and develop supplies in remote areas and in deeper fields. As a result, pressure for development in Alaska and the Outer Continental Shelf will continue. Low-cost fields in the conflict-laden Middle East, location of the world's largest oil reserves, will reap large economic rents under these conditions, only underscoring how oil security concerns will become even more important than peak oil.

Petroleum markets will increasingly experience supply constraints that are geopolitical and technological in nature (as more nations peak in production). Only a few areas of production growth exist outside the Middle East.[15] None of these areas, however, will likely be able to sustain increased production for more than five years. Most surplus oil from Russia, the largest oil producer outside of the Middle East and the United States, is sold in Europe because of closer trade ties. Despite strong trade ties, Mexico—the second-largest supplier of oil to the United States after Canada—is limited by its own needs. Moreover, rapidly rising demand for petroleum products in China and India could make these geopolitical patterns problematic for the United States.

The United States has been in this situation before. Starting with the oil embargo from the Arab members of the Organization of the Petroleum Exporting Countries (OPEC) in October 1973, the U.S. government spent nearly a decade actively exploring a large range of domestic energy options. Among these were oil shale, tar sands, and coal gasification and liquefaction.[16] By the time pilot projects for these synthetic fuels got off the ground, high energy prices suppressed demand growth, and policy support for these projects all but disappeared when gasoline prices tapered off.[17] In addition to their increasingly high price tag, synthetic fuels development in the United States has been hampered by serious concerns over water requirements, land cover disruption, waste generation, CO_2 emissions, and other environmental problems. Even so, with higher oil prices today there is renewed interest in oil shale development in the western United States, especially through in-situ conversion. While U.S. oil shale reserves exceed those of domestic oil, it is still a non-renewable resource, and significant environmental questions remain. The same can be said for tar sands, which have been successfully developed in Canada, while receiving less interest in the United States.

SUSTAINABLE TRANSPORTATION PRINCIPLES

15 S. Dees, P. Karadeloglou, R. K. Kaufmann, and M. Sanchez, "Modeling the World Oil Market," *Energy Policy*, 35 (2007): 178-91; Heinberg, note 13 above, pages 116-17.

16 Oil shale and tar sands are low-grade geologic repositories of hydrocarbons that yield usable oil through high-temperature pyrolysis and/or distillation. Coal gasification and liquefaction convert coal into a synthetic gas under high temperature and pressure for further processing into commercial gas or oil fuels.

17 W. D. Constain, "Energy Policy and Boom and Bust Cycles: Government Action and Instability in the Development of Oil Shale," *Policy Studies Journal* 13, no. 2 (1984): 401-11; and H. R. Linden, "The Evolution of an Energy Contrarian," *Annual Review of Energy and the Environment* 21 (1996): 31-67.

For transportation to be sustainable, greenhouse gas emissions need to be reduced, as do emissions of conventional air and water pollutants. To do this, it is vital to procure a sustainable physical fuel supply (though the two are linked).[18] Thus renewable fuels, such as biomass and biodiesel, need to be managed in an environmentally sound and sustainable manner.

Sustainability, however, encompasses much more, such as investments in poverty alleviation; clean water; transportation accessibility; and adequate diet, health care, and education.[19] Social concerns must also be taken into consideration: For example, walking and bicycling are sustainable and generally socially desirable, but people's opinions about these modes of transportation are colored by their perceptions of social class or economic forces like the supply of fuel. Many people may feel forced to use these options because of their low income or fuel supply shortages and would drop them if their income rose or more fuel became available. Based on these considerations, several principles of sustainable transportation emerge.

The U.S. transportation sector today is far from sustainable—note the paucity of renewable energy use in the sector. For example, while the use of corn-based (and environmentally problematic) ethanol in the United States is growing rapidly, in 2006 it accounted for less than 2 percent of total transportation energy consumption, or 5.5 billion gallons (including imports).[20] This contrasts with Brazil, which is 40 percent reliant on sugarcane-based ethanol. No other nation approaches Brazil and the United States in their rate of renewable transportation fuel use. Based on the composite measurements of the Environmental Sustainability Index of Nations (2005) and the Pilot Environmental Performance Index (2006), developed by the Yale Center for Environmental Law and Policy, the United States ranks poorly.[21] The indices, however, do not include specific measurements for the transportation sector, only broader measurements of sustainable energy use. Furthermore, carbon neutrality, total greenhouse gas emissions, and net energy gained from biofuels are contested, with a few lifecycle analyses concluding that the fossil fuel energy and global greenhouse gas emissions saved in ethanol and biodiesel production do not compensate for carbon used or emissions generated by the input, accounting for the crop grown, method employed, inputs, and the energy it takes to produce various useful coproducts such as animal feed, residual fuel sources, or chemical byproducts.[22]

18 Projecting global emissions to 2054, and accounting for expected increase in electricity and fuel use, Princeton University professor of mechanical and aerospace engineering Robert Socolow and his colleagues estimate that we would need to eliminate 7 billion tons of carbon dioxide (CO_2) per year just to stabilize at the 2001 emissions level. See R. Socolow, R. Hotinski, J. B. Greenblatt, and S. Pacala, "Solving the Climate Problem: Technologies Available to Curb CO_2 Emissions," Environment, 46 no. 10 (December 2004): 8-19.

19 J. D. Marshall and M. W. Toeffel, "Framing the Elusive Concept of Sustainability," *Environmental Science & Technology* 39, no. 3 (2005): 673-82; J. D. Sachs and W. D. Reid, "Investments Toward Sustainable Development," *Science*, 19 May 2006, 1002-03; and M. K. Heiman, "Community Attempts at Sustainable Development through Corporate Accountability," *Journal of Environmental Planning and Management* 40, no. 5 (1997): 631-43.

20 Ethanol production statistics by nation are reported by the Renewable Fuels Association: http://www.ethanolrfa.org/industry/statistics/(accessed 9 April 2007).

21 D. Esty, M. Levy, T. Srebotnjak, and A. de Sherbinin, 2005 *Environmental Sustainability Index* (New Haven: Yale Center for Environmental Law & Policy, 2005); and D. Esty et al., *Pilot 2006 Environmental Performance Index* (New Haven: Yale Center for Environmental Law & Policy, 2006).

22 D. Pimentel and T. W. Patzek, "Ethanol Production Using Corn, Switchgrass, and Wood: Biodiesel Production Using Soybean and Sunflower," *Natural Resources Research* 14, no. 1 (March 2005): 65-76; and M. Giampietro, S. Ulgiati, and D. Pimentel, "Feasibility of Large-Scale Biofuel Production," *BioScience* 47, no. 9 (1997): 587-600.

Many candidate transportation fuels and technologies can reduce reliance on motor gasoline. These include more efficient autos; several renewable energy options; other non-renewable fuels (including diesel, which has a higher energy density than unleaded gasoline) that could be used as transitional fuels, especially if they are coupled with carbon capture and storage; and electric and hybrid vehicles. Although many are competitors with hydrogen energy and hydrogen fuel cell vehicles (HFCVs), others, such as renewable energy and hybrid technology, can be linked with hydrogen. While all these options need to be carefully assessed—it is safer for society to diversify its energy sources—sustainable priorities emerge.

TRANSPORTATION FUEL ALTERNATIVES TO PETROLEUM

Four categories of fuels can be derived from renewable energy sources, and these are only sustainable if they are managed as such: grain-based ethanol, biomass (cellulosic) ethanol, biodiesel, and biomass (woody) methanol. At present, 95 percent of U.S. liquid biofuels production consists of ethanol, with the rest being biodiesel. Ethanol has been heavily subsidized with a 40–60 cents per gallon federal tax exemption or credit since 1978. Additional credits and grants are available through many states and the federal government for ethanol production, fuel blending, and equipment purchase, including pump installation. As encompassed in the 2005 Energy Policy Act, the U.S. goal is to produce 7.5 billion gallons of this "renewable fuel" by 2012 and 1 billion gallons of cellulosic ethanol by 2015, thereby reducing U.S. petroleum consumption by 0.8 to 1.6 percent and anticipated CO_2-equivalent greenhouse gas emissions by 0.4 to 0.6 percent.[23]

More than 95 percent of U.S. ethanol production is derived from corn. This fuel is blended with gasoline at levels ranging from 5 to 85 percent. While most analyses show a modest net fossil fuel-derived energy gain and CO_2 emissions reduction from ethanol and especially biodiesel, these debates hinge on several assumptions regarding the feedstock used, conversion technology, and value of coproducts.[24] Even so, corn production usually exacerbates problems of soil erosion; loss of biodiversity; dependence on gas and oil-based fertilizers, pesticides, and herbicides; increased nitrous oxide emissions (another greenhouse gas); water loss through irrigation; and water and air pollution.[25] Furthermore, current ethanol refineries usually require large fossil fuel inputs. Similar to the situation for oil-dependent agriculture, ethanol production is thus not sustainable at the present time. Domestic production of cellulosic ethanol, in contrast, has three times the resource potential, can avoid most fossil fuel inputs by burning plant lignin (an

23 The House Committee Print of the Energy Policy Act of 2005 can be found at http://www.govtrack.us/congress/bill-text.xpd?bill=h109-1640 (accessed 30 June 2007); and P. Leiby, *Estimating the Energy Security Benefits of Reduced U.S. Oil Imports*, ORNL/TM-2007/028 (Oak Ridge, TN: Oak Ridge National Laboratory, February 2007).

24 See, for example, J. Hill, E. Nelson, D. Tilman, S. Polasky, and D. Tiffany, "Environmental, Economic, and Energetic Costs and Benefits of Biodiesel and Ethanol Biofuels," *Proceedings of the National Academy of Sciences* 103, no. 30 (25 July 2006): 11206-10; and EPA, *Regulatory Impact Analysis: Renewable Fuel Standard Program*, EPA420-R-07-004 (Washington, DC: EPA, April 2007), particularly chapter 6.

25 D. Pimentel, "Ethanol Fuels: Energy Balance, Economics, and Environmental Impacts are Negative," *Natural Resources Research* 12, no. 2 (June 2003): 127-34.

organic polymer), and is a more energy-efficient product. According to DOE, cellulosic ethanol has the potential to displace more than one-third of the petroleum used in the United States. Owing to these advantages, cellulosic ethanol could possibly reduce CO_2 emissions by more than 90 percent and lessen other environmental effects, if it is made from residues or grasses that are not required for field fertilization.[26] The first commercial cellulosic ethanol plants opened in late 2007. Feedstocks include agricultural and forestry residues, short-rotation woody crops such as hybrid poplar and willow, municipal solid waste, and perennial grasses.

Biodiesel production and use, while also highly attractive and common in Germany and France, are limited to a potential of 0.4 billion gallons a year in the United States based on the feedstock supply.[27] It is defined as a renewable fuel for diesel engines derived from animal fats or vegetable oils such as soybean and palm, which meets the specification of the American Society for Testing and Materials. The fuel is blended with an oil-based diesel distillate at levels ranging from 2 to 99 percent. Finally, biomass methanol, another alternative that can be made from forest residues (such as tree stumps, branches, and leaves) or wood would be an alternative product for up to a quarter of the biomass ethanol feedstock supply. However, methanol and MTBE (methyl tertiary butyl ether—an increasingly banned gasoline additive made from methanol and isobutylene)—are well known for their toxic effects. In addition, methanol has a lower energy content than ethanol (both are lower than gasoline) and is more corrosive. These problems may limit the pursuit of this fuel.

Four sources of fossil fuels could also be substituted for petroleum-based gasoline and diesel—compressed natural gas (CNG), oil shale, tar sands, and coal liquefaction. Two combined-cycle coal gasification electric power plants have been built in the United States, but neither produces transportation fuels. A fifth option, methanol derived from natural gas, is usable today in many flex-fuel vehicles but has been limited by concerns over its toxicity and thus is used mainly to make MTBE, formaldehyde, and other industrial chemical products. CNG is a low-cost, clean-burning fuel, emitting about half the CO_2 of gasoline or diesel per gallon equivalent. It could be seen as a transitional fuel or one that could be coupled with CO_2 sequestration. Use of CNG requires vehicles to have a large gas storage tank and a much more developed refueling network than the one currently in place, since these vehicles have a maximum range of 200–250 miles and only about 1,200 fueling stations exist in the United States. In addition, most of the gas supply is given a higher priority for applications such as heating, industrial use, and electricity generation than for transportation.

The other nonrenewable fuels have high CO_2 emissions, and thus carbon sequestration would have to be considered. Among these, while oil shale and coal

26 C. E. Wyman, "Biomass Ethanol: Technical Progress, Opportunities, and Commercial Challenges," *Annual Review of Energy and the Environment* 24 (1999): 191; B. D. Solomon, J. Barnes, and K. E. Halvorsen, "Grain and Cellulosic Ethanol: History, Economics, and Energy Policy," *Biomass and Bioenergy* 31. no, 6 (June 2007): 416-25; and R. D. Perlack et al., *Biomass as Feedstocks.for a Bioenergy and Bioproducts Industry*, report prepared by Oak Ridge National Laboratory for the U.S. Department of Agriculture and DOE, DOE/GO-102005-2135 (Washington, DC: DOE, Transportation and Climate Division, Office of Transportation and Air Quality, April 2005), 38.

27 Perlack et al., ibid., page 30; and E. Martinot, "Renewable Energy Gains Momentum: Global Market and Policies in the Spotlight," *Environment*, July/August 2006, 26-43.

gasification/liquefaction have only been assessed in the United States in recent years, commercial projects have existed in Brazil, Estonia, China, and elsewhere. Shell Exploration and Production Co. anticipates that a commercial oil shale project in the Green River Formation of western Colorado may be viable after 2015.[28] Meanwhile, the first coal gasification-liquefaction plant in the United States is planned for eastern Pennsylvania. Employing the Fischer-Tropsch process first used by Nazi Germany and South Africa when their access to global oil was blocked, this facility will use waste coal from more than 150 years of anthracite mining to produce 40 million gallons per year of clean-burning diesel fuel and 41 megawatts (MW) of electricity. In the process, 2.5 to 3.5 times more CO_2 is generated than if the coal was burned directly—a major release not being controlled through carbon sequestration.[29]

Finally, potential low- or no-carbon options to gasoline vehicles include more efficient autos, increased use of diesel fuel and vehicles, gasoline (or diesel)-electric hybrids, all-electric vehicles, "plug-in" hybrids, HFCVs, and direct combustion of hydrogen. Diesel autos can travel roughly 30 percent farther on a gallon of fuel than a comparable gasoline model. Diesel models, such as the Volkswagen Jetta, can get more than 40 miles per gallon. While many more options are available in Europe, where diesel sales may soon overtake those of gasoline cars, most energy-efficient diesels do not yet meet U.S. air quality standards. Thus, despite their better mileage, diesels account for less than 5 percent of U.S. motor vehicle sales and could be much better promoted. The most popular of the growing options for hybrid cars is the Toyota Prius; almost 400,000 have been sold in the United States since 2000.[30] The Prius gets 50 or more miles per gallon under certain driving conditions, and new models that get 100 miles per gallon are possible with plug-in hybrids. Further development of all-electric vehicles, while stagnant over most of the last decade, can be expected to take off again with increased interest in plug-in hybrids, improved battery management, and electricity storage.

The CO_2 emissions of electric vehicles, as is the case with hydrogen, are a function of the energy source, ranging from zero or low (hydro, biomass, wind, geothermal, and nuclear) to high or higher (natural gas, oil, and coal). Nuclear power, while an emissions-free source of electricity, raises concerns of weapons proliferation, plant safety, waste disposal, and high cost. These concerns temper any prospects of a nuclear power revival. Thus, limited funds might be better spent on hybrid and diesel fleet conversion, energy efficiency, and truly renewable sources of energy. According to the carbon stabilization wedge theory,[31] nuclear power does not have to play a major role in reducing global CO_2 emissions, given

28 A. Paist et al., "Potential of Biomass Fuels to Substitute for Oil Shale in Energy Balance in Estonian Energy Sector," *Oil Shale* 22, no. 4 (Special Issue 2005): 369-79; S. Raabe, "Shell is Going to the Wall for Oil," *Denver Post*, 22 October 2006, available at: http://www.denverpost.coin/business/ci-4530946 (accessed 29 October 2006), http://usinfo.state.gov/joumals/ites/0706/ijee/ijee0706.htm (accessed 26 June 2007). Even with sequestration, a full lifecycle coal diesel analysis would generate as much carbon emissions as would generation and use of a comparable amount of conventional petroleum-based fuel; see J. Deutch and E. J. Moniz, *The Future of Coal: Options for a Carbon-Constrained World* (Cambridge, MA: Massachusetts Institute of Technology, 2007), 154.

29 K. A. McGinty, "Pennsylvania: Changing the Way America Thinks about Energy," *eJournal USA* 11, no. 2 (2006).

30 S. Duffy, "Hybrid Car Sales Figures," *Hybrid Car.com*, 8 June 2007, http://www.hybridcar.com/information-center/hybrid-car-overview/hybridcar-market-sales-figures.html (accessed 8 June 2007).

31 Socolow, Hotinski, Greenblatt, and Pacala, note 18 above, page 16.

the alternatives.

THE BUSH ADMINISTRATION'S HYDROGEN ECONOMY

As with electricity, the sustainability of hydrogen fuel, whether directly burned in an engine or used to feed an HFCV, depends on the feedstock used, the technical ability to sequester CO_2 emissions, overall conversion efficiency, infrastructure, cost, and other factors.

In his 2003 State of the Union Address, President Bush announced $1.2 billion in research funding intended to ensure that the United States will lead the world with development of clean hydrogen-powered vehicles. Developed over the previous year as a public-private partnership between DOE and the three major U.S. automakers, Bush's "FreedomCar and Fuel [Cell] Initiative" was promoted by DOE as allowing freedom from petroleum dependence while also enabling Americans to "drive where they want, when they want, and in the vehicle of their choice" through use of affordable and convenient fuel. An anticipated reduction of more than 500 million metric tons of carbon equivalent greenhouse gases per year by 2040—an amount equivalent to what the U.S. released from transportation in 2001—was portrayed as a convenient, yet secondary, benefit to energy security and affordability.[32]

Not to be outdone, then-EC President Romano Prodi announced that he wanted his presidency to be remembered for only two things: expansion of the European Union eastward and hydrogen energy.[33] The EC's High Level Group for hydrogen and fuel cells released a 2003 report calling for a public-private partnership with increased funding for research and development and installation of basic hydrogen transport and delivery infrastructure.[34] Bush and Prodi then issued a joint statement proclaiming that Europe and the United States would work together, as hydrogen was the key to sustained economic growth[35]—a goal somewhat short of sustainable development. Back in the United States, California Governor Arnold Schwarzenegger allocated funds for two dozen hydrogen fueling stations along state highways—the first step in what he envisioned as a future statewide system—and pledged to convert one of his five Hummers to hydrogen.[36]

Optimistic projections notwithstanding, the U.S and European policy directives calling for a "hydrogen economy" (a term first coined by General Motors) were noticeably vague on the source of the hydrogen. Acknowledging that hydrogen is merely an energy carrier and not a primary fuel, the directives accepted the current

32 Bush, note 5 above; G.W. Bush, "Hydrogen Fuel Initiative Can Make 'Fundamental Difference,'" press release (Washington, DC, 6 February 2003); White House, "Fact Sheet: Hydrogen Fuel: A Clean and Secure Energy Future," press release (Washington, DC: 6 February 2003), http://www.whitehouse.gov/news/releases/2003/02/20030206-2.html (accessed 25 August 2007); and DOE, *Hydrogen, Fuel Cells and Infrastructure Technologies Program: 2003 Annual Progress Report* (Washington, DC: DOE, 2003), bttp://wwwl.eere.energy.gov/hydrogenandfuelcells/annual-report03.ht ml (accessed 26 June 2007).

33 Prodi, note 5 above.

34 V. V. Vaitheeswaran, *Power to the People* (New York: Farrar, Straus and Giroux., 2003), 228; and European Commission, note 2 above.

35 White House, "Joint Statement on Hydrogen Cooperation," joint statement by President George W. Bush, European Council President Konstandinos Simitis, and European Commission President Romano Prodi on Hydrogen Cooperation, press release (Washington, DC: 25 June 2003).

36 M. Llanos, "Green Hummer for Schwarzenegger?" *MSNBC News*, 3 October 2003, http://msnbc.msn.com/id/3180817/ (accessed 26 June 2007).

practice of hydrogen extraction directly from fossil fuels—principally from natural gas but eventually from coal—and through nuclear-driven electrolysis. Renewable sources of hydrogen through electrolysis were portrayed as desirable, more so in Europe than in the United Stales, but in both cases, they were considered relatively insignificant for another 30 or 40 years.[37]

In September 2003, the collaborative research and development effort between DOE and its private partners was renamed the FreedomCar and Fuel Partnership.[38] With the addition of the major oil companies, the mission was defined as assisting development of a "clean and sustainable energy future," with hydrogen technology far enough advanced by 2015 to allow the private sector to make an informed decision on whether to move forward with large-scale commercialization. While new funding was earmarked for development of reliable hybrid electric vehicles and the batteries they depend upon, the central focus of the partnership remains development of HFCVs with supporting infrastructure. A primary objective is for hydrogen to be cost equivalent with gasoline per gallon delivered to the consumer, independent of generation pathway. Auxiliary goals address improvements in overall fuel efficiency as, for example, through a 50 percent reduction in vehicle weight, improvements in vehicle life expectancy, and development of on-board hydrogen storage systems of a high enough energy density to compete with gasoline-driven internal combustion engines (ICEs).

President Bush released his Advanced Energy Initiative in February 2006 as part of the Energy Policy Act of 2005. Designed to increase U.S. energy security through greater reliance on coal, nuclear, natural gas, and renewable energy sources, the initiative was justified by the president as a reaction to increased demand by China and India for oil supplies in a more competitive global economy while maintaining "reasonable" consumer energy prices. Among other things, the initiative implements Title VI of the act authorizing DOE to construct a prototype next-generation nuclear power plant at its Idaho National Laboratory for the specific purpose of producing hydrogen.[39]

ONLY AS GREEN AS ITS SOURCE

With more than 4 million "flexible-fuel" vehicles already on the road capable of running on ethanol, gasoline, CNG, or a gasoline-ethanol blend, hydrogen

---

37 European Commission, note 2 above; DOE, *A National Vision of America's Transition to a Hydrogen Economy: To 2030 and Beyond* (based on the National Hydrogen Vision Meeting, Washington, DC, November 15-16, 2001) (Washington, DC: DOE, 2002), http://www.eere.energy.gov/hydrogenandfuelcells/pdfs/visiondoc.pdf (accessed 26 June 2007); and J. A. Turner, "Sustainable Hydrogen Production" *Science*, 13 August 2004, 972-74.

38 DOE, *Partnership Plan: FreedomCar & Fuel Partnership* (Washington, DC: DOE, 2006).

39 White House, "President's Letter" (Washington, DC: 20 February 2006), http://www.whitehouse.gov/stateoftheunion/2006/energy/index.html (accessed 26 June 2007); White House, "Fact Sheet: The Advanced Energy Initiative: Ensuring a Clean, Secure Energy Future," (Washington, DC, 24 May 2006), http://www.whitehouse.gov/news/releases/2006/05/20060524-4.html (accessed 26 June 2007); and United States Senate, *Energy Policy Act of 2005*, Senate Report 109-078, 9 June 2005 (1st. Session 109th Congress) (Washington, DC: The Library of Congress, Thomas Database). See also P. Crofton, "Emerging Issues Relating to the Burgeoning Hydrogen Economy," *Energy Law Journal* 27, no. 1 (2006): 39-64.

is promoted by the current Bush administration as the fuel of the future.[40] The Energy Policy Act of 2005 sets a goal of 100,000 hydrogen-fueled vehicles by 2010 complete with a viable supporting infrastructure and mass-market penetration through two-and-a-half million vehicles by 2020.[41] Increased support for renewable energy notwithstanding, it appears that the vast majority of hydrogen produced today and envisioned for the immediate future will be "brown" insofar as hydrogen from fossil fuel sources will generate CO_2 as a byproduct. Electrolysis will largely come through conventional fossil fuel–derived electricity and especially nuclear power. These U.S.-based hydrogen sources are promoted as the key to energy independence due to abundant supply—240 years of proven reserves at current consumption rates for coal and no foreseeable near-term limits for uranium reserves.[42] They are also presented as "green," anticipating mass application of carbon sequestration for coal sources and the assumption that nuclear power results in no net CO_2 emissions. The latter point ignores fuel mining, fuel enrichment, fabrication, and other components of the nuclear fuel cycle that generate 5–10 percent of the carbon output of coal per unit of energy output.[43]

At present, more than 95 percent of U.S. hydrogen is generated through steam reformation of natural gas, a high-temperature, energy-intensive, nickel-catalyzed process with a net thermal efficiency of only 60–70 percent compared to 70–85 percent yield for electrolysis. However, limited supply, volatile market prices, and significant CO_2 emissions render natural gas an unreliable and unsustainable hydrogen source. With 27 percent of the world's coal supply, the United States may ultimately designate coal as its preferred source for hydrogen despite a net thermal efficiency of only 48 percent, even less than that of natural gas. The result is that more CO_2 is released per unit of energy generated from the reformation of fossil fuel to generate hydrogen than is derived from burning the fossil fuel directly for energy. This leaves electrolysis derived from renewable resources as the only sustainable way to generate hydrogen without significant carbon emissions and/or radioactive wastes. However, as explained, even though electrolysis can attain a higher thermal energy conversion efficiency for hydrogen production, not considering the cost of controlling carbon dioxide release and other pollution control measures, the least expensive renewable electrolysis of hydrogen is almost four times as expensive as natural gas when used to create hydrogen, twice that of coal per unit of hydrogen produced, and more than five times the cost of gasoline as a fuel per unit of energy produced.[44]

40 T. B. Mello, "Fueling Up With Ethanol," 7 February 2006, http://www.edmunds.com/advice/fueleconomy/articles/109194/article.html (accessed 26 June 2007). At present flexible-fuel vehicles are largely limited to sport utility vehicles, light trucks, and luxury cars. They average 27 percent lower mileage per gallon when running on an E85 (85 percent ethanol) blend due to ethanol's lower energy density than gasoline; see *Consumer Reports*, "The Ethanol Myth," October 2006, 15-19.

41 United States Senate, note 39 above.

42 White House, 20 February 2006, note 39 above.

43 See DOE, note 38 above; DOE, note 32 above; and Oko-Institut, "Global Emission Model for Integrated Systems," Version 4.3 (Darmstadt, Germany: Institute for Applied Ecology, 2006).

44 D. A. J. Rand and R. M. Dell, "The Hydrogen Economy: A Threat or an Opportunity for Lead-Acid Batteries?" *Journal of Power Sources* 144, no. 2 (2005): 568-78; P. B. Stronberg, "Policy Statement: Renewable Hydrogen" (Boulder, CO: American Solar Energy Society, 2004), http://www.ases.org/programs/policy/hydrogen.pdf (accessed 30 June 2007); and U. Bossel, B. Eliasson, and G. Taylor, "The Future of the Hydrogen Economy: Bright or Bleak?" (Oberrohrdorf, Switzerland: The European Fuel Cell Forum. Original 15 April 2003, updated 26 February 2005), http://www.efcf.com/reports/E08.pdf (accessed 26 June 2007).

The programs in the United States and Europe optimistically predict the problem of carbon emissions from fossil fuel reformation will be solved through sequestration, likely in depleted underground oil and natural gas fields or through deep-sea injection.[45] According to DOE, hydrogen produced through the nation's abundant coal reserves, together with coal gasification and carbon capture and storage, holds the promise of "near-zero greenhouse gas emissions."[46] Carbon sequestration, however, is a very expensive proposition, as the carbon oxides must be separated from other flue gases, compressed, and transported long distances if not injected on site. Although coal gasification is a promising way to produce hydrogen from a fossil fuel (because the flue gas is already purified), carbon capture and sequestration remains a potential deal-breaking expense. To achieve commercial viability, it will have to significantly come down in price, encouraged through targeted research, development, and demonstration projects, and perhaps ultimately through the as-yet politically unpopular imposition of carbon taxes.

With steam reforming of natural gas, more than 10 kilograms (kg) of CO_2 are released per kg of hydrogen generated. This figure doubles if the source is coal. Again with electrolysis, hydrogen is only as green as its source: Coal-based electrolysis of hydrogen generates about 7.4 times the CO_2 per net unit of useful energy than if an energy-equivalent unit of gasoline were used directly as the energy source for automobiles.[47]

As a result, if coal and natural gas are to be viable sources for hydrogen production, CO_2 must be sequestered. The two main methods entail biological sequestration—a process that may be enhanced through forest expansion, improved fertilization, and other measures designed to promote a net short-term gain in plant photosynthesis—and more permanent geological sequestration. Long-term geologic sequestration projects under development envision injection of liquid CO_2 into secure formations—perhaps linked with enhanced oil and natural gas recovery, as is currently practiced, or in deep saline aquifers—as well as deep-sea (deeper than 3,000 meters below sea level) placement. Here the high pressure and cold temperatures are expected to keep the CO_2 liquid and secure.

At present more than 20 small-scale federally subsidized carbon sequestration demonstration projects are under development in the United States. Three larger projects already in progress are associated with gas recovery in the North Sea and Algeria and coal gasification with enhanced oil recovery along the Saskatchewan-North Dakota border. Moreover, in May 2007, General Electric and BP announced a global joint venture to develop at least five 500-MW coal-and/or petroleum coke-based[48] hydrogen electric power plants, each with carbon capture and geologic storage. While the goal of this partnership and the smaller carbon sequestration projects is to achieve competitive market acceptance within a decade, the

45 See Prodi, note 5 above; European Commission, note 2 above; and DOE, note 37 above.

46 DOE, Hydrogen Production: Coal Gasification, http://www.1.eere.energy.gov/hydrogenandlfuelcells/production/coal.gasification.htiml (accessed 26 August 2007). See F. Keith and A. Farrell, "Rethinking Hydrogen Cars," *Science*, 18 July 2003: 315 for a dissenting opinion about the virtues of hydrogen as a viable transportation fuel.

47 Muradov and Veziroglu, note 9 above; and R. Wurster, "Hydrogen: Bridges Towards a Lasting Energy World?" *BWK* 56, nos. 1-2 (2004), S18-23.

48 Petroleum coke is a solid hydrocarbon residual derived from oil refining. As with coal, petroleum coke can be a source of hydrogen with CO_2 as a residual byproduct.

challenges, when extended to the generation of transportation fuels, are significant. For example, carbon capture and sequestration is only feasible at a large-scale hydrogen production facility, thereby penalizing distributed generation that may consume less energy for fuel transportation and result in less fuel loss.[49] In addition, a sudden release, as occurred in 1986 at Lake Nyos in Cameroon when the super-saturated, cold, deep lake released a massive quantity of the gas, may not only undo the desired sequestration, but it may also cause deaths among nearby populations. Furthermore, as with any underground storage of a gas or liquid under pressure, permanence is contextual with geological sequestration. Routine escape is anticipated depending on the formation in question (for example, from fractured oil and gas fields), the initial pressure achieved, and chemical interaction with the surrounding material. However, while permanence cannot be assured, some scientists contend that leakage might be slow enough—particularly if sequestration occurs below the ocean floor—to allow deep oceanic absorption and re-equalization of atmospheric carbon almost back to pre-industrial levels over the ensuing centuries.[50]

The permanence of sequestration notwithstanding, CO_2 liquefaction is a costly and inefficient process, significantly reducing the net yield obtained. So while carbon sequestration and coal-based hydrogen production remain promising technologies that deserve further research funding, they still support non-sustainable use of fossil fuels. However, given the reality of abundant coal supply and use, large-scale sequestration, once proven, will likely serve as an unavoidable bridge to a more sustainable system based on renewable sources of energy.

PROVIDING INFRASTRUCTURE FOR THE HYDROGEN ECONOMY

The United States uses more than 1 million metric tons of gasoline per day. It would take the equivalent of the nation's entire existing electric output to generate through electrolysis the 3.77 billion cubic meters of hydrogen necessary for replacement. This figure does not even cover what it would take to replace with hydrogen the 230,000 metric tons of jet fuel and 497,500 metric tons of petroleum distillates, including diesel, consumed daily.[51] Whatever the source, serious energy inefficiencies and logistical barriers are associated with the production, compression or liquefaction, transport, and storage of hydrogen before conversion back to electrical and then kinetic energy in an HFCV.

Once isolated, hydrogen is transported, stored, and made ready for use in a vehicle as a compressed gas, chilled liquid, or through a combination of the two. Metal hydrides can also be used to carry hydrogen, but their substantial weight per volume carried and the high heat required to release the gas make them cur-

49 General Electric Energy, "GE and BP Form Alliance to Develop and Deploy Hydrogen Power Technologies," press release (24 May 2007), http://www.gepower.com/about/press/en/2007-press/052407b.htm (accessed 26 June 2007).

50 D. Schrag, "Preparing to Capture Carbon," *Science*, 9 February 2007, 812-13. See Deutch and Moniz, note 29 above for a strong defense of the inevitable role coal must play in our energy future and for public funding of large-scale carbon capture and sequestration demonstration projects.

51 J. Wilson and G. Burgh, *The Hydrogen Report: An Examination of the Role of Hydrogen in Achieving U.S. Energy Independence* (Grosse Pointe, MI: The Management Group (TMG), 2003), http://www.tmgtech.com/pages/7/index.htm (accessed 26 June 2007).

rently impractical for transportation applications. As is the case with natural gas, compressed hydrogen gas through pipeline delivery for urban areas and nearby concentrated use (as at a refinery) is the least expensive method but is prohibitively expensive for dispersed rural application. In addition, hydrogen can embrittle metal pipes, which are already prone to leaks due to the high pressure required for hydrogen transport given its low energy density and atomic weight. Securing the right-of-way for new pipelines presents additional problems.

Preparation of hydrogen for transport and storage consumes a large amount of energy. Here the gaseous pathway comes out ahead, though still well behind conventional storage and transport of natural gas and gasoline. A temperature of -253°C is needed to liquefy hydrogen. Roughly 30 percent of the energy available through the process is needed just for initial liquefaction, and an additional 10 percent is necessary for maintenance of the liquid or to achieve the volumetric equivalent energy density (at 800 atmospheres or 11,760 pounds per square inch (psi)) in a compressed gas. Additional energy is required to maintain pressures and/or the liquid state, especially over long distances and time periods. Yet liquefied hydrogen has only 7 percent the density of water and just 2.5 percent the energy of gasoline per unit of volume at an ambient pressure of 1,000 psi, while as a compressed gas, hydrogen contains only 30 percent the energy of methane at an equivalent pressure of 11,600 psi.[52]

With both liquefaction and compression, very heavy steel-walled tanks, trucks, and pipelines are required to store and transport the hydrogen. This further cuts down on end-use efficiency. According to an expert panel assembled by the American Physical Society, storage may well be the largest roadblock for President Bush's hydrogen initiative.[53] While transport inefficiencies can be reduced through direct piping from source of generation to dispersed fueling stations or by on-site hydrolysis or reformation of natural gas, and vehicle weight can be reduced through a new generation of lightweight filament-wound carbon fiber tanks, the situation remains that due to its low weight per unit of energy delivered, the process of generation, compression or liquefaction, and transport of hydrogen requires a substantial amount of energy. To carry the equivalent amount of energy transported by a single, light gasoline delivery truck, liquid hydrogen would require 5 trucks, and compressed hydrogen would require 19.

Switching to pipelines to avoid the safety problems, traffic congestion, and inefficiencies associated with trucking, major barriers still arise from the physical nature of hydrogen. For a 3,000-km pipeline—conceivable for a hydrogen plant at the mouth of a well or mine with requisite on-site carbon sequestration—due to the higher compression and lower volumetric energy density for hydrogen, the mass fraction (compressor) consumption for hydrogen is 50 percent of the energy transferred versus only 20 percent for natural gas. In addition, we can expect much more leakage for hydrogen compared to methane due to its smaller molecular

52 Ibid.; Bossel, Eliasson, and Taylor, note 44 above; Lovins note 8 above.

53 American Physical Society, *The Hydrogen Initiative* (College Park, MD: American Physical Society, Panel on Public Affairs, March 2004).

size.[54]

Finally, physical laws also limit delivery of hydrogen to end-use vehicles. For example, liquid fuels can be transferred by gravity alone, while hydrogen gas requires additional pumping pressure to empty a supply tank and account for the fact that the pressurized gas, as it is released from a holding tank, cools and thus condenses in the supply tank from which it was transferred. On-board reforming of hydrogen, an alternative to off-site hydrogen formation and delivery, is no longer considered a viable option due to unacceptable start-up requirements, the lack of carbon sequestration if the source were natural gas, and even higher energy loss than with off-site formation.[55] An often-cited European report concluded that the total energy needed to generate, compress, transport, and store hydrogen at a distributed filling station—thereby reducing energy loss associated with long-distance transport—would still consume 40–80 percent of the original fuel's energy, and even more for liquid hydrogen, depending on the size of the filling station and the source of the electricity employed. By comparison, the current well-to-lank loss for gasoline is only 12 percent, and for natural gas, it is a mere 5 percent.[56] Even if the hydrogen were derived from less-expensive and more energy-efficient natural gas instead of through electrolysis, it makes more environmental and economic sense to use methane directly as a hybrid vehicular fuel than to convert it first to hydrogen for that purpose.[57]

NET ENERGY YIELD AND CO_2 EMISSIONS

Analysts speak of "well-to-wheels" analysis when calculating the lifecycle energy demand and environmental costs of different transportation fuels. While results vary widely according to input assumptions, geographically specific fuel pathways, and vehicle employment, sophisticated modeling is being conducted through an ongoing collaborative effort headed by the Joint Research Center of the European Commission (JRCEC).[58] Research suggests that energy and greenhouse gas emissions savings are only achieved through more efficient HFCVs (30–40 percent), as natural gas-derived hydrogen, burned directly, consumes more net energy than a

54 European Commission Joint Research Center, CONCAWE, and EUCAR, *Well-to-Wheels Analysis of Future Automotive Fuels and Powertrains in the European Context* (Version 2 b, May 2006, and Version 2c, March 2007) (Ispra, Italy: Institute for Environment and Sustainability, JRC, 2006), http://ies.jrc.ec.europa.eu/WTW (accessed 26 June 2007); and Bossel, Eliasson and Taylor, note 44 above.

55 National Academy of Engineering, Board on Energy and Environmental Systems, *The Hydrogen Economy: Opportunities, Costs, Barriers, and R&D Needs* (Washington, DC: The National Academies Press, 2004); and J. Gluot, "U.S. DOE, Automakers Give Up on On-Board Reforming," *Octane Week* 19, no. 3 (2004): 1.

56 Bossel, Eliasson, and Taylor, note 44 above.

57 D. Crea, "Twenty Hydrogen Myths: A Physicist's Review," http://www.hydrogennews.org/hydrogen/crea.htm (accessed 26 June 2007).

58 European Commission Joint Research Center et al., note 54 above. In the United States, a similar effort is under way through a public-private collaboration headed by General Motors and Argonne National Lab, see N. Brinkman et al., *Well-to-Wheel Analysis of Advanced Fuel/Vehicle Systems—A North American Study of Energy Use, Greenhouse Gas Emissions, and Criteria Pollutant Emissions* (Argonne, IL: Argonne National Laboratory, May 2005). See also S. Ramesohl and F. Merten, "Energy System Aspects of Hydrogen as an Alternative Fuel in Transport," *Energy Policy* 34, no. 11 (2006): 1251-59; and M. Granovskii, I. Dincer, and M. A. Rosen, "Life Cycle Assessment of Hydrogen Fuel Cell and Gasoline Vehicles," *International Journal of Hydrogen Energy* 31 (2006): 337-52. The well-to-wheels analysis is not a full lifecycle analysis, as it does not consider emissions or energy involved with facility and vehicle construction nor end-of-life disposition.

conventional internal combustion engine and offers only minimal greenhouse gas savings. Preliminary well-to-wheels analysis from energy source procurement to final use of the fuel in an HFCV or similar-sized gasoline-driven internal combustion engine suggests that the CO_2-equivalent greenhouse gas emissions generated per distance driven are roughly half for compressed hydrogen made from natural gas compared to gasoline, and the energy consumed per 100 km driven is just 68 percent. The differences are less, however, if long-distance hydrogen delivery, gasoline hybrid and diesel vehicles, liquefied hydrogen, and hydrogen from electrolysis are considered. So, while the net greenhouse gas emissions are lower when natural gas displaces petroleum as a fuel in any powertrain, the net well-to-wheels efficiency of an HFCV using natural gas-derived hydrogen is roughly 21 percent, close to that of present-day high-performance hybrid ICEs, and the total fossil fuel energy consumed is just 7 percent less.[59]

With coal-derived hydrogen, CO_2 emissions and fossil energy consumption are greater in an HFCV than with the conventional gasoline-driven or hybrid internal combustion engine. Although carbon sequestration, if practical and affordable, would lower the CO_2 emissions, it would also raise the energy consumed. On the other hand, wind-derived hydrogen through centralized electrolysis has almost no carbon emissions as long as the energy used for hydrogen compression or liquefaction and delivery is also wind derived. Working with the JRCEC data and projecting the current rate of technological advance to 2050, researchers estimated that the final CO_2 emission from HFCVs when using methane-derived hydrogen would be slightly lower (8 percent) than that from ICEs, much higher if the hydrogen comes from coal, and a moot comparison if natural gas is no longer an available or affordable hydrogen source.[60]

Thus, the available data suggest that hydrogen derived from natural gas and used in an HFCV offers a modest (30 percent) advantage with regard to greenhouse gas emissions compared to an advanced hybrid gasoline internal combustion engine. Moreover, there is an energy consumption advantage for the HFCV over the internal combustion engine when we consider the entire fuel lifecycle. Should nuclear or coal energy through electrolysis be used for the hydrogen, the HFCV pathway is approximately half as energy efficient as the internal combustion engine and consumes significantly more energy per distance driven.[61]

This comparison also sets aside the fact that HFCVs are currently nowhere near commercial application, costing more than 10 times more per rated unit of power compared to the internal combustion engine.[62] Nonetheless, current costs, efficiencies, and affiliated CO_2 emissions notwithstanding, a sustainable transportation system ultimately must be based on renewable energy. Although achieving a sustainable transportation system requires renewable energy and much lower CO_2 emissions, if slowing climate change is the primary justification for the transition, it does not necessarily follow that renewable energy at present should be diverted

59 Rand and Dell, note 44 above; and European Commission Joint Research Center et al., note 54 above.

60 See Ramesohl and Merten, note 58 above.

61 Rand and Dell, note 44 above; and European Commission Joint Research Center et al, note 54 above.

62 There is also an economy of scale with fuel cell efficiency favoring large stationary application and by boats and trains rather than for smaller cars and trucks.

to hydrogen production.

THE BEST USE FOR A PRECIOUS RESOURCE?

Large-scale hydropower is a less expensive source for hydrogen, yet most U.S. hydropower resources are already committed for direct electricity production, and additional sites are limited. Another option, reformed biomass, is at present the lowest-cost renewable source of hydrogen after hydropower and figures prominently in many proposals for a hydrogen economy. However, the amount of land required to replace current fossil fuels with biomass is enormous and not without major environmental concerns. This leaves wind and solar power as the only viable renewable energy sources for hydrogen. Yet the cost of solar power rivals the prohibitive expense of hydrogen derived from nuclear-powered electrolysis, while wind power is best used directly to substitute for coal-based electricity from the standpoint of energy efficiency, cost, and CO_2 reduction.[63]

If the primary goal is to reduce greenhouse gas emissions, it is more effective to employ renewable energy to replace conventional coal-fired electricity, currently responsible for 32 percent of total U.S. CO_2 emissions. Using renewable energy directly to replace coal-fired electricity displaces approximately 2.7 times as much CO_2 when used for the new generation of "clean" coal plants—described as such because they involve some combination of coal washing, gasification, flue gas desulphurization, carbon dioxide purification with sequestration, and other measures designed to enhance efficiency, reduce environmental impact, and possibly recover hydrogen—and 3.4 times as much when used to replace electricity from conventional power plants, compared with using renewable energy to replace gasoline with hydrogen. Even substituting natural gas directly for coal-based electricity displaces 2.7 times more CO_2 than if the gas were converted to hydrogen as a first step.[64]

Up to 90 percent of the electricity generated by wind turbines enters the grid and is delivered to consumers, with transmission and distribution averaging a 2–8 percent loss.[65] With the second law of thermodynamics working against it, hydrogen as an energy carrier from wind power cannot match this efficiency because it depends on additional energy conversions—from electrical to chemical, and back to electrical. Taking into account energy loss for compression or liquefaction and for transport, the net energy delivered to the consumer falls to 30 percent or less.

63 Significant wind power deployment has been demonstrated in Denmark and Northern Germany with 18-25 percent grid penetration; see M. K. Heiman and B. D. Solomon, "Power to the People: Electric Utility Restructuring and the Commitment to Renewable Energy," *Annals of the Association of American Geographers* 94 (2004): 109-10. Even when backed up by conventional natural-gas driven spinning reserve, the additional cost for wind power is far less than if the wind were first used to generate hydrogen and then converted back to electricity through a fuel cell; see D. Milborrow and L. Harrison, "Hydrogen Myths and Renewables Reality," *Wind Power Monthly* 19, no. 5 (2003): 47-52. Ramesohl and Merten, note 58 above, estimate that 145 gigawatts of wind power would be needed to meet Germany's transport requirements exclusively from hydrogen, an amount greater than that nation's total electricity capacity from all sources.

64 P. Mazza and R. Hammerschlag, "Carrying the Energy Future: Comparing Hydrogen and Electricity for Transmission, Storage and Transportation" (Seattle, WA: Institute for Lifecycle Environmental Assessment, 2004), 39, http://www.ilea.org (accessed 26 June 2007); and D. Morris, "A Better Way to Get Front Here to There: A Commentary on the Hydrogen Economy and a Proposal for an Alternative Strategy," (Minneapolis, MN: Institute for Local Self-Reliance, 2003), http://www.newrules.orgelectricity-betterway.html (accessed 3 April 2007).

65 Mazza and Hammerschlag, ibid.; and Bossel, Eliasson, and Taylor, note 44 above.

Due solely to conversion inefficiencies and not taking into account the cost of fuel cells or other infrastructure expenses, the actual cost of hydrogen-generated electricity at the point of end use through a fuel cell is roughly four times that for conventional sources of electricity from the grid.[66] Hydrogen's low energy density limits its potential as a fuel for long-distance travel, such as by trains, planes, and boats. Alternatively, synthetic hydrocarbons derived from biomass and organic waste could be more sustainably used for long-distance transport, with local driving powdered through electricity based on other renewable resources. This combination is brought together through a "plug-in" hybrid electric vehicle.

HYBRID VEHICLES: A HYDROGEN ECONOMY ALTERNATIVE?

Building the infrastructure necessary for a U.S. system of hydrogen generation, distribution, and fueling requires resources comparable to those currently employed for natural gas and petroleum systems—in short, a very ambitious and expensive undertaking. Moreover, were the current fleet of petroleum-based vehicles replaced by HFCVs, the latter would have to come down in price by a factor of 10 or more with cost and maintenance to bring them within the cost range of today's motor vehicles.[67] Optimistic projections in Europe for scale economies with mass production suggest that it will take 30–40 years of continued research and development focusing on lowering the cost and improving the efficiency of HFCVs and an aggressive, heavily subsidized program to introduce the requisite infrastructure before an active consumer market emerges.[68]

If we achieve a transportation system where the majority of vehicles are fueled by hydrogen, the problem of CO_2 emissions will remain until the hydrogen is derived from renewable energy sources and/or the challenge of secure and permanent carbon sequestration is addressed. In the interim, alternatives to achieve the goals of energy independence and security, while also reducing the CO_2 emissions and radioactive wastes associated with the hydrogen economy envisioned by the Bush administration and reluctantly accepted as an unavoidable transitional state by the EC, should be considered. Chief among these are the already-proven and consumer-tested highly efficient diesel automobiles and, most recently, the hybrid gas-electric vehicles (HEVs) pioneered by Toyota, Honda, and Ford.

Many hydrogen advocates point to reported HFCV efficiencies 3–4 times that of conventional internal combustion engines (50–60 percent as opposed to 15 percent for a typical car) to bolster the claim that despite higher fuel prices and lower conversion efficiencies for hydrogen production than for gasoline derived from oil, HFCVs are already competitive with gasoline in terms of net useful en-

66 Bossel, Eliasson, and Taylor, note 44 above.

67 American Physical Society, note 53 above; and Wilson and Burgh, note 51 above.

68 European Commission, note 2 above. For a review of the literature and progress toward the hydrogen economy, see W. McDowall and M. Eatnes, "Forecasts, Scenarios, Visions, Backcasts and Roadmaps to the Hydrogen Economy: A Review of the Hydrogen Futures Literature," *Energy Policy* 34, no. 11 (2006): 1236-50; and National Research Council, *Review of the Research Program of the Freedom CAR and Fuel Partnership: First Report* (Washington, DC: National Academies Press, 2005), Executive Summary.

ergy output. Therefore, one can drive several times farther on a gallon-equivalent of hydrogen in an HFCV than on a gallon of gasoline. Actual efficiencies notwithstanding, this comparison fails to consider that light HEVs with large battery packs are already increasing gasoline mileage by more than 50 percent and that one can go even farther on a gallon in a diesel hybrid vehicle.[69]

With renewable energy used to replace fossil fuel-derived electricity, a more effective way to reduce CO_2 emissions than conversion to hydrogen, the main rationale for hydrogen production comes as a transportation fuel to replace insecure and unsustainable oil. Yet as an energy carrier, hydrogen has a net yield of only 51 percent when derived from renewable energy through electrolysis, compared to 75–85 percent for electricity stored in a battery. Moreover, the CO_2 emissions from an HEV are at least equivalent to those from an HFCV when the hydrogen is derived from natural gas.[70]

Moving beyond HEVs that rely on fossil fuels, the plug-in hybrid electric vehicle (PHEV) provides a viable alternative. With larger battery packs, PHEVs are designed to run primarily on electricity for a 20–60 mile daily commute, only switching over to gasoline, ethanol, or biodiesel for longer trips. Charging at night with off-peak electricity that costs the equivalent of 50 cents per gallon for gasoline, existing nickel-metal hydride HEVs have a 20-mile electric charge range (lithium ion PHEVs should perform better). Experimental PHEVs have reached 100–180 mpg for the typical car used primarily for short-range commuting, while costing only one-fourth per mile of a conventional car to operate. PHEVs should also be able to travel 3–4 times farther than an HFCV on a kilowatt-hour of renewable electricity. This is due to the cost for, and more efficient use of, electricity and does not consider vehicle costs or future innovations in HFCVs or PHEVs. If an HFCV were employed, it would still be more efficient in terms of economics, energy, and the environment to couple HFCV technology with a regenerative battery, saving the more costly hydrogen for power backup—in short, a plug-in hybrid electric HFCV.[71]

Building upon the concept of stabilization wedges,[72] modelers working with the U.S. Environmental Protection Agency estimate that it would take 4.3 wedges of approximately 5 billion metric tons of CO_2-equavalent gas reduction each to flatten U.S. passenger vehicle emissions back to 2007 levels from those projected for 2050. Assuming 30 percent market penetration each, 2.7 wedges could be had from existing technology through cellulosic ethanol, 1.1-to-2.2 wedges from PHEVs, and

69 See Lovins, note 8 above; Wilson and Burgh note 51 above; and U.S. DOE, *Fuel Economy Guide Model Year 2007* (Washington, DC: DOE, 2006), http://www.fueleconomy.gov/feg/FEG2007.pdf (accessed 26 June 2007). The 2007 Toyota Prius is rated at 60 mpg city and 51 highway compared to 24 city and 33 highway for the comparable size four-cylinder Camry model.

70 Morris, note 64 above; R. Hammerschlag and P. Mazza, "Questioning Hydrogen," *Energy Policy* 33, no. 16 (2005): 2039-43; and Romm, note 2 above, pages 149-50.

71 Mazza and Hammerschlag, note 64 above; J. Carey, "Giving Hybrids a Real Jolt," *Business Week,* 11 April 2005, 70-72; W. Kempton and J. Tomic, "Vehicle-to-Grid Power Fundamentals: Calculating Capacity and Net Revenue," *Journal of Power Sources* 144, no. 1 (2005): 268-79; J. J. Romm and A. A. Frank, "Hybrid Vehicles Gain Traction," *Scientific American* 294, no. 4 (2006): 78-79; G. J. Suppes, "Roles of Plug-In Hybrid Electric Vehicles in the Transition to the Hydrogen Economy," *International Journal of Hydrogen Energy* 31, no. 3 (2006): 353-60. While hybrid fuel cell vehicles should be more efficient and release less greenhouse gas than conventional fuel cell vehicles, the savings are lower than for comparable hybridization of the internal combustion engine vehicle due to the greater efficiency and smaller size of the fuel cell engine to begin with.

72 For more on the wedge theory, see Socolow, Hotinski, Greenblam, and Pacala, note 18 above.

a 0.8-to-1.0 wedge from hybrid diesel and gasoline vehicles. Combining the low greenhouse gas fuels with anticipated advances in vehicle technology could generate the additional wedges necessary for stabilization and even generate a surplus to assist with stabilization from trucking, aviation, and rail transportation or to offset passenger vehicle emissions below current levels. With smarter urban planning, car-pooling, and other measures designed to reduce carbon-emitting travel 15 percent, another four wedges could come through travel demand management.[73]

HYDROGEN: BRIDGE TO THE FUTURE?

Distributed hydrogen fuel cells may be a useful substitute for expensive coal- or natural gas-driven peaking power plants used to stabilize the electricity grid and appear ideal to store intermittent wind and solar energy. As such, continued funding for research and development on fuel cells and associated advances in vehicle and fuel tank construction and carbon sequestration applicable across a wider variety of fuel pathways is warranted. The potential of fuel cells to power the transportation sector is limited, however, by the laws of physics as well as economic and environmental considerations. The so-called "hydrogen economy" may well prove feasible for isolated regions, far from existing energy infrastructure and blessed with abundant renewable resources, such as Iceland. Yet even Iceland's once-vaunted dream of a hydrogen economy may be stalled.[74] In the meantime, it is imperative that the world, led by the industrialized nations, commits to sustainably provided energy sources and technologies to stem global climate change. For a hydrogen economy to work, it would have to compete with electricity, a well-established energy carrier supported by an infrastructure already in place. For the transportation sector, the growing market today for hybrid gasoline-electric vehicles is a logical first step, along with more efficient gasoline and diesel-powered automobiles and, very soon, all-electric vehicles and PHEVs.

Coupling renewable fuel sources necessary for a sustainable transportation system (such as cellulosic ethanol) with electricity used through PHEVs, rather than through conversion first to hydrogen for HFCV use, may be the next step. Thus PHEVs would rely on synthetic liquid hydrocarbon fuels derived from atmospheric carbon in the form of biomass ethanol, wood-based methanol, or biodiesel fuel. Biofuels at this reduced level of use are feasible given the much lower backup requirements for PHEVs that are powered by renewable electric energy as compared to biofuels that are used to produce hydrogen for an HFCV.

Renewable energy is a necessary precondition for a sustainable hydrogen future, and not the other way around. A focus on hydrogen first, at least as envisioned by the Bush administration—with reliance on carbon sequestration to permit fossil fuels as the primary sources—threatens to detract attention from energy ef-

73 EPA, note 1 above. See also Socolow, Hotinski, Greenblatt, and Pacala, note 18 above. Where there is a range, higher wedges for carbon pathways may be attributed to anticipated carbon sequestration and use of integrated combined cycle power plants for fuel production.

74 F. Sverrisson, "Missing in Action: Iceland's Hydrogen Economy," *WorldWatch* 19, no. 6 (November/December 2006): 20-25.

ficiency and renewable energy. The latter are necessary measures that are already proven as the fastest way to achieve energy security and reduced greenhouse gas emissions.[75]

The vast majority of U.S. funding already allocated for the hydrogen economy does not sufficiently differentiate between green or brown sources of hydrogen and thus makes a questionable contribution to sustainability. Public and private funds might be better spent on research and development for energy efficiency and conservation, backed by a federal renewable portfolio standard of 20 percent or more for electricity, a parallel renewable fuels standard for hydrogen from other sources with accompanying support limited to appropriate pathways, and a national carbon tax. Already adopted or under consideration in Europe, these measures are desirable, though the carbon tax is considered politically unacceptable for the United States at the present time.

Proponents of the hydrogen economy tend to focus on the lack of political will, or technical and socioeconomic barriers that must be overcome as the main obstacles to this transformation.[76] However, the hydrogen economy is not close to being ready. It should be noted that the United States experienced this level of dislocation during the 1970s in response to the OPEC oil embargo, when the national speed limit was lowered to 55 mph, fuel-efficiency standards were established, and major state and federal tax credits were extended for energy conservation and renewable energy supply. These measures worked quickly, and energy demand dropped dramatically before picking up again in the 1980s when energy prices fell and the restrictions were removed.

Ultimately, the U.S. public may also have to accept global climate change rather than energy prices as the driving force behind national energy policy, a shift that is currently under way in Europe. While pursuing a variety of long-term energy options, including hydrogen, primary attention should be given to appropriate transportation pathways and technologies that are already within our grasp.[77]

---

75 The German government is having second thoughts about the emphasis on hydrogen as a bridge to a renewable future. In June 2003, the state secretary announced that Germany considers solar- and even renewable-based hydrogen as poor investments and will commit to developing fuel cells that can run on more efficient fuels, such as biogas and even coal gas; see "High Level Group on Hydrogen and Fuel Cells Conference in Brussels," *HyWeb-Gazette* (Newsletter of L-B-Systemtechnik GmbH (LBST) and the German Hydrogen Association (DWV)), Third Quarter, 2003, htip://www.hyweb.de/News/arcv303e.html (accessed 26 June 2007).

76 McDowall and Eames, note 68 above; Lovins, note 8 above; Rifkin, note 2 above; and P. R Edwards, V. L. Kuznetsov, and W. I. E David, "Hydrogen Energy," *Transactions of the Royal Society* A, Vol. 365 (April 15, 2007): 1043-56.

77 The Energy Policy Act of 1992 and the Freedom Car and Fuel Partnership earmark modest funding for development of reliable hybrid gas-electric vehicles and the batteries they depend upon, even as the central focus remains development of hydrogen fuel cell vehicles with supporting infrastructure; see DOE, note 38 above; and White House 20 February 2006, note 39 above. In 2006 General Motors became the first U.S. automaker to commit to bringing out a rechargeable plug-in hybrid gas-electric vehicle based on a lithium battery platform; see S. Freeman, "GM Pledges to Make Plug-In Hybrid Vehicle," *The Washington Post*, 30 November 2006; and D. Shepardson, "GM May Revive the Electric Car; Automaker Expects Future Success With Technology of Hybrids, Batteries and Hydrogen Fuel Cells," *Detroit News*, 10 November 2006.

Beyond Batteries*

Portable Hydrogen Fuel Cells

By Carol Potera
Environmental Health Perspectives, January 2007

Mention hydrogen fuel cells, and most people envision hydrogen-powered cars as an alternative to the gas-guzzling and polluting internal combustion engine. In fact, many much smaller applications also could benefit from this nonpolluting technology. However, despite the billions of dollars being poured into the research and development of hydrogen fuel cells, few products have been commercialized.

To jump-start the hydrogen fuel cell economy, Larry Bawden and Lee Arikara cofounded Jadoo Power Systems in 2001. While demonstrating their technology at a convention in 2002, an observer remarked that the creation of electricity from hydrogen seemed like magic. The company's name grew from that comment—Jadoo means "magic" in Hindi. "We wanted a nontechnical name to brand ourselves as a provider of solutions, not another technical house," says Bawden, Jadoo's president and CEO.

A small company with 40 workers, Jadoo searches for applications that require 100-500 watts of power (a hydrogen car, for comparison, needs 50,000–100,000 watts to give it the pep of a typical gasoline-powered car). Jadoo first targeted the cumbersome and inefficient batteries hauled around by television news crews. Television camera operators typically carry three rechargeable "brick" batteries, each weighing about six pounds and costing $500. An additional battery charger costs $1,500. According to Arikara, Jadoo's vice president of business development, television stations spend an average of $3,500 per camera to outfit them with batteries. Further, while swapping out a dead video battery, all power stops, and critical film footage can be lost.

This made the broadcast industry an ideal niche market to demonstrate that hydrogen fuel cells could do the job better and cheaper. The experts at Jadoo designed and manufactured a 100-watt hydrogen fuel cell system, called N-Genr™, to fit professional video cameras. N-Gen weighs five pounds, and it's fueled by a two-pound hydrogen-filled canister called N-Stor™. A small reservoir retains enough hydrogen to power the cameras for up to 30 seconds while replacing an empty hydrogen canister, allowing the camera to run continuously. Rechargeable batteries lose capacity with each recharge and eventually are discarded, adding to landfill contamination with metals such as nickel and cadmium. But fuel cells do not discharge and degrade over time. Theoretically, the metal hydride should not wear out, though in practical use it could deteriorate. The company recommends that customers return the canisters every five years so the metal hydride can be checked.

A new rechargeable brick battery runs for about two hours, whereas N-Gen can last four to five hours before needing a refill of hydrogen. A brick battery takes about six hours to recharge, up to six times longer than it takes to refill an N-Stor canister. In short, television camera operators can replace three inefficient six-pound brick batteries with one highly efficient N-Gen system at a total of seven pounds. Moreover, at $2,050, the N-Gen portable power system costs about one-third less than three brick batteries and a battery charger.

The CBS affiliate in Sacramento, California, is testing the Jadoo system. "We've had zero problems, and it delivers smooth, steady voltage far longer than any battery pack," says Kalo Alexandra, remote systems engineer. He'd like Jadoo to reduce the size of the fuel cell and hydrogen canister and add hookups for other equipment like lights and microphones. Overall, the Jadoo system "gives every indication of sounding the death knell for brick batteries in the broadcast industry," Alexandra says.

Video engineer Dave Titchenal adopted Jadoo's technology for his video production company in Modesto, California. His crews set up cameras and video projection equipment in large auditoriums and football stadiums, connected to outlets by hundreds of yards of taped-down electrical cords—which feels like miles when you're on your knees taping it down. He's replaced all those cords with Jadoo fuel cells. "It's fabulous to know that you don't have to be tied to a power grid," says Titchenal.

HOW IT WORKS

"The basic difference between a battery and a fuel cell," Bawden notes, "is that a battery stores electrons, but our fuel cells make electrons." Inside a fuel cell, hydrogen and oxygen from the air combine to produce electricity and water vapor, which stays confined to the surface of the N-Stor cartridge until it evaporates. No fuel is burned in this electrochemical process, so no polluting by-products (such as carbon dioxide) are emitted. As long as there's a supply of hydrogen, electricity flows in a fuel cell.

The N-Gen power system measures about 4 inches by 4 inches by 7 inches, and the N-Stor canisters come in two sizes, holding 130 or 360 watt-hours of energy. The smaller canister, which is used on TV cameras, is about the size of a 12-ounce soda can; the larger size is the same diameter but twice as tall. The fuel canister quickly snaps into a port on the N-Gen. A digital display tells how much fuel remains and the amount of power (watts) being used.

Inside the N-Stor canister, metal hydrides soak up the hydrogen gas like a sponge, tripling the amount of canister that can be packed into the same space. Since the hydride absorbs the hydrogen, no compression is required.

The company is exploring alternative ways to store hydrogen, such as sodium borohydride made from borax. A borohydride canister would weigh significantly less than the current metal hydride type. Because sodium borohydride generates hydrogen simply by adding water, it would not need hydrogen gas refills. Customers would "add water to borohydride packs to activate them, just like astronauts make Tang," says Bawden.

In the meantime, when a canister needs refilling, it is inserted into Jadoo's FilOne™ station, which hooks up to a hydrogen tank through a hose. The FillOne station calculates and displays the refill time, usually about two hours for a 130 canister or four hours for a 360. A larger FilPoint™ station refills four 130 canisters simultaneously in about an hour. Or users can ship empty N-Stor canisters to Jadoo for refilling.

As fuel cells are becoming accepted at TV stations, most are buying the larger FillPoint at a cost of about $1,700. The Jadoo system uses industrial-grade hydrogen that is easy to buy through local welding supply stores. A "K-cylinder" of compressed hydrogen, enough to fill about 55 to 60 N-Stor 130 canisters, costs around $50.

Because the original N-Gen system was created for the broadcast industry, it contains the same interface found on rechargeable brick batteries to attach it to video cameras. To make N-Gen more versatile, Jadoo has since added a 12-volt direct current interface (like the one that plugs into a car cigarette lighter) and a 110-volt alternating current interface for use with appliances that plug in to the wall. In independent testing of N-Gen for the FuelCellWorks.com news website, the system powered a fan, electric screwdriver, fax machine, electric razor, bug zapper, food mixer, and laptop and desktop computers.

EXPANDING MARKETS

The company's early success earned Bawden and Arikara the 2006 Ernst & Young Entrepreneur of the Year Award for emerging markets in Northern California. Jadoo's solutions also caught the attention of the military. Soldiers in the U.S. Army's Special Operations Command carry 80 pounds of heavy batteries to power field radios that transmit life-and-death messages. Jadoo will be replacing the batteries with a 24-pound fuel cell, and is working to further reduce the weight to 12 pounds. Jadoo's fuel cells can also power military devices such as robots and unmanned armored vehicles.

Kuchera Defense Systems in Windber, Pennsylvania, uses Jadoo's fuel cells to power its T2 inspection robots that check for explosives under military and civilian vehicles. Bob Unger, program manager of advanced systems at Kuchera, says Jadoo's N-Gen system operating on one hydrogen canister extends the life of a T2 robot approximately threefold over the commonly used BA-5590 lithium battery.

"The military is in need of smaller and lighter power sources for portable devices, and Jadoo's technology ideally suits them," Unger says. At the new Center for Excellence for Advanced Energy Systems in Manufacturing, funded by the Pennsylvania Energy Development Authority and located at the Kuchera facility, researchers will create environmentally friendly commercial products that integrate Jadoo's fuel cell systems and other advanced energy devices.

Jadoo recently introduced the XRT system designed for first responders in emergency preparedness situations. The system includes the N-Gen fuel cell and six 360 canisters. Hurricane Katrina highlighted the tragic effects of lost electrical power—batteries powering the radios of first responders died the first day, and there was no electricity to recharge them. The XRT weighs only 50 pounds, yet furnishes the same energy as the 200 pounds' worth of lithium ion batteries that commonly power emergency equipment. The XRT can power portable radios, laptop computers, emergency lighting, satellite phones, and modems during electrical failures. "Fuel cells with enough hydrogen canisters could have supplied power during the entire time that the power was out in New Orleans," says Bawden.

In Jadoo's vision for the future, fuel cells will power home appliances or even entire houses. Moreover, fuel cells could supply steady electricity for residents, travelers, and humanitarian aide workers in regions throughout the world that do not have electricity or a reliable power source.

BUILDING THE HYDROGEN ECOSYSTEM

Jadoo was the first, and remains the only, company to receive approval from the U.S. Department of Transportation to ship hydrogen fuel cells as air cargo. Bawden says misconceptions about the safety of hydrogen gas initially made regulators skeptical about the safety of the metal hydrides in the N-Stor canisters. However, after enduring dozens of tests showing that the canisters safely withstood bonfire burning, forced overfills, and being shot with rifles, the N-Stor canister gained legal shipping status.

A lack of understanding about the safety of hydrogen is also "slowing the fuel cell economy down," Bawden says. As a member of the Hydrogen Technical Advisory Committee, which makes recommendations to the Secretary of Energy, he hopes to educate people and change attitudes and policy. "Propane gas in a grill is more dangerous," he says.

The trailblazers at Jadoo are spearheading the hydrogen economy by continuing to find niche markets for portable fuel cells to prove their commercial feasibility. Experts generally agree that although large-scale environmental gains are not immediate, they will follow when fuel cells are widely accepted. Jadoo's specialty applications "will drive the price point down, making hydrogen technology commonplace," predicts Bawden.

"We're building the ecosystem for the hydrogen industry," says Arikara. In fuel cell parlance, "ecosystem" refers to the many potential players, such as electronics and valve manufacturers, who are sitting on the sidelines and watching the technology. "They want to see commercialization to ensure a return on their investment in parts, tools, and equipment," Arikara explains. As more companies become involved, he adds, "prices will become competitive, and the technology will make significant environmental impacts."

The portable fuel cell market "doesn't get much attention, but it's an enabling sector with products available today that are paving the way for consumers to accept hydrogen vehicles," says Patrick Serfass, director of technology and program development at the National Hydrogen Association, a trade organization. With reduced use of fossil fuels and release of hazardous emissions, Serfass says the widespread acceptance of fuel cells "will bring benefits to the environment, energy security, and economic growth."

5

Hydroelectric and Wave Power Viable Alternatives?

Editor's Introduction

Hydropower is among the oldest energy sources on earth. Since human civilization began, we have relied on water to fuel our energy needs. Despite this long history, at present, less than ten percent of the power used in the United States is derived from hydroelectricity. However, hydropower remains the country's chief source of renewable energy, accounting for around half of the total. In addition, hydroelectricity is not a major contributor to CO_2 emissions. Nevertheless, it does have negative environmental implications. Hydroelectric dams destroy ecological habitats, impeding the migration of fish, for example. Moreover, when water is sequestered in reservoirs and the like, the vegetation underneath decays, releasing methane, a greenhouse gas, into the atmosphere. Though wave or tidal power avoids some of these excesses, such technology is not widely applied and consequently composes only a small proportion of the total amount of hydroelectricity generated globally. The selections in this chapter, "Hydroelectric and Wave Power: Viable Alternatives?," explore the science behind hydropower as well as the environmental toll associated with it. Entries also consider how hydroelectricity and wave power can be deployed to counteract climate change and the other side effects of traditional energy sources.

William Arthur Atkins charts the history of hydropower in the United States in "Hydroelectric Power," the first piece in this section. While small-scale waterpower in the form of waterwheels spurred the industrial revolution, Atkins writes that three principle factors contributed to the evolution of this energy source at the turn of the 20th century: greater electricity demand, the invention of the electric generator, and better hydraulic turbine technology.

In "Ending a Dammed Nuisance," a writer for *The Economist* charts the excesses of hydroelectric dams as well as recent improvements in turbine technology that may alleviate some of these dilemmas, if not the need for these dams altogether.

As with solar and wind energy, hydroelectric power has small-scale, or "microhydro" applications that can trim one's electricity bill and soften one's carbon footprint. Steve Maxwell discusses some of these options in "Homestead Hydropower." While microhydro systems are readily available to those who can afford them, the most important component of a home-scale hydropower installation is the water source and the volume and speed at which the water flows.

Much like other forms of hydropower, tidal energy has been used as a fuel source for centuries. However, wave power has not enjoyed the same widespread, and large-scale application as hydroelectricity. Indeed, as David C. Holzman notes in "Blue Power: Turning Tides Into Electricity," wave energy today is still in the early stages of development. Nevertheless, as Holzman's analysis of tidal power illustrates, "the field is heating up fast."

In "Wave Master," this section's final article, Stuart Nathan profiles Stephen Salter, one of tidal power's foremost pioneers, charting the life and achievements of the singular researcher.

Hydroelectric Power*

By William Arthur Atkins
Water: Science and Issues, 2003

The damming of streams and rivers has been an integral part of human civilization from its early history. Controversy paralleled this use because impounding and diverting water for upstream users affects those who live downstream, and also modifies the local habitats of plants and animals. Dams are built to control floods, improve navigation, provide a drinking-water supply, create or enhance recreational opportunities, and provide water for irrigation and other agricultural uses. A small percentage of dams (less than 3 percent in the United States) are used to generate power.

Waterpower was the impetus that powered manufacturers who were building a growing nation during the U.S. Industrial Revolution of the nineteenth century. Waterwheels used the power of river water flowing downstream to turn machinery. Water continued to produce the largest part of industrial power until after the Civil War (from 1861 to 1865) when it diminished in importance. Yet waterpower would soon experience a rebirth in the form of hydroelectric power. The modern terms "hydroelectric power" and "hydropower" generally have the same meaning.

COMING OF AGE

At the beginning of the twentieth century, hydroelectric power in the United States came of age with three events: the development of the electric generator; improvements in the hydraulic turbine; and a growing demand for electricity. The first commercial hydroelectric power plant was built in 1882 on the Fox River in Appleton, Wisconsin, in order to provide 12.5 kilowatts of power to light two paper mills and a residence. Paper manufacturer H. F. Rogers developed the plant after seeing Thomas Edison's plans for an electricity power station in New York.

EARLY TWENTIETH CENTURY

Commercial power companies soon began to install a large number of small hydroelectric plants in mountainous regions near metropolitan areas. By 1920, hydroelectric plants accounted for 40 percent of the electric power produced in the United States.

The creation of the Federal Power Commission in 1920 increased development of hydroelectric power plants. The development of larger and more cost-efficient power plants showed that monetary support by the federal government was necessary for such hydroelectric plants to compete effectively with other power-generating plants. Then in 1933 the government saw that besides power production, hydroelectric power plants could also be effectively used for flood control, navigation, and irrigation. As a result, the government created the Tennessee Valley Authority in the southeastern United States to develop large-scale waterpower projects. In the Pacific Northwest, the Bonneville Power Administration, created in 1937, similarly focused on electrifying farms and small communities with public power.

TODAY

Hydroelectric power plants generally range in size from several hundred kilowatts to several hundred megawatts, but a few enormous plants have capacities near 10,000 megawatts in order to supply electricity to millions of people. According to the National Renewable Energy Laboratory, world hydroelectric power plants have a combined capacity of 675,000 megawatts that produces over 2.3 trillion kilowatt-hours of electricity each year; supplying 24 percent of the world's electricity to more than 1 billion customers.

In many countries, hydroelectric power provides nearly all of the electrical power. In 1998, the hydroelectric plants of Norway and the Democratic Republic of the Congo (formerly Zaire) provided 99 percent of each country's power; and hydroelectric plants in Brazil provided 91 percent of total used electricity.

In the United States, more than 2,000 hydropower plants make hydroelectric power the country's largest renewable energy source (at 49 percent). The United States increased its hydroelectric power generation from about 16 billion kilowatt-hours in 1920 to nearly 306 billion kilowatt-hours in 1999. It runs a close second to Canada in the total amount of hydroelectric power produced worldwide. However, only 8 percent of the total U.S. electrical power was generated by hydroelectric power plants in 1999.

The largest U.S. hydropower plant is the 6,800-megawatt Grand Coulee power station on the Columbia River in Washington State. Completed in 1942, the

Grand Coulee today is one of the world's largest hydropower plants, behind the 13,320-megawatt Itaipu hydroelectric plant on the Parana River between Paraguay and Brazil.

Canada is the world's largest hydroelectric power producer. In 1999, it generated more than 340 billion kilowatt-hours of power, or 60 percent of its electric power, far outdistancing the U.S. hydropower percentage. The former Soviet Union, Brazil, China, and Norway are among the other top hydroelectric-generating countries.

FUNCTION

Hydropower functions by converting the energy in flowing water into electricity. The volume of water flow and the height (called the head) from the turbines in the power plant to the water surface created by the dam determines the quantity of electricity generated. Simply, the greater the flow and the taller the head means the more electricity produced.

The simple workings of a hydropower plant has water flowing through a dam, which turns a turbine, which then turns a generator. A hydropower plant (including a powerhouse) generally includes the following steps:

The dam holds water back, and stores water upstream in a reservoir, or large artificial lake. The reservoir is often used for multiple purposes, such as the recreational Lake Roosevelt at the Grand Coulee Dam. Some hydroelectric dams do not impound water, but instead use the power of the flowing river, and are known as run-of-the-river. Gates open on the dam, allowing gravity to pull the water down through the penstock. An intake conduit carries water from the reservoir to turbines inside the powerhouse. Pressure builds up as water flows through the pipeline. The water then hits the large blades of the turbine, making them turn. The vertical blades are attached through a shaft to a generator located above. Each turbine can weigh as much as 172 tons and turn at a rate of 90 revolutions per minute. The turbine blades turn in unison with a series of magnets inside the generator. The large magnets rotate past copper coils, which produce alternating current (AC). The transformer inside the powerhouse takes the AC and converts it to higher-voltage current so as to allow electricity to flow to customers. Out of every power plant exit four power lines consisting of three wires (associated with three power phases) and a neutral (ground) wire. Used water is carried through outflow pipelines, which reenters the river downstream.

IMPACTS AND TRENDS

Hydroelectric power is a clean source of renewable energy where an adequate water source is readily available. Hydropower plants provide inexpensive electricity without environmental pollution such as air emissions or waste byproducts.

And, unlike other energy sources such as fossil fuels, water is not consumed during electrical production, but can be reused for other purposes.

However, hydropower plants that rely on impoundments can negatively affect the reservoir site and the surrounding area. New reservoirs will permanently flood valleys that may have contained towns, scenic locations, and farmland. The permanent inundation also destroys fish and wildlife habitat that once existed at the reservoir site; however, new and different habitat is created. Hydropower operations that use run-of-the-river dams can block the passage of migrating fish, such as salmon. For example, many large dams in the Columbia River Basin impede Pacific salmon during their annual migrations through the river system.

Only 2,400 of the 80,000 dams in the United States are used for hydroelectric power. It is costly to construct a new hydroelectric power plant, and construction uses much water and land. In addition, environmental concerns have been voiced against their use. According to the U.S. Geological Survey, the likely trend for the future is toward small-scale hydroelectric power plants that can generate electricity for single communities.

Ending a Dammed Nuisance*

The Economist, February 19, 2008

In today's green world, hydroelectric dams are often unwelcome. Though their power is renewable and, on the face of it, carbon-free, there are lots of bad things about them, too. Blocking a river with a dam also blocks the movement of fish upstream to spawn and the movement of silt downstream to fertilise fields. The vegetation overwhelmed by the rising waters decays to form methane—a far worse greenhouse gas than carbon dioxide. The capital cost is huge. And, not least, people are often displaced to make way for the new lake. The question, therefore, is whether there is a way to get the advantages without suffering the disadvantages. And the answer is that there may be.

The purpose of a dam is twofold. To house the turbines that create the electricity and to provide a sufficient head of water pressure to drive them efficiently. If it were possible to develop a turbine that did not need such a water-head to operate, and that could sit in the riverbed, then a dam would be unnecessary. Such turbines could also be put in places that could not be dammed—the bottom of the sea, for example. And that is just what is starting to happen, with the deployment of free-standing underwater turbines.

The big disadvantage of free-standing turbines is that they are less efficient in transforming the mechanical energy of water into electrical energy than turbines in dams are. They are also subject to more wear and tear than turbines protected by huge amounts of concrete. They can be hard to get at to repair and maintain. And the generators they run, being electrical machines, need to be protected from the water that surrounds the rest of the turbine.

A discouraging list. But in the past three decades computing power has become cheaper, helping developers to simulate the behaviour of water and turbine blades—something that is hard to do with paper, pen and formulas. Moreover, prototypes can be built directly from the computer model. All this has helped scientists and industry to solve the weaknesses inherent in free-standing turbines.

The first new design was by Alexander Gorlov, a Russian civil engineer who worked on the Aswan High Dam in Egypt. He later moved to America where, with the financial assistance of the Department of Energy, he produced the first prototype of a turbine that could extract power from free-flowing currents "without building any dam". The Gorlov Helical Turbine as it is known, allows you to use any stream, whatever the direction of its flow. The vertical helical structure, which gives the device its name, provides a stability that previous designs lacked. It increases the amount of energy extracted from a stream from 20% to 35%. In addition, as the shaft is vertical the electric generator can be installed on one end above the water—without any need of waterproof boxes.

In 2001 Mr Gorlov won the Edison patent award for his invention, and the turbines have now been commercialised by Lucid Energy Technologies, an American company, and are being tested in pilot projects in South Korea and North America.

A second design is by Philippe Vauthier, another immigrant to America (he was originally a Swiss jeweller). The turbines made by his company, UEK, are anchored to a submerged platform. They are able to align themselves in the current like windsocks at an aerodrome so that they find the best position for power generation. As they are easy to install and maintain, they are being used in remote areas of developing countries, as well.

Finally, a design by OpenHydro, an Irish company, is not just a new kind of turbine but also a new design of underwater electric generator. Generators (roughly speaking) consist of magnets moving relative to coils. Why not have the magnets encapsulated in the external, fast moving part of a turbine? The turbine is then installed in an external housing, containing the coils. The result looks like an open-centre turbine contained within a tube. OpenHydro's generators do not need lubricant, which considerably reduces the need for maintenance, and are said to be safer for marine life.

These new designs, combined with the fashion for extracting energy from the environment by windmills and solar cells, means money that previously shied away from the field is now becoming available. According to New Energy Finance, a specialist consultancy, investments in companies proposing to make or deploy free-standing turbines have risen from $13m in 2004 to $156m in 2007. Projects already underway include the installation by American Verdant Power of a tidal-turbine in New York's East River and pilot projects in Nova Scotia with UEK, OpenHydro and Canadian Clean Current.

And that, optimists hope, is just the beginning. Soon, many more investors will be searching for treasures buried in the ocean sea beds—or, rather, flowing above them.

Homestead Hydropower*

By Steve Maxwell
The Mother Earth News, February/March 2005

Home-scale hydroelectric power systems offer an opportunity for humans to forge an intelligent and sustainable partnership with sunshine, rain and running water. Sometimes dubbed "microhydro," this approach uses low-impact mechanical systems to harness moving water to generate clean, reliable electric power. Unlike the intermittent power from wind or solar systems, hydroelectric power can flow night and day from year-round streams.

A hydroelectric system converts the force from flowing water into electricity. You take the kinetic energy of water flowing downhill from a stream or river and direct it onto a wheel in a turbine that converts the rotational energy to electricity. The amount of power produced depends on the volume of water flowing onto the turbine and the vertical distance it falls through the system. Equipment costs range from about $1,000 for the smallest, to $20,000 for a system large enough to power several modern homes.

"Many microhydro systems generate 75 to 350 kilowatt hours (kWh) per month," Scott Davis explains in his book, *Microhydro: Clean Power from Water*, a new title in the *Mother Earth News* "Books for Wiser Living" series. Davis is a renewable energy developer with decades of microhydro experience. In fact, it's his life's work, and he's gathered all his knowledge, experience and enthusiasm into this concise, easy-to-understand manual. His book covers the entire subject, from the essentials of site selection to the nitty-gritty of hardware choices and installation.

THE BASICS

To implement a successful microhydro system, you will need the following basic requirements:

- At least 2 gallons per minute of flowing water, and a lot of drop; or 2 feet

* Excerpted from *Mother Earth News* magazine. Read the full story at www.MotherEarthNews.com or call (800) 234-3368.

of drop and 500 gallons per minute of water flow.
- A proper turbine, alternator and shelter from bad weather.
- Permission from the relevant authorities, even if the project is entirely on your own land.
- A water intake and enough pipeline or "penstock" to divert water to the turbine and return it to the stream.
- A transmission line to move the power from the alternator to the point of use.
- Batteries and a power inverter subsystem to convert the electricity to an alternating current (AC), and a controller for the electrical system.

SITE ASSESSMENT

If you're lucky enough to have an abundance of flowing water, you may be tempted to envision projects that are larger than what is normally required. Davis stresses that you should plan to produce only the power you need, not the maximum amount possible. If you don't have an obvious microhydro location—but you still have access to running water—you still may be able to set up a system.

In its simplest form, the energy potential of flowing water depends on its flow rate (usually measured in gallons per minute) multiplied by the pressure behind that flow (related to the overall distance of water drop, called "head" in the business). Davis recommends a multistep approach to assess your microhydro potential before buying any equipment. Accurate site assessment is key because it identifies the total energy potential that's available, and it all begins with a measurement of water-volume flow rates. "Most microhydro systems use between 2 and 1,000 gallons of water per minute," Davis says. "If you have a spring or very small creek, the amount of available water may be the factor that limits your power output."

One of the ways to find the total amount of available water, Davis says, is to use the "container method." Find a spot where the potential stream's water enters a culvert and time how long it takes to fill up a container of a known size. The stream's flow in gallons per minute equals the size of the container in gallons divided by the time it takes to fill in seconds, times 60. For example, if a 5-gallon bucket fills up in 10 seconds, the stream flows at 30 gallons per minute (gpm).

Next, you need information on the pressure behind that flow, which relates to the amount of vertical drop the water undergoes as it travels through your site. Pressure measurement combines with flow rate to determine the raw energy potential of a location. In turn, this defines the universe of choices for the hardware necessary to produce the electricity you need at wall sockets, light fixtures and appliances. Flow rate multiplied by pressure equals power.

You won't get very far in the microhydro adventure before you realize something important: There's more to a good system than just flowing water. You also are dealing with terrestrial conditions, and that's why creating a stream profile is essential and should be the third factor to consider when choosing your optimum site.

"A completed stream profile sounds something like this," Davis says. "The first 100 feet drops 20 feet. The second 100 feet are not as steep, and drops 16 feet, and so on." What you're aiming for is an accurate representation of the water flow over natural landforms, and how those characteristics can be used to good advantage in your plans. By using a surveyor's transit, a water level or a laser level, you can produce a side-view profile—or cross-section—of the entire stream landscape as water runs from pipeline intake to output port.

A stream profile also helps you determine the best location for the water-intake end of the pipe. This is where most of your regular maintenance will happen (cleaning out brush and stream debris, for instance), so you need to choose a spot with easy access, if possible. Also, if the flow rate of your stream is more than a few gallons per minute, you may find several possible locations for the turbine itself. The stream profile often makes it easier to identify optimal turbine placement, which usually consists of a stable water level, accessibility and water relatively free from debris. Another important consideration is to place the turbine in an area where it won't be affected by freezing water.

Most microhydro installations include a pipeline that diverts water over land down from an area of high elevation, connecting to an enclosed water wheel (that's the turbine) at some lower level. This situation raises key questions: Will a 2-inch-diameter pipe give you the best energy potential in relation to the cost of the material and its flow rate? How does this compare with a 4-inch pipe? Will your energy expectations be met with a 500-foot pipeline, or do you need a 1,000-foot pipe to get more head (water pressure)? How will flow volume, vertical drop and friction in the pipe affect the amount of power generated? All these questions are important because they each can have a tremendous effect on power output.

Davis cites one case study where variations in pipe size, flow rate and static head yielded a 350-percent output difference across the four options examined.

THE HARDWARE

Most people who choose hydropower are attracted to the fascinating variety of unusual hardware that makes clean, low-cost electricity.

Turbines complete the first part of the energy-conversion process, and in many ways, they're the heart of any hydropower system. Many designs are available, but most include some kind of fanlike wheel on a shaft—set within a metal case—that contains and directs water flow to spin the blades. Turbines are designed for both low- and high-pressure applications.

High-head impulse turbines are the most versatile—used for situations with heads ranging from 6 to 600 feet—and can generate enough power to sustain most any requirement given the right conditions. The Turgo impulse turbine uses a jet of water to strike the enclosed water wheel at an angle. Because the impulse turbine uses more water, significant power can be generated with less head, which may result in shorter penstocks. The Pelton impulse turbine sends a jet of water to strike the enclosed water wheel along its circumference, which can be slightly more efficient than the Turgo turbine, Davis says, and is used especially for low-flow, high-head situations.

Low-head turbines are meant for heads under 10 or 12 feet. These turbines are ideal candidates to charge batteries a long way from the powerhouse at low expense. The LH-1000—made by Energy Systems and Design—will produce power from as little as 2 feet of head, and the Powerpal—made by Asian Phoenix Resources—is a complete small-scale AC system.

Constructing your own microhydro system also can be a viable option. Many different methods can be good alternatives to purchasing commercially produced turbines and alternators, but the efficiency and effectiveness of a homemade system depends much on its design. A centrifugal pump can be made into a backward-running Francis turbine (in which water flows through the turbine runner); an induction motor can be used as an alternator; and a crossflow turbine can be fabricated with readily available materials common to Third World situations, Davis says. Go to www.otherpower.com for ideas on how to make homemade systems.

The electrical side of any hydropower facility always includes a device to convert the mechanical energy of a spinning shaft into electrical energy (either a generator for direct current or an alternator for AC). That electrical energy is then sent through a series of components called the "balance of system" equipment, which saves and regulates the electricity once it's generated. But before you tackle the electrical side of hydropower, you need to understand something about the two basic types of electricity: direct current (DC) and AC.

DC is the sort of electricity delivered by a battery. Imagine a whole bunch of electrons piled up against one pole of a battery, desperately trying to get to the other pole. When you close the circuit across both poles, energy flows in one direction and can spin a motor or light a bulb in the process. DC electricity is more complicated to generate than AC, and it travels less efficiently. That said, you can store DC power in a battery, and that makes it more useful for small hydropower applications that need to build up a stockpile of energy to meet large intermittent loads.

AC is the type you get from the grid; just think about it as a series of rising and falling voltage waves. In a typical grid-delivered power system, this rise-and-fall cycle happens 60 times a second. Most appliances are designed to run on AC power only.

Smaller hydropower systems might include a series of deep-cycle batteries for storing DC energy for intermittent high demand, though having a DC foundation to your system doesn't necessarily rule out the option of AC output, as well. The secret is something called an inverter. "These convert direct-current battery power (DC) into the kind of alternating current (AC) that we're all familiar with," Davis says.

If your energy needs are medium to high, you should consider a microhydro system that generates AC power with an alternator right from the start. At that level, you're nearing the point where electrical space heating can be part of your plans. "A 10-kilowatt system that runs in the winter," Davis says, "can provide heat that is the equivalent of burning 12 cords of firewood in a six-month heating season."

To understand how a microhydro setup operates in real life, it's often useful to look at examples. At the smaller end of the microhydro spectrum, a remote homestead in British Columbia wanted to produce enough electricity to run lights, radio, radiophone and stereo with an existing 1¼-inch domestic water supply pipe. The residents had doubts they would still have enough water to run their showers and toilets after the conversion, given the water's static pressure only amounted to 65 pounds per square inch (psi). They installed a Harris hydroelectric turbine with a Ford alternator close to the house that produces a modest output of 50 kWh per month. They chose a 500-watt inverter as the electrical subsystem. This system provides for the homestead's lights, radio and stereo, but propane provides other vital home services such as refrigeration and cooking.

And at the larger end of the microhydro spectrum, a remote First Nations American Indian community in British Columbia needed a high-output system, but the area's geography challenged the development of a microhydro system. Using an excavator, Davis and his crew dug a usable trench and laid a 4-inch-diameter pipeline, traveling over 900 feet and delivering 350 gpm over 315 feet of vertical head. This hydroelectric system generates a whopping 7,200 kWh per month at a continuous output of 10,000 watts using an 8-inch Pelton turbine wheel, directly driving a brushless 12-kilowatt alternator.

Microhydro is a clean, sustainable source of power for homesteads in the right location. By considering some of the preceeding requirements, you'll know if it can be a possibility for you. If it is, Davis' book and other resources will give you a more thorough look at the systems and companies on the market, plus a sound foundation for further development.

Blue Power*

Turning Tides into Electricity

By David C. Holzman
Environmental Health Perspectives, December 2007

Water has been used by humans as an energy source in the form of tide mills and water wheels for nearly 2,000 years. As a large-scale power source, however, tidal and wave energy is at roughly the same stage of development that wind power was at in the 1980s, numerous observers say, with many concepts but few installations—a situation that reverses as a technology matures. And the field is heating up fast, which is good news given the wealth of human and environmental health effects that follow traditional fossil fuel-fired power plants.

Tidal turbines capture the energy of the currents, as well as that of rivers, irrigation canals, dam tailraces, and possibly even ocean currents such as the Gulf Stream, in much the same manner that wind turbines transduce air currents. The diverse taxonomy of wave devices, meanwhile, could convert the ocean's roiling into grid-ready electrons. Wave and tidal energy, known collectively as "marine energy," is currently capable of supplying electricity equivalent to 10–25% of today's world's production, according to various estimates, or about 2–5% of end-use energy.

In the United States, wave energy conversion alone could supply the equivalent of 6.5% of electricity at current consumption rates, according to one fairly conservative estimate by the Electric Power Research Institute (EPRI), the research arm of the electric utility industry. This is equivalent to the electricity generated by all conventional U.S. hydroelectric plants. Tidal power could furnish another 3–3.5% of electricity needs.

In the United Kingdom, the Carbon Trust, a government-funded company promoting climate change mitigation, estimates somewhat more optimistically that in the long run, wave and tidal power together could supply 15–20% of British electricity needs. According to the 2006 Carbon Trust report *Future Marine*

Energy, the United Kingdom could be using these technologies to produce two to five U.S. nuclear plants' worth of electricity by 2020.

The zero-emission cleanliness of wave and tidal energy technologies is comparable to that of wind, and marine energy is arguably the least aesthetically disruptive method of producing electricity. Unlike the proposed Cape Wind offshore wind farm, for example, which currently has some legislators in Massachusetts saying "not in my backyard," wave and tidal technologies are often invisible from shore.

For purposes of energy capture, water is similar to wind, except that seawater is more than 800 times denser than air, essentially making it easier to capture energy. Moreover, whereas the wind can come from any direction, in most locations the tides flow only in and out, reducing the complexity of the mechanisms required to harvest that energy.

Tidal power is readily predictable, which makes coordinating the flow of electricity in the grid quite manageable. The keys to a strong tidal current are a large rise and fall in the tides and geographical features that funnel the water through a narrow channel. As with wind, the energy available in a tidal current varies as the cube of the current's speed. Six knots (about 6 mph) is the threshold for economic viability, according to the 200 EPRI report *North America Tidal In-stream Energy Conversion Technology Feasibility Study*. But tides this swift are uncommon. Viable wave resources are more widely distributed.

THE TECHNOLOGIES

The biggest new wave project is in Portugal, where Pelamis Wave Power is building the world's largest wave farm. In its first phase the plant will produce up to 2.25 MW, enough to power 450 average U.S. homes. The ultimate goal is 20 MW (enough for 4,000 homes). The first commercial-scale pre-production Pelamis outfit off of Scotland currently contributes up to 750 peak kW to the U.K. grid.

Like the sea snake for which it is named, the Pelamis floats atop the ocean's surface. Each of the Pelamis converter's segments is about the size of a train car. Passing waves bend the Pelamis at the joints. Hydraulic rams work like bicycle pumps to resist that bending, pushing oil at high pressure through hydraulic motors to drive electrical generators.

Another leading wave technology, Finavera Renewables' AquaBuOY, sits atop a long cylinder that hangs down into the ocean. The cylinder contains a solid steel piston, sprung from each end with a hose made of steel-reinforced rubber. As the buoy bobs up and down, the heavy piston's inertia stretches one segment of the hose while compressing the other. The potential energy thus captured, once released, pumps water through a turbine in the buoy, generating electricity. Finavera is conducting a pilot study in Washington State to be completed in 2009, with 50- and 100-MW systems eventually planned for Oregon, California, and Portugal.

Another commercial-scale system currently in operation is the 500-kW LIMPET (Land Installed Marine Powered Energy Transformer). Wavegen, its manufacturer, installed this shoreline energy converter on an island off of Scotland in 2000. The LIMPET shunts incoming waves into a shore-mounted container. The "oscillating water column" within forces air back and forth through a turbine, driving a generator.

There are 25 concepts for capturing energy from tidal currents. One of the leaders is the tidal turbine manufactured by OpenHydro Group, which was chosen by Nova Scotia Power for projects in the exceptionally harsh but potentially abundant reservoir of energy that is the Bay of Fundy. The bay is home to some of the world's strongest tides, rising and falling nearly 50 feet, and its Minas Passage has the fastest tides in the world at 8 knots, says Margaret Murphy, manager of public affairs for Nova Scotia Power. That speed is both good and worrisome. "Picture a ton of ice, encrusted with sand, moving at eight knots, [and crashing into the turbine]," she says.

Nova Scotia Power plans to begin testing a 1-MW OpenHydro unit in the Minas Passage starting in late 2009. "The eventual dream would be to deploy three hundred megawatts in this one passage," Murphy says—enough for an average capacity of around 170 MW.

Another tidal generator, manufactured by Ocean Renewable Power Company, has the advantage of being able to continue reaping tidal energy without any mechanical repositioning as the tide shifts. The blades of these large turbines—two of which fit into a tractor trailer–sized module with a generator between them—trace the outline of a cylinder as they rotate, rather than a circle. Their spinning turns a shaft at the central axis of the cylinders.

The company hopes to develop tidal farms in Maine, Alaska, and possibly the Gulf Stream, although the latter's distance from shore currently renders it economically marginal for less than a gigantic farm. The company's Maine subsidiary and the city of Eastport plan to have a full-scale prototype operating early in 2009, with 40 MW of commercial power planned for the state and more installed elsewhere.

Perhaps the most radical concept in tidal power is the use of vortex-induced vibrations—the same phenomenon that toppled the Tacoma Narrows Bridge in 1940—to generate power. Vortex-induced vibrations occur whenever a current flows around a flexible cylindrical structure. Vortices are shed sequentially from alternate sides of the cylinder, causing the cylinder to oscillate. A tidal current device dubbed VIVACE (Vortex Induced Vibrations for Aquatic Clean Energy) transduces that oscillation into electricity.

This approach, if proven successful, could greatly expand the tidal and ocean/river resource because it can harvest ample power from the vast majority of currents that fall well below the EPRI economic viability threshold of 6 knots. Currently, the engineering firm Vortex Hydro Energy is developing a pilot project to generate 3 kW from a current of less than 2 knots on the Detroit River for the Detroit Power Authority, with the power to be used to light a wharf.

COSTS AND BENEFITS

At this early stage in development, electricity from wave and tidal generators is not inexpensive. Wavegen is peddling its wares to Pacific Island nations, where the cost of wave power—40–50 cents per kWh—competes with local diesel generators. In Scotland, the cost is 18–21 cents per kWh, says Dave Gibb, "wavegen's general manager. By comparison, in the mainland United States, the per-kWh cost of electricity averages around 7–8 cents, but can reach 20 Cents in some regions. Roger Bedard, the ocean energy leader at the EPRI, notes that wind started out around 40 cents per kWh, and has declined to around 7 cents. He expects wave and tidal costs to drop similarly, eventually costing even less than wind.

Marine energy is notably environmentally benign. The 2004 EPRI report *Offshore Wave Power in the US: Environmental Issues* states that "given proper care in site planning and early dialogue with local stakeholders, offshore wave power promises to be one of the most environmentally benign electrical generation technologies."

Like hydroelectric dams, wave and tidal technologies are nonpolluting. But unlike dams, which block whole rivers, tidal turbines do not require water impoundments nor do they appear to interfere with migration of fish or other animals or otherwise interfere with the ecology. A study by Oak Ridge National Laboratory published in the October 2005 issue of *Hydro Review* placed the probability of migrating fish being injured by the tidal turbine project in New York City's East River at 0.004–0.457%.

"I haven't heard of any specific environmental concerns with [wave and tidal power] yet, but it's something we will continue to follow," says John H. Rogers, senior energy analyst and Northeast Clean Energy Project manager at the Union of Concerned Scientists. Rogers asserts that any environmental impact must be balanced against the impact of forgoing these technologies—for example, the construction of more coal or other fossil fuel plants, with their attendant environmental impacts.

Nonetheless, some genuine environmental concerns need to be studied, says Keely Wachs, environmental communications manager at Pacific Gas and Electric, which is aggressively pursuing renewables. Along the West Coast, he says, the majority of gray whale migration routes run within 2 nautical miles of shore, coinciding roughly with the likely siting of wave power plants relative to shore. Installing such devices could destroy the kelp forests where migrating mother-calf pairs shelter. Wave machines could also conceivably interfere with local fishing industries, says Wachs. Again, however, careful siting could obviate many if not all these concerns.

REGULATING THE TIDES

About one-third of U.S. states have production goals and incentives for renewable energy, including marine energy. One of the most ambitious states, Oregon, has set a goal of 25% renewable electricity by 2025. Oregon also provides a state tax credit of 50% per installation, up to $20 million, as well as low-interest loans for wave and tidal projects.

The European Union is pursuing wave and tidal energy even more aggressively. Whereas the United States offers federal subsidies for renewable electricity of 1.9 cent per kWh, Portugal, the most generous of the European countries, offers nearly 30 cents per kWh.

In the United States, the biggest roadblock to swift adoption of wave and tidal technologies is regulation. It takes around five years and millions of dollars' worth of studies to gain permission to plant a prototype turbine in a tidal current or in offshore waves. "It took us more than four years to get approval to put six turbines in the water," says Trey Taylor, president of Verdant Power, which is testing its tidal turbines in the East River. During those four years, "we had to keep the engineering team together, and pay salaries." The cost of permitting alone was more than 50% of the total project costs to date.

The problem is that there are few baseline environmental impact data "since none of these projects have been deployed before," says Mary McCann, a fish biologist who is manager of environmental services at Devine Tarbell and Associates, a consulting firm in Portland, Maine. "How do you get projects in the water to collect information to answer these questions when you are supposed to have the answers first, in order to get approval to put them in the water?"

"A sense of proportionality needs to be built into the process," says Sean O'Neill, president of the Ocean Renewable Energy Coalition, the national trade association for marine renewable energy. "Treating these technologies as though they are utility-scale projects is causing companies like [Verdant] to devote the majority of their capital on permitting instead of new technology development."

The problem is not so much with the Federal Energy Regulatory Commission, which regulates licensing, as with all the other agencies that get their say, says McCann. Furthermore, says Tim Oakes, a senior regulatory advisor with Kleinschmidt Energy and Water Resource Consultants in Strasburg, Pennsylvania, wave and tidal projects frequently are held to higher standards than conventional power projects, because they are located in waterways and offshore, thus falling under federal regulatory jurisdiction. In contrast, he says, conventional power plants are usually subject to the much milder state regulation.

McCann believes the federal government should provide assistance and research funds for wave and tidal development, with the information gained to be shared with all. Although there is currently no wave or tidal energy program within the U.S. DOE, legislative efforts to establish such are flowering across Capitol Hill, says Walter Musial, a senior engineer at the DOE National Renewable Energy Laboratory.

Some of these problems may soon be resolved, says Oaks. On 2 October 2007, the Federal Energy Regulatory Commission held a workshop in Portland, Oregon, where it proposed a program to complete licensing for several types of pilot projects within six months.

Wave Master*

By Stuart Nathan
The Engineer (London, England), April 9–22, 2007

Wave Power is on the rise. As concerns grow over the need for diverse ways to generate electricity without boosting greenhouse gas emissions, dozens of new devices are taking shape in wave tanks and slipping into the water for testing.

But wave power's history dates back more than three decades and, if anyone can claim to be its founding father, it is veteran design engineer Stephen Salter. His Salter's Duck is still the most efficient wave power converter. Now an emeritus professor at Edinburgh University, Salter is still working on ambitious designs for marine power systems—some of which may help reduce global warming in unexpected ways.

According to Neil Kermode, director of the European Marine Energy Centre in Orkney (*The Engineer*, 26 March), Salter can claim much of the credit for the resurgence of wave power.

'Stephen was a lone voice in the wilderness as far as wave power was concerned,' he said.

'I remember seeing him on TV when I was at school; he was very inspiring. He had such a clever concept that was so unusual'—the words 'wave' and 'energy' were never associated in the public mind before that. Waves were something you went surfing on. Energy was something that came out of a socket. But after Stephen spoke about it, it became something people connected with, and that's never really gone away.

'Now there's a change in the political climate and Stephen and the people who were associated with his research are forming a critical mass of expertise.'

Born in South Africa just before World War II, Salter's career as a design engineer has led him into several unexpected places. He was an instrumentation engineer on the first hovercraft and on Black Knight, the UK's rocket project of the early 1960s. Later he moved to the University of Edinburgh to work on robot mechanics and electronics in the School of Artificial Intelligence.

Soon after moving to Scotland, Salter became concerned about the finite nature of oil resources. He turned his attention to renewable energy and wave power in particular.

Forming his own research group, he designed the first generation of his now-famous wave energy converter. Shaped like a flattened cam with the narrow end facing into the waves and the rounded end rotating around a flexible spine, the device resembled the head of a duck, nodding up and down as the waves passed underneath it. Salter's Duck was born.

To develop the Duck, Salter designed a revolutionary wave tank whose wave maker was driven by digital drives and incorporated force feedback and water velocity sensors.

The Duck works by absorbing about 90 per cent of the energy from incoming waves, leaving a calm sea behind the cam. The nodding motion of the cam operates pistons that compress hydraulic oil. Once pressure has built up, the pressurised oil is released through a hydraulic motor that generates electricity, converting 90 per cent of the captured power. To date, it is the most efficient wave-energy converter ever designed.

Initially, Salter said, enthusiasm for the Duck was high. 'Cost predictions were impossibly high but the people in charge of the programme were very optimistic. Their enthusiasm diminished as costs came down.'

In the early 1980s, the government closed the wave-energy project. Salter thinks this was politically motivated; the nuclear industry was heavily represented on the panel awarding energy grants and its members became concerned as the cost projections came down. 'When the programme manager predicted that with development, the cost would be 3.3p/kWh, which was getting close to being economically viable even then, they excluded him from the next important meeting of the key committee,' said Salter. 'They basically killed the project because it was going to threaten the expansion of the nuclear industry,' he claimed.

Salter agrees that initial costs for a Duck system would be high, and that his proposals for a functional string were ambitious. 'We'd been told to build a 2,000MW station, equivalent to two really big power stations, in the first go, so we designed something exactly aimed at that. It's too big an initial investment. The very smallest system we could do would be about 600MW, and that would be 10 Ducks, each 45m wide, with a gap of 60m between them—about 600km of sea. They're set in a row and the longer the row the more power you get, because they also assist each other in a variety of nice, complicated ways.'

However, such a large, complex system was ahead of its time. 'It's a bit like somebody saying in 1905 that they had a really good idea for a huge aircraft like the Airbus A380 when people didn't believe that biplanes would fly.'

Salter is encouraged by the current high profile of wave power, particularly with the Pelamis device, which was developed by one of his former students, Richard Yemm, at Edinburgh's Ocean Power Delivery (OPD).

Pelamis uses a similar, high-pressure, oil-based system to generate power but rather than using a wide, flat cam to absorb the power of the waves it is based on a long, narrow tube, which flexes with the waves, absorbing less energy. The trade-off, OPD believes, makes the device more able to survive in high seas than the Duck, which was believed to be vulnerable to very large waves (although Salter disputes this).

'OPD has done a really thorough job, and started in our wave tank,' Salter said. 'It's done some fantastic computer modelling of how Pelamis behaves, and I'm full of admiration and very proud of it.'

However, he sees Pelamis as an intermediate technology to restore faith in practical wave power; if it succeeds, he believes, people will look at the more efficient version of the technology. 'When you look at the power per unit mass [from Pelamis] it's very nice but it doesn't make good use of the wave front. It's the right thing to do at this stage but we'll start looking at Ducks again when we think "There's only 400km of sea here, we would get a bigger energy resource if we used it more intensively"'.

Salter remains convinced of the potential for marine renewables. 'You could run continents on this sort of power,' he said. 'The long-term dream for the Duck stream is that you run a long line of them from the Hebrides down to the west coast of Ireland, with a break to allow shipping through, then you build out from Cape Wrath [the most westerly point on the northern coast of Scotland], past the Faroes and all the way to Iceland. You can use hydro electrics and the Icelandic geothermal to back that up when there aren't any waves.'

'So you get a very high-capacity factor of wave power coming into Scotland and Norway and feeding on down into the rest of Europe. That's a really enormous resource.'

The prospects for tidal power are equally large, he said, particularly from the Pentland Firth, the channel between Scotland and Orkney that is estimated to hold half of Europe's tidal power resource. 'I think we could get 10-20GW out of Pentland, using tidal stream turbines,' he said, which is more than is generated in the UK by nuclear power stations. 'You could run a distribution system down the east coast of the UK, with spurs going off it for Newcastle, York and Birmingham down to London. Then you'd link the Iceland string into the top.'

Now approaching 70, Salter is still active in engineering research and his concepts are as ambitious as ever. His current project, in collaboration with atmospheric physicist John Latham of the US National Centre for Atmospheric Research, is to design a fleet of renewably-powered, remote-controlled yachts that would spray a mist of sea water into the air to create low-level clouds with a high albedo (reflectivity). These clouds, Latham believes, would reflect solar energy away from the Earth and provide a global cooling effect to counteract the warming caused by greenhouse gases.

Salter has developed plans for the yachts, which would be propelled by 60ft high vertical rotors. Known as Flettner rotors, these interact with the wind to propel the yacht, acting like sails, but with far greater efficiency. The yachts would drag two 3m-diameter turbines that would generate the electricity to spin the Flettner rotors and spray water droplets from their tops. He and Latham believe a fleet of 50 such yachts, guided to the required locations by GPS, would be needed to produce an appreciable effect.

'There's no funding for this, but we're going ahead quite quickly. We're working on the full-scale design and we've got work going on predicting how much we need to spray—it's an amazingly small amount,' said Salter. Calculations indicate a spray-rate of about 10kg of water per second. 'But we do need to get information on atmospheric conditions and cloud-cover fractions.'

Despite the difficulties, Salter is driven by the need to ameliorate the effects of climate change—as he has always been. 'We're in a massive state of denial about this,' he said. 'And we need to take action.'

6

Geothermal Energy

Editor's Introduction

Frequently overlooked in discussions of alternative energy, geothermal power, derived from the heat stored beneath the planet's surface, offers clean and renewable energy at increasingly affordable prices. In fact, geothermal currently generates as much energy as both solar and wind power combined. Still, few believe geothermal is capable of fundamentally transforming our current energy structure in the way hydrogen fuel cells or solar power might. Nevertheless, if properly deployed, geothermal could serve as a vital tool in lessening our dependence on fossil fuels and reducing our greenhouse gas emissions. The entries in this section, "Geothermal Energy," discuss the potential of this fuel source and the efforts currently underway to harness it.

The western United States is particularly rich in geothermal energy. James Yearling details the situation in "Geothermal Energy, Power from the Underground," observing that only a small portion of the available energy is currently being exploited. However, he believes that geothermal may be utilized more widely in the future, citing a recent study by the Massachusetts Institute of Technology (MIT) that concludes that technological innovations could lead to geothermal supplying 10 percent of the total energy consumed in the United States by 2050.

Blessed with extensive hot springs and lava flows, Iceland possesses a wealth of geothermal capital. In "Deep Heat" Caroline Williams discusses the Iceland Deep Drilling Project (IDDP), which seeks to indirectly harvest energy from the Earth's magma. Unlike most geothermal endeavors, the IDDP will not access the magma itself, but rather a reservoir of water adjacent to it. Due to its proximity to the magma and the intense air pressure at such depths, this water has become a "supercritical" liquid, unstable but extremely energy intensive. Experts believe that a supercritical geothermal well could produce up to 10 times more energy than a traditional well. Despite this vast potential, supercritical liquids are notoriously difficult to handle, consequently the success of the IDDP is by no means a certainty. Indeed, William states, "When the words 'supercritical and 'drilling' go together, they are usually followed by 'incident'."

Like solar and wind energy, geothermal has small-scale applications that can reduce one's reliance on outside power sources. In "Geothermal Technology: A Smart Way to Lower Energy Bills," Scott Calahan describes his experience outfitting his home with a geothermal pump.

Geothermal Energy, Power from the Underground*

By James Yearling
High Country News, February 25, 2008

The thought of Nevada's cities—lighting up the desert landscape with neon lights, all-you-can-eat buffets and noisy slot machines—makes most environmentalists cringe. It's not just aesthetic: These gambling hubs are seen as gluttonous resource gulpers.

One of them, however, is gaining praise for its production of renewable energy. The city of Reno, north of Las Vegas, is a "hotspot" for geothermal power production.

Geothermal plants now provide enough electricity to serve all 200,000 residents. And energy analysts say Reno's success barely scratches the surface: Projects slated for the West could nearly double the nation's geothermal generating capacity in the next few years, according to a new survey from the Geothermal Energy Association.

Geothermal sources now generate nearly 3,000 megawatts per year in the U.S.—more than any other nation, but still only 0.4 percent of total energy use, roughly equivalent to two large coal-fired power plants.

The investment risk is still too high for a commercial-scale geothermal industry to flourish, according to Jefferson Tester of the Massachusetts Institute of Technology; the projects take years of planning and construction and don't get the large government subsidies that other energy producers do.

But adequate federal funding for research and development would smooth out operational kinks, slash the risk and give investors more confidence, he says.

"We know the resources are there, it's just a matter of developing them," says Karl Gawell, executive director of the Geothermal Energy Association. "The solution isn't black-and-white, and we have a long way to go, but we have all the pieces—they just have to be put together."

The West is prime for geothermal development because its underground reservoirs of steam, hot water and hot rocks tend to lie close to the surface, especially in places like the Pacific Northwest's Cascade Mountains and Southern California's Imperial Valley.

Half of all geothermal energy production in the nation is in the West, and 90 percent of the identified geothermal resources are on Western public lands. In its infancy, geothermal electricity production required extremely hot water, over 360 degrees Fahrenheit.

New technology, however, allows the use of water as cool as 165 degrees, greatly expanding opportunities for power production. Geothermal energy can also be tapped directly as a heating source. In some places, geothermal heating districts have been established; one such system uses hot water pipes to heat 37 buildings in San Bernardino, Calif. More than 80 geothermal power projects are in the works across the West, in every state except Montana and Colorado.

READY TO SUPPLY POWER

In Nevada, Idaho, Utah and California, geothermal plants already supply power to the grid. By 2050, advances in geothermal technology could supply 100,000 annual megawatts of power, according to a 2006 MIT study—10 percent of U.S. energy consumption.

And by 2015, the cost of geothermal electricity should be competitive with that of coal, which currently provides about half of the country's energy, according to the Department of Energy. Consumers generally pay between 3 and 5½ cents for a kilowatt hour of coal power and between 5 and 8 cents for a kilowatt hour of geothermal power.

Not only will geothermal costs come down as technology improves, coal costs will continue to rise, due to the cost of transporting coal and complying with eventual greenhouse gas legislation. Unlike other renewable energy sources that depend on the vagaries of wind or sun, geothermal plants produce consistent power.

"Geothermal plants generate power 24 hours a day, year-round, and don't face hazards like tropical storms that plague other energy industries," says Paul Thomsen of Reno-based geothermal developer Ormat. "And the plants release hardly any carbon emissions."

ENVIRONMENTAL IMPACT

But no energy source is entirely free of environmental impacts. Although geothermal development is prohibited in national parks and wilderness areas, development on other public lands could alter viewsheds and geothermal features and pollute surface water.

A typical natural-gas-fired plant sucks up 361 gallons of freshwater per megawatt hour, compared to less than 5 gallons for geothermal plants—but even that could cause conflicts with other water users in drought-stricken areas. Vents around geothermal operations can release objectionable gases such as ammonia, methane and hydrogen sulfide, which smells like rotten eggs, and some projects have induced small earthquakes. Still proponents say these side effects are minimal when stacked against the environmental costs of traditional energy production.

To help developers unleash geothermal potential on public lands, the Bureau of Land Management and the Forest Service are jointly investigating the environmental impacts of expanding geothermal leasing. (The BLM issues all geothermal leases and permits.) Once the final assessment comes out this fall, the agencies will allow additional leasing on lands with high potential.

Currently, there are about 420 geothermal leases on federal land, 55 of which are producing geothermal energy. Interest in leasing has increased sharply in the last decade; the BLM has issued nearly 300 geothermal leases since 2001, compared to only 25 between 1996 and 2001. Last summer, the agency launched an effort to speed up the leasing process.

Of the approximately 100 geothermal lease requests pending as of January 2005, the BLM has pledged to process at least 90 percent of them by August 2010. But even after a geothermal company leases public land, the process of actually acquiring a permit to develop the resource remains painful. The BLM is so overrun with oil, gas and coalbed methane permit requests that geothermal interests get pushed to the back burner.

"The BLM doesn't have adequate resources or personnel to deal with geothermal, so permits get delayed for years," Gawell says. "I literally know people who have died waiting."

GEOTHERMAL POLITICS

Geothermal development has benefited from bipartisan support in the House and Senate, but the Bush administration's commitment has been less than robust. The Energy Act of 2005, touted as renewable-friendly, created the Geothermal Technologies Program in an attempt to boost the industry.

The administration requested $26 million for the program the first year and $23 million the next—for 2007 and 2008, it didn't request a dime, leaving industry experts, environmentalists and policymakers angry and confused. The 2009 budget, though, asks for $30 million.

Questioned by Congress, the Department of Energy justified the 2007 budget cut by saying that geothermal was a "mature technology" that didn't need additional funding. The department also cited an Office of Management and Budget grading system in order to claim that the geothermal program wasn't performing well enough to justify extra dollars.

But funding for the clean-coal technology program was upped, even though its performance was rated lower than that of the geothermal program. Meanwhile, federal subsidies for the nuclear and fossil fuel industries still range in the hundreds of millions of dollars. In 2005, federal production tax credits previously tied to wind and solar power were expanded to include geothermal projects. But the credits are set to expire at the end of this year, even though over 100 geothermal development companies recently sent letters to the White House calling for an extension.

By one vote, the Senate recently declined an extension that would have lasted through 2012. Those tax credits have been the deciding factor as to whether developers can afford to break ground on new geothermal projects, says Lisa Shevenell, director of the Great Basin Center for Geothermal Energy.

For 10 years after plant construction, the tax credits pay geothermal developers 2 cents for every kilowatt-hour of electricity generated. That substantially lowers the cost of generating power, leading to lower costs for consumers and lower risks to investors.

"Without an extension of the tax credit deadline, most likely, projects will be downsized or put on hold altogether," says Gawell. But geothermal may get a boost from the Energy Independence and Security Act of 2007, which Bush signed in December.

The legislation includes the Advanced Geothermal Energy Research and Development Act, which directs the Department of Energy to authorize up to $95 million annually for research and development. And most of the Western states, with the exception of Wyoming, Utah and Idaho, have established renewable portfolio standards, which require electric utilities to produce a certain percentage of their energy (usually 10 to 15 percent) from renewable sources, including geothermal, by a certain date.

As with any power source, access to transmission facilities is key. In November 2007, the Bush administration proposed 6,000 miles of "energy corridors," rights of way for distributing oil, gas, hydrogen and electricity.

Although some environmentalists disapprove of corridors in national parks and monuments, others welcome the plan because it could minimize the time it takes to site and approve projects. Success stories like Reno prove that, although geothermal is by no means a cure-all for the nation's energy problems, it is definitely part of the solution.

"Interest in geothermal has really blossomed," says Shevenell. "And in the next few years, I think that the industry will, too." Tapping energy from underground could make the barren Nevada desert a land of plenty—and someday soon, it could power millions of households in the West.

Deep Heat*

By Caroline Williams
New Scientist, August 14, 2004

"This is our gold," Gudmundur Omar Fridleifsson beams, as steam rising from the ground mists up his glasses. "Geothermal, hydrogen . . . and fish." The wind changes direction and we get a sulphurous lungful. "In Iceland we call this 'the pleasant smell'," he adds.

The first thing you notice about Iceland are the bleak, moss-covered lava flows overlooked by black, snow-tipped volcanoes. The second is the smell. The shower in the hotel, much like the steam enveloping us now, has a distinctly eggy whiff. Hardly surprising when you consider that most of Iceland's domestic hot water is heated deep underground and piped straight to the bathroom. According to Fridleifsson, sulphur is good because it helps stop the water pipes from rusting. It certainly stops visitors spending too long in the shower.

In a way, it is pipework that has brought me here: Fridleifsson is the manager of the Iceland Deep Drilling Project (IDDP). This ambitious scheme of extreme plumbing aims to bring unfeasibly hot fluids to the surface where we can reap the benefits of their energy. And it will make the geothermal well we're standing beside, and every other well, seem like little more than a scratch on the Earth's surface.

The project aims to drill down 5 kilometres and extract energy from magma. Rather than dealing with molten rock directly though, Fridleifsson wants to tap into a reservoir of water which has come into contact with the magma and, thanks to the high temperatures and pressures at this depth, gone beyond steam to form a "supercritical" fluid. This is tricky stuff to handle: it has properties of both liquid and gas, and is an excellent solvent. In fact, this fluid will be chock-full of metals and minerals, which can precipitate out at the drop of a hat, blocking pipes and creating a risk of blowout. But most important, this supercritical fluid has a greater heat content per unit of mass than steam from conventional wells. The

---

*Article by Caroline Williams from *New Scientist*, August 14, 2004.

sums suggest that a supercritical well should yield anything up to 10 times more energy than its steam-based counterparts. And while drilling down 5 kilometres has been done before, this will be the first time anyone in the world has set out to go supercritical.

The project also promises to tackle some of the world's biggest geological and environmental questions. Thanks to the chemistry of supercritical fluids, this well could kick-start the global hydrogen economy and create the first sustainable mine—one that squirts precious metals and minerals up from the depths like a fountain. It will even give geologists their first peek inside the mid-Atlantic ridge and reveal the chemistry of mysterious vents called black smokers, which are usually only found deep beneath the ocean, without the need to touch the delicate ecosystems they support.

The IDDP started life in a mid-blizzard chat between Fridleifsson, then working as a well-site geologist, and Albert Albertsson, of the Icelandic energy company Sudurnes Regional Heating. "It was about 11 pm, and the weather was very dramatic," Fridleifsson recalls. "Albert and I were chatting at a well site. We started talking about deep drilling and supercritical fluids and it turned out that we were both really keen on the idea. Albert was the one who wanted to tame the beast," he says. The pair were so taken with the idea that they proposed the project at the World Geothermal Congress in Japan in 2000.

Since then, feasibility studies have shown that drilling into this kind of hot, high-pressure liquid is technically possible. The project has also won support from a consortium of Iceland's three largest energy companies, including Sudurnes Regional Heating, and in December 2003, Sudurnes Regional Heating agreed to allocate one of its planned wells to the IDDP, in effect stumping up a fifth of the $S5 million it will take to complete the project. The first 2.5 kilometres will be drilled in January next year. It will be extended to 4 kilometres in 2006, and to the final depth of 5 kilometres in 2007.

As test sites for deep drilling go, Iceland is one of the best. Formed where a mantle plume coincides with the mid-Atlantic ridge, an underwater mountain range where new crust is constantly created, it is one of the most geologically active regions in the world (*New Scientist*, 8 March 2003, p 32). The Icelanders have made good use of this: the first geothermal well was drilled in1928 and today 99 per cent of the people in the capital, Reykjavik, and nearly 90 per cent of the entire population, use geothermal energy to heat their homes. Fruit and vegetables are grown in geothermally heated greenhouses. They even farm fish, using naturally heated water.

HEALTHY EFFLUENT

On our way across the Reykjanes peninsula in the south-west, we stop at the Svartsengi power station which provides water and electricity for the Sudurnes region and take a dip in the plant's famously healthy effluent, the Blue Lagoon.

Somehow we manage to carry on talking science while covered in an exfoliating mixture of white silica mud and algae.

A couple of hours later and looking 10 years younger, we reach the IDDP site. There is not much to see yet except a colony of Arctic terns nesting amid the lava flows, but by next year it will be the scene of a very different activity.

Reykjanes was chosen because it is here that the mid-Atlantic ridge makes landfall. As a result, molten lava is closer to the surface here than almost anywhere else. Frequent earthquakes have cracked the rock, allowing rain and seawater to seep downwards to where it is heated. The evidence for this is all around us. Mud boils on the surface and steam escapes from every fissure. It is easy to see why Viking settlers named this flat expanse of lava Reykjanes—"the steamy peninsula."

Most geothermal wells tap energy from a mix of boiling water and steam formed underground at temperatures between 200 °C and 340 °C. The steam is separated and passed through a turbine at the surface. However, Fridleifsson plans to drill through this region and go straight to the source of the heat. To extract energy from magma he must devise a convenient way of getting its heat to the turbine: the magma itself is far too hot. So, says Grimur Bjornsson, an engineer at the Reykjavik-based research institute Iceland Geosurvey, the IDDP will use water that sits in a reservoir directly on top of the magma. The extreme conditions encountered here change it into a supercritical fluid: a mix of liquid-like, hydrogen-bonded clusters of water molecules dispersed in a gas-like phase that makes an excellent solvent for all kinds of chemicals. It is this supercritical fluid that will be sent up through the well to the turbine, Bjornsson says.

Tapping this resource will be far from easy. When the words "supercritical" and "drilling" go together, they are usually followed by "incident." A well in Nesjavellir, just outside Reykjavik, accidentally hit supercritical fluid in 1985 and had to be plugged with 600 metres of gravel to stop the system blowing out. Supercritical conditions have also caused problems in high-temperature wells in Japan and Italy.

So the IDDP well head will be designed to handle fluid pressures of more than 220 bars and the well itself will be lined with three layers of cemented steel casing for over half its length. The casing will have to be carefully designed to handle the expansion caused by temperatures ranging from 30 °C to more than 500 °C. Geologists usually try to avoid drilling into material at high temperatures. Recently, one well in Iceland accidentally drilled into high-pressure steam at 380 °C, "although we didn't know it at the time," Bjornsson says.

At each stage of drilling, the well fluid will be sampled, and the flow rate through the well measured. These will be crucial moments; if there isn't enough pressure from below to drive the fluid upwards, the well will be useless. If the fluid is too cool, they'll end up with a very expensive, but conventional, geothermal well. But if all goes to plan and they hit supercritical conditions as expected, the fluid will be piped up for testing. Then all they have to do is work out how to deal with it.

"Part of the problem is that we don't know what temperatures and pressures to expect, and even less what the chemical composition will be," says Jon Orn Bjarnason of Iceland Geosurvey. "We've been drilling to 2 kilometres for decades so we pretty much know what the fluids will be at that depth. What we find at 5 kilometres—that's a little different."

Most speculate that they will meet hot, high-pressure seawater modified by boiling and reacting with surrounding rock. It will contain all kinds of chemicals such as potassium, chlorides and calcium, plus pretty much any metal you care to think of. This could cause some headaches.

Conventional wells get slowly furred up by mineral deposits in the pipes, leaving them blocked like old arteries. But supercritical fluid could turn out to be the hard water from hell. If its temperature or pressure drops too far, or it mixes with cooler steam, minerals and metals could suddenly precipitate out. This could seal the pipes entirely, causing a build-up of pressure and a blowout that could destroy the well. The trick will be to control the pressure at the top of well and the speed of fluid flowing to the surface. "It's not a case of keeping out the harmful minerals, it's a matter of controlling the conditions of production so that they don't precipitate where you don't want them to," says Robert Fournier of the US Geological Survey, one of the project's scientific advisers.

If they manage to tame the fluid, converting its energy into electricity using a turbine should be relatively easy. "If we can convert supercritical fluid to superheated steam we are in business," says Fridleifsson. "Steam is something we are used to." The only difference is that while a flow of 2 kilograms per second of conventional steam produces 1 megawatt of power, the same flow rate of supercritical steam could, theoretically, generate 10 megawatts.

With an energy source this efficient, it will be even cheaper to produce hydrogen, by electrolysing water, to fuel Iceland's clean-energy revolution. Iceland's commitment to hydrogen is already clear. The world's first hydrogen filling station opened just outside Reykjavik in April 2003 to fuel three city buses. There are plans to convert the entire fishing fleet, and eventually the whole country, to run on hydrogen. But could going supercritical convert the rest of the world too?

Possibly. Turning hydrogen into a global commodity relies on finding a cheap way to produce it and a safe way to transport it. Supercritical fluids could offer a solution to both problems. "At temperatures above 400 °C, what are known as 'supercritical water processes' become possible," says Dan Fraser of the University of Manitoba in Canada.

Fraser thinks it should be possible to use a process called "supercritical water partial oxidation" to catalyse a reaction that transforms organic material—present in the fluid from the mine or added later—to create hydrogen directly. He also believes it is possible to efficiently convert carbon dioxide and hydrogen into methanol, which can be shipped around the world and is easily broken down into hydrogen when required.

GLOBAL HOTSPOTS

Better still, geothermal hotspots like Reykjanes are not unique to Iceland. Fraser's group is working on a similar project in the Aleutian Islands, and other potential sites exist in the Great Rift Valley in Africa, Italy, Mexico, Costa Rica, Hawaii, California, Nicaragua, Japan and New Zealand: in fact, wherever there are young volcanic rocks. If the IDDP is successful, its technology could be applied worldwide.

But there is much more to the IDDP than just cheap energy and hydrogen production. The same metals that could cause problems in the plumbing might turn out to be as profitable as the production of energy—if not more so. Fraser's group is awaiting a patent on a system to extract metals from supercritical fluids, based on the sudden precipitation that occurs when supercritical fluid meets cold water. This process has already been observed around black smokers. If geologists can recreate it at the well head, geologically active countries could become huge stores of clean energy, as well as finding themselves quite literally sitting on a gold mine—and a sustainable one at that. "If you're drilling supercritical, pretty much the whole periodic table could come up. Third World countries could suddenly have resources of gold, silver, copper and zinc," Fraser says.

But no one is certain that this form of mining will succeed, and for now the ever-pragmatic IDDP team is focusing on the job in hand: to reach a depth of 5 kilometres safely. Geologists, engineers and environmentalists are all watching closely. Listening to the international experts who have gathered in Iceland to discuss the science, it is clear that no one is sure what they will encounter at that depth. "After hearing so many eminent scientists with different views, you think, well, we just don't know," Bjarnason says at the end of the two-day meeting. Like everyone else involved, he can see only one way of finding out—by drilling that hole.

Geothermal Technology*

A Smart Way to Lower Energy Bills

By Scott Calahan
Tech Directions, February 2007

Heating costs for both natural gas and oil have risen dramatically in recent years—and will likely continue to do so. Consequently, it's important that students learn not only about traditional heating technology, but also about the alternative methods that will surely grow in use in the coming years. I've had personal experience with one such method—geothermal—and share what I've learned in this article for the benefit of other technology educators and their students.

CHOOSING GEOTHERMAL

In 1999, I began some major remodeling to a "starter" home my wife and I had purchased a few years earlier. As part of the remodel, I decided get rid of the electric baseboards and wood stove then used to heat the home. After exploring many options, it appeared the best economic choices called for installing either a heat pump or a natural gas furnace. We decided to go with natural gas.

By 2001, our family had outgrown that home and we wanted to build a new one. The "obvious" choice was to use natural gas to heat our new home as well. In addition, my wife wanted to add air conditioning to our new home, since the summer temperature in our area often reaches the 90s, sometimes going as high as 100° F. Early in the construction process, our builder approached us with the option of putting in a geothermal heating and cooling system. At first, the upfront costs seemed prohibitive. After much thought and research, though, we decided that geothermal made good economic and environmental sense.

THE BASICS

The term geothermal comes from the Greek words geo (earth) and therme (heat) (Geothermal Education Office, 2000). Use of geothermal energy is certainly not a new idea since archaeological evidence shows that people have used it for over 10,000 years. In North America, the Paleo-Indians used hot springs for cleansing and as a source of warmth. In the 1800s, people saw the opportunity to pipe hot water into homes and businesses.

In the 1960s, France began heating up to 200,000 homes using geothermal water. Later, in the mid-1990s, Carl Nielsen developed the first ground-source heat pump for use in his residence (U.S. Department of Energy [DOE], History, 2004). Years ago, the upfront cost of heating a home geothermally seemed cost prohibitive. Now, the economic benefits make it a wise choice for many reasons.

The earth maintains a constant temperature between 42–80° F in the United States (generally in the 45–50° F range in the northern latitudes) (Geothermal Heat Pump Consortium, date unknown). Consequently, it proves much more efficient to use the temperature of the earth to heat and cool rather than using the sometimes extreme outside temperatures, as is the case with ordinary heat pumps that sit outside a building.

To heat and cool your home, geothermal heat pumps (GHPs) (also known as "ground-source heat pumps" or "geoexchange systems") are used. According to the Environmental Protection Agency (EPA), they offer the most energy efficient, environmentally clean and cost-effective space-conditioning system available (Geothermal Heat Pump Consortium, 1997).

A GHP system moves heat from the earth (or groundwater source) into the home in the winter. In the summer, the GHP pulls heat from the house and discharges it into the ground. A standard heat pump works the same way, though it must rely on varied temperatures from the outside air. In winter, the heat pump sits outside in the cold air. The colder the air, the more difficult it is to extract heat from it. In summer, the heat pump sits outside in the hot air. The hotter the air, the more difficult it is to transfer heat to it.

In other words, a standard heat pump's operating efficiency is lowest when the demand is highest. A geoexchange system does not have this problem because of the relatively constant temperature of the earth that it uses to heat or cool. Assuming installation of piping below the frost line (approx. 5' in Washington State), the temperature would be around 45–50° F. So in winter, a geoexhchange unit extracts heat from ground that is much warmer than the outside air, which could be 20° F or much lower. In summer, it can discharge heat to ground that is much cooler than the outside air, which could easily be 90–100° F.

SYSTEM COMPONENTS

Although today's market features numerous geothermal heat pumps, geoexchange systems generally comprise three main components: (1) an earth connection system, (2) a heat pump system and (3) a heat distribution system (DOE, Geothermal, 2004).

The earth basically serves as either a heat source or heat sink, depending on whether you are trying to heat or cool. The mechanism used to transfer and extract heat to or from the earth is the ground loop, a series of high density, polyethylene or polybutylene pipes thermally fused together. The loop is buried in the ground or placed in an existing pond or lake. The loops circulate a mixture of water and antifreeze that act as the heat exchanger.

The ground-source heat pump works much like common heat pumps and air conditioners. They all make use of a refrigerant to help transfer heat into and out of a home. The refrigerant helps geoexchange systems take advantage of one of the primary principles of heat transfer: Heat energy always flows from areas of higher temperature to areas of lower temperature (Geothermal Heat Pump Consortium, no date). In there words, the system takes existing heat and moves it from a lower-temperature location to a higher-temperature location.

Inside the home, conventional ductwork distributes heated or cooled air from the GHP throughout the home. This makes installation a simple process for both new construction and retrofit.

TYPES OF SYSTEMS

Basically two types of systems exist: closed loop and open loop. In closed loop systems, the pipe forms a continuous loop that acts as the heat exchanger. The pipe connects to the indoor heat pump to form a sealed loop. An antifreeze solution circulates through the loop, recirculating its heat-transferring solution in a pressurized pipe.

Closed loop systems can either be placed in horizontal trenches, vertically bored holes or an existing lake or pond. In a horizontal closed loop system, the pipe is typically laid in trenches at least 4' deep. A well-insulated 2,000 square foot home would require laying at least 1,500'–1,800' of pipe.

If land space is not available, a run of pipe could be laid at 5' and looped back over itself at 3' with no adverse effect on system efficiency. If enough land is not available for a horizontal system, a vertical closed loop system would work. In this case, holes are typically bored 125'–150' or more deep, depending on the heat pump capacity needed. A third closed loop system uses a water source (pond or lake) at least 6' deep at its lowest level.

Open loop systems use groundwater from a conventional well as a heat source. Since this method does not use a continuous loop, it requires use of a discharging method. The water can be released into a stream, pond, ditch, drainage tile or return well. A return well is a second well bore that returns the water to the ground aquifer. The amount of groundwater needed by the system varies, but the average system will use 6–10 gallons per minute while operating. Since the water simply absorbs heat (cooling) or gives up heat (heating), it is not polluted or otherwise altered.

The primary cost difference between systems comes in the installation. Horizontal loops are less expensive to install than vertical loops, providing the availability of adequate land space. Vertical loops do not require much land, but boring the holes can be very expensive. An existing pond requires little excavation and may have the lowest installation cost.

Once installed, the net results in operating cost and efficiency run about the same for open and closed loop systems. However, over a period of years, a closed loop system will require less maintenance because it is sealed and pressurized, which eliminates the chances of mineral build up or iron deposits.

ADDITIONAL BENEFITS

In addition to the energy savings involved in heating and cooling a home, many geoexchange systems come with de-superheaters that transfer excess heat from the GHP's compressor to a water heater, which reduces the energy needed to heat the water. While air conditioning during summer, waste heat extracted from interior air produces virtually free hot water. A de-superheater does not provide hot water when the system is not operating. However, because the GHP is so much more efficient than other means of water heating, manufacturers now offer "full demand" systems that use a separate heat exchanger to meet all of a household's hot water needs. These units cost-effectively provide hot water as quickly as any competing system (DOE, Geothermal, 2004).

COST

Factors that affect the type of system to install include the heating and cooling "load," the design and construction of the home, the land available and the region's climate. Generally speaking, an average-size home of about 2,000 square feet would require about a three-ton system. On average, a GHP system costs about $2,500 per ton of capacity, or roughly $7,500 for a three-ton unit.

In comparison, other HVAC systems would cost about $4,000, including air conditioning. The extra $3,500 added on to a mortgage might raise the mortgage payment by $30 per month, but energy savings may well exceed that, leaving you with a positive cash flow (Office of Geothermal Technologies, 1999).

Several GHP systems carry the Department of Energy and Environmental Protection Agency ENERGY STAR label. Many financial institutions offer special ENERGY STAR loans with lower interest rates, longer terms or both (Office of Geothermal Technologies, 1999). Many states also offer rebates or other incentives to homeowners who install geoexchange systems. GeoExchange.org currently lists 22 states with incentives for installing geoexhange systems.

ENVIRONMENTAL BENEFITS

The Geothermal Heat Pump Consortium and the Department of Energy's Office of Geothermal Technologies (1999) had a lofty goal of increasing the annual installation of GHP systems to 400,000 by the end [of] 2005. This could save consumers over $400 million per year in energy bills and reduce U.S. greenhouse gas emissions by over one million metric tons of carbon each year. The Geothermal Heat Pump Consortium (2004) lists several other environmental impacts:

- The use of geoexchange lowers electricity demand by nearly 1kW per ton of capacity.
- For every 100,000 homes with GHP systems, there is a reduction of foreign oil consumption by 2.15 million barrels annually and a reduction of electricity consumption by 799 million kW hours annually.
- GHPs generate no on-site emissions and have the lowest emissions among all heating and cooling technologies.
- GHPs represent savings to homeowners of 30 to 70 percent in the heating mode and 20 to 50 percent in the cooling mode compared with conventional systems.
- More than 900,000 geoexchange systems have been installed in the U.S., resulting in the elimination of more than 5.2 million metric tons of CO_2 annually and more than 1.4 million metric tons of carbon equivalent annually.
- These 900,000 installations have also reduced electricity demand by 2.3 million kW and have saved more than 36 trillion BTUs of fossil fuels annually.

FINAL THOUGHTS

As a personal testament, my wife and I are extremely pleased with every aspect of our geoexchange system. Our new home has nearly double the square footage of our starter home, yet our heating bills have never exceeded any bill we had for heating with natural gas in the much smaller home.

Surveys by utility companies show that more than 95 percent of homeowners like their GHP system and would recommend a system to their family or friends (Office of Geothermal Technologies, 1999). We are definitely among the 95 percent who would recommend a geoexchange system for both economic and environmental reasons! I encourage you to inform your students about this important technology.

Bibliography

Books

Blume, David, R. Buckminster Fuller, and Michael Winks. *Alcohol Can Be a Gas! Fueling an Ethanol Revolution for the 21st Century*. San Cruz, Calif.: International Institute for Ecological Agriculture, 2007.

Boyle, Godfrey, ed. *Renewable Energy*. New York: Oxford University Press, USA, 2004.

Busby, Rebecca L. *Hydrogen and Fuel Cells: A Comprehensive Guide*. Tulsa, Okla.: PennWell Corp., 2005.

Chiras, Dan. *The Homeowner's Guide to Renewable Energy: Achieving Energy Independence through Solar, Wind, Biomass and Hydropower*. Gabriola Island, B.C., Canada: New Society Publishers, 2006.

Davis, Scott. *Microhydro: Clean Power from Water*. Gabriola Island, B.C., Canada: New Society Publishers, 2003.

Dickson, Mary H. and Mario Fanelli, eds. *Geothermal Energy: Utilization and Technology*. London, U.K.: Earthscan Publications Ltd., 2005.

DiPippo, Ronald. *Geothermal Power Plants: Principles, Applications and Case Studies*. Oxford, U.K.: Elsevier Science, 2005.

Ewing, Rex A. *Got Sun? Go Solar: Get Free Renewable Energy to Power Your Grid-Tied Home*. Masonville, Col.: PixyJack Press, LLC, 2005.

Gibilisco, Stan. *Alternative Energy Demystified*. New York: McGraw-Hill Professional, 2006.

Gipe, Paul. *Wind Power, Revised Edition: Renewable Energy for Home, Farm, and Business*. White River Junction, Vt.: Chelsea Green Publishing Company, 2004.

Gupta, Harsh K., and Sukanta Roy. *Geothermal Energy: An Alternative Resource for the 21st Century*. Oxford, U.K.: Elsevier Science, 2006.

Hoffmann, Peter. *Tomorrow's Energy: Hydrogen, Fuel Cells, and the Prospects for a Cleaner Planet*. Cambridge, Mass.: The MIT Press, 2002.

Holland, Geoffrey, and James Provenzano. *The Hydrogen Age: Empowering a Clean-Energy Future*. Layton, Utah: Gibbs Smith, Publisher, 2007.

Intergovernmental Panel on Climage Change. *Climate Change 2007 - The Physical Science Basis: Working Group I Contribution to the Fourth Assessment Report of the IPCC*. New York: Cambridge University Press, 2007.

Kemp, William H. *Biodiesel Basics and Beyond: A Comprehensive Guide to Production and Use for the Home and Farm*. Tamworth, Ont., Canada: Aztext Press, 2006.

———. *The Renewable Energy Handbook: A Guide to Rural Energy Independence, Off-Grid and Sustainable Living*. Tamworth, Ont., Canada: Aztext Press, 2006.

Nelson, Willie. *On the "Clean" Road Again: Biodiesel and the Future of the Family Farm*. Golden, Col.: Fulcrum Publishing, 2007.

Nersesian, Roy L. *Energy for the 21st Century: A Comprehensive Guide to Conventional and Alternative Sources*. Armonk, N.Y.: M.E. Sharpe, 2006.

Pahl, Greg. *Biodiesel: Growing A New Energy Economy.* White River Junction, Vt.: Chelsea Green, 2005.

Podobnik, Bruce. *Global Energy Shifts: Fostering Sustainability in a Turbulent Age.* Philadelphia, Pa.: Temple University Press, 2005.

Rajeshwar, Krishnan, Stuart Licht, and Robert McConnell, eds. *Solar Hydrogen Generation: Toward a Renewable Energy Future.* New York: Springer, 2008.

Rifkin, Jeremy. *The Hydrogen Economy.* New York: Tarcher, 2003.

Scheer, Hermann. *The Solar Economy: Renewable Energy for a Sustainable Global Future.* London, U.K.: Earthscan Publications Ltd., 2004.

Simon, Christopher. *Alternative Energy: Political, Economic, and Social Feasibility.* Lanham, Md.: Rowan & Littlefield Publishers, Inc., 2006.

Sweet, William. *Kicking the Carbon Habit: Global Warming and the Case for Renewable and Nuclear Energy.* New York: Columbia University Press, 2006.

Web sites

Readers seeking additional information about alternative energy may wish to refer to the following Web sites, all of which were operational as of this writing.

Alternative Energy News

www.alternative-energy-news.info

The mission of Alternative Energy News is to "raise awareness about clean energy sources using any means necessary." Their Web site serves as a portal for news and information related to renewable and alternative energy.

American Coalition for Ethanol (ACE)

www.ethanol.org

Formed in 1988, the American Coalition for Ethanol (ACE) is the largest nonprofit in the United States dedicated to fostering ethanol use and production. Their Web site features links to news articles about the industry as well as in-depth explanations of ethanol technology and its benefits

American Solar Energy Society (ASES)

www.ases.org

The American Solar Energy Society (ASES) is a nonprofit organization founded in 1954 that is "dedicated to increasing the use of solar energy, energy efficiency, and other sustainable technologies in the U.S." In addition to serving as a clearinghouse for clean energy news, the organization's Web site provides links to its *Sunbeam* newsletter and the magazine *Solar Today*.

American Wind Energy Association (AWEA)

www.awea.org

The American Wind Energy Association (AWEA)'s mission is to "promote wind power growth through advocacy and communication, and education." Their Web site offers a host of resources for researchers, including news reports, extensive information on legislation and policy, and how-to-guides for small-scale wind projects.

International Geothermal Association (IGA)

iga.igg.cnr.it/index.php

Since its founding in 1988, the International Geothermal Association (IGA) has worked to encourage the use of geothermal energy throughout the globe. In addition to informative articles and diagrams on geothermal technology, the IGA Web site features an interactive map detailing geothermal energy use by nation.

National Biodiesel Board (NBB)

www.biodiesel.org

The National Biodiesel Board (NBB) is the trade association of the American biodiesel industry.

Its multimedia Web site provides a wealth of vital information and statistics, including a biodiesel buying guide.

U.S. Department of Energy: Hydrogen Program

www.hydrogen.energy.gov

The U.S. Department of Energy's Hydrogen Program, in conjunction with the private sector, academia, as well as international organizations, works to advance hydrogen technology, in order to make hydrogen feasible as a renewable fuel source while addressing the public's safety concerns. The Program's Web site discusses a host of hydrogen-related issues, including storage, manufacture, and delivery.

Additional Periodical Articles with Abstracts

More information about alternative energy and related subjects can be found in the following articles. Readers who require a more comprehensive selection are advised to consult Readers Guide Abstracts and other H.W. Wilson Publications.

Going Green by Empowering Choice. Deron Lovaas. *The Futurist* v. 41 p27 January/February 2007.

There needs to be a role for public policy in the marketing of alternative fuels in the United States, Lovaas contends. Oil combustion is weighing the United States down, and oil's contribution is bound to grow disproportionately as companies and countries develop higher-pollution substitutes such as tar sands and oil shale. Fortunately, the price-driven search for oil substitutes is also driving the development of cleaner technologies. The United States must invest in infrastructure that levels the playing field for competing alternatives, and performance standards for these alternatives must be linked to investment to guarantee that taxpayer money is being put to effective use. Programs to promote alternative fuels must guarantee large, rapid cuts in the combustion of oil-derived fuels; boost the fuel-efficiency of the nation's vehicle fleet; produce incentives to commercialize clean alternatives; and advocate rail transit and other alternatives to driving in urbanized areas.

Wet and Wild: Microhydro for the Home. Starre Vartan. E: The Environmental Magazine v. 18 p44 May/June 2007.

Small-scale hydropower systems may be an ideal and affordable option for homeowners who wish to generate their own electricity, Vartan reports. These systems, which are known as "microhydro" and produce from 100–300 kilowatts, have negligible environmental impact if a "run of river" arrangement is used. This setup, which is the most common, includes an intake pipe, which directs some of the water into a turbine that generates power. Most systems do not require large volumes of water, and the water that is returned to the stream after it has passed through the turbine is as clean as when it entered at the top. Vartan also provides advice on installing a microhydro system.

Big Is Beautiful. Utility-Scale Solar Energy. Christine Woodside. *E: The Environmental Magazine* v. 18 pp20, 22 May/June 2007.

Utility-grade solar energy is becoming a viable option, according to Woodside. Concentrating solar power has been around for decades but is still seen as new technology. Florida Power & Light Energy, an independent energy producer, has been operating a concentrating solar power plant in the Mojave Desert of California for about 20 years, and in 2007, power companies in the United States, Germany, Spain, South Africa, and elsewhere are planning or constructing major solar electricity plants employing the technology. In "Tackling Climate Change in the U.S.," a report issued in January by the American Solar Energy Society, experts forecast that solar photovoltaic panels, installed everywhere from people's roofs to parking lots to brownfield sites, could supply 7 percent of total U.S. electricity needs by 2030.

Renewable Hydrogen Goes Maine-Stream. Curtiss P. Martin. E: *The Environmental Magazine* v. 17 p12 November/December 2006.

The writer reports that a $250,000 demonstration project recently unveiled in Maine could provide the pathway to a clean hydrogen future. In August the Chewonki Foundation's environmental education center in Wisacasset, Maine, unveiled the country's first hydrogen backup system, which kicks in when grid power goes down and runs totally on renewable energy. The Chewonki hydrogen system can generate backup power for the 11,000-square-foot visitor's center for four days in the event of a power outage. Liberating hydrogen from its molecular bonds can be a dirty process, but energy sourced from solar panels installed on the center's roof combines with "green power" purchased from hydroelectric dams in the state before entering into an Avalence electrolyzer. The electrolyzer is novel because it generates hydrogen at high pressures, doing away with the need for expensive compressor and moisture-control equipment.

Power Puffs. Tom Arrandale. *Governing* v. 21 p64 December 2007.

Wind power is currently experiencing a renaissance across the nation, Arrandale contends. Federal and state officials are relying on massive arrays of high-tech turbines to capture energy from wind to help replace fossil fuels and offset global warming. Rural cities and counties are fascinated by the prospects of creating new jobs and producing electricity from the wind. For all wind energy's clean and green appeal, however, even the most well-intentioned technologies can have harmful consequences. Wind-swept communities are likely to be in for some difficulties as large-scale wind power development extends to new areas. Officials will need to strike a balance between energy demands and preserving the local community's unique character.

Starving for Gas? Lester R. Brown. *The Humanist* v. 66 pp30–31 September/October 2006.

Cars rather than people will benefit most from the increase in world grain consumption this year, Brown notes. The U.S. Department of Agriculture predicts that world grain use will rise by 20 million tons in 2006, 14 million tons of which will be used to manufacture auto fuel in the United States, leaving only 6 million tons to satisfy the world's growing food needs. As oil prices rise, it becomes increasingly profitable to convert crops into automotive fuel, either ethanol or biodiesel, meaning that the price of oil in effect becomes the support price for food commodities: When the fuel value of a commodity exceeds its food value, the market will convert it into fuel. As a result, the stage is being set for a head-on collision between the world's wealthy automobile owners and food consumers.

Where the Gas Is Greener. Laura Putre. *Indianapolis Monthly* v. 29 pp72+ January 2006.According to Putre a biofuel experiment in Reynolds, Indiana, may revolutionize the way people fuel their cars and heat their houses. The locus of a large-scale science study called "BioTown USA," Reynolds is slated to become the first U.S. municipality to run entirely on renewable energy, with the first stage being the addition of a "bio island" to the town's sole gas station to provide corn-derived E85 fuel (85 percent ethanol and 15 percent gasoline) as well as biodiesel fuel that is 20 percent soybean oil. The next two phases of BioTown USA will investigate converting livestock waste into electricity and natural gas. One reason Reynolds was chosen is its location—near West Lafayette, where Purdue University is conducting research into renewable fuels. However, a more significant reason is that there are 150,000 hogs in a 15-mile radius of Reynolds—roughly 270 for each resident.

The Hype About Hydrogen. Joseph J. Romm. *Issues in Science and Technology* v. 20 pp74–81 Spring 2004.

The long-term potential of hydrogen technology should not be used as an excuse to avoid taking action on lowering greenhouse gas emissions, Romm believes. Despite the promise of hydrogen-powered fuel-cell vehicles for reducing pollution, the transition to a hydrogen economy would take many decades, and any reductions in the use of fossil fuels are likely to be minor in the short term. Given the availability of few potential zero-carbon replacements for oil, the Department of Energy (DOE) is not spending too much on hydrogen R&D, but given the urgent need for lowering greenhouse gas emissions, the DOE is spending far too little on energy efficiency and renewable energy. For now, the priority is to deploy existing clean-energy technologies and to prevent any expansion of the inefficient carbon-emitting infrastructure.

Would You Use Vegetable Oil to Fuel Your Vehicle? Tim Wacker. *The Mother Earth News* pp111–115 December 2007/January 2008.

It is possible to run a diesel car or truck on vegetable oil and almost eliminate one's use of traditional gas or diesel, Wacker reports. Moreover, doing so can also save drivers money. Known as "veggie cars" or "grease cars," the vehicles have fuel systems adapted to burn both diesel fuel and straight vegetable oil, but even proponents acknowledge that vegetable oil is not for everyone because of the extra work it requires. The writer discusses the technicalities of converting a vehicle to run on vegetable oil and associated legal problems. Also presented is an interview with William Kemp, author of *Biodiesel Basics and Beyond*, in which he discusses the limitations of biodiesel and vegetable oil technologies.

The Big Dig. Jeff Persons. *The Mother Earth News* pp52–54+ May 2001.

Installing a geothermal-energy system allows homeowners to cut their electricity bills by using the temperature of the earth to heat and cool their homes, Person contends. He goes on to outline the history of domestic geothermal energy and discusses the two main types of geothermal systems: open-loop and closed-loop.

Hydrogen: Saviour or Fatal Distraction. James Randerson. *New Scientist* v. 183 p12 August 21 2004.

According to Randerson energy experts are still bitterly divided over what should be the top priority for meeting long-term energy needs and reducing emissions. He notes that in a recent *Science* article, a writer argued that the use of energy from renewable sources to generate hydrogen is the only green way to produce energy for cars and trucks. However, other researchers maintain that this approach is not economically feasible and that strategies to reduce greenhouse gases are needed immediately.

The Energy Fix. Tom Clynes. *Popular Science* v. 269 pp47–51+ July 2006.

Clynes describes 10 renewable energy technologies and policies that could lessen the dependence of the U.S. on fossil fuel. Accompanying the article is an illustration detailing energy-saving innovations.

Windmills in the Sky. Michael Behar. *Popular Science* v. 267 pp38–39 September 2005.

An engineer at the University of Technology in Sydney, Australia, may have a solution to the drawbacks associated with wind power, Behar reports. Wind energy is often regarded as noisy and aesthetically unappealing, and it can also interfere with television reception. Now, Bryan Roberts proposes bypassing these problems by floating wind turbines in the jet stream—an extremely fast air current that circles the world at altitudes of 15,000 and 45,000 feet. As envisioned by Roberts, airborne turbines will generate an electrical current that will be transmitted along extremely strong tethers to ground stations linked to the utility grid. Roberts and three other engineers have formed the company Sky WindPower, based in San Diego, California, to develop the so-called Flying Electric Generator.

Oceans of Electricity. Peter Weiss. *Science News* v. 159 pp234–36 April 14, 2001.

The generation of energy from waves is attracting increasing interest, Weiss reports. Waves are driven by winds produced by solar heating of the Earth's surface, and the best wave-energy regions tend to be coasts subjected to waves driven by the wind across long stretches of water. Although the potential for wave energy varies between locales and seasons, ocean waves overall constitute a huge global energy reserve. The first patent for a wave-power device was filed in 1799 by two French inventors and envisioned the direct use of wave power to mechanically drive machinery. However, in modern devices, converted wave momentum spins coils of wire within ring-shaped magnets to generate a current. Across the world, wave-power innovators are developing potentially effective technologies for both onshore and offshore generators that they expect could compete with other power sources and contribute to more electric grids within the next few years

Is Solar Power for You? Joyanna Laughlin. *Sunset* v. 216 pp114–15 June 2006.

With energy bills increasing, nonrenewable fossil fuels declining, and federal and state tax incentives available, solar energy systems are becoming increasingly popular, according to Laughlin. The research company Solarbuzz reports that the American market for solar photovoltaic (PV) systems is expanding by 25 percent to 30 percent per year. Financial incentives are part of the attraction. Thanks to the Energy Policy Act of 2005, a federal tax credit of up to $2,000 is currently available for installing a PV system on a residence. In addition, many states are offering extra tax credits and rebates, from lower permit fees in San Diego to cash back in many cities, that can reduce the cost significantly. Laughlin also provides information and advice on selecting the best solar energy system for a house.

It's Not Too Early. Marty Hoffert. *Technology Review* (Cambridge, Mass.: 1998) v. 109 p69 July/August 2006.

In this article, part of a special section on energy technologies that might forestall global warming, Hoffert contends that it is time to begin building a sustainable carbon-free energy infrastructure. The world currently uses about 13 terawatts of power, about 80 percent of it from carbon-dioxide-emitting fossil fuels, and if Earth's average temperature is to be kept low enough to prevent eventual large sea-level rises and accommodate continued 3 percent annual economic growth, between 10 and 30 terawatts of new carbon-free power will be required by 2050. To achieve this, an Apollo-type research effort is required, beginning perhaps with the funding of radical programs along the lines of ARPA-E, an initiative proposed by the National Academy of Sciences and modeled on the U.S. Advanced Research Project Agency. The writer also discusses other potentially fruitful avenues of energy research.

Wind Power Upgrade. David Talbot. *Technology Review* (Cambridge, Mass.: 1998) v. 108 pp21–22 May 2005.

Wind power has become the planet's fastest-growing source of electricity, and it is continuing to pick up even more momentum, Talbot reports. As a way of both boosting and serving demand, manufacturers are at work on massive new offshore wind turbines with blade spans bigger than the length of a football field. The largest commercial wind turbine currently in operation has a blade span of 104 meters and produces as much as 5.6 megawatts of electricity, which is sufficient to power 1,000 average U.S. homes. Now, Germany's Repower Systems has tested a demonstration turbine that produces 5 megawatts and has a blade span of 125 meters, and General Electric is at work on a design for a 70-meter blade, which would result in a total blade span of more than 140 meters.

Fossilized Policy: Summary of Wind Power Upgrade. David Talbot. *Technology Review* (Cambridge, Mass.: 1998) v. 108 pp17–18 May 2005.

Even though alternative electricity sources are viable, the United States does not have a consistent national policy to bring these technologies into common use, Talbot maintains. Alternative energy technologies have improved in effectiveness and could soon mitigate some of the numerous geopolitical, health, and environmental problems that have their roots in society's reliance on fossil fuels. Nonetheless, the United States lacks a dependable, long-term policy to provide renewables with a firmer footing through initiatives such as federal financing, tax credits, grid-connection mandates, and streamlined construction regulations. This is unfortunate given that certain technologies are ready for commercialization, notably wind turbines, which are efficient and reliable enough to be a match for fossil fuels in some areas.

Wave Power. Tracy Staedter. *Technology Review* (Cambridge, Mass.: 1998) v. 105 pp86–87 January/February 2002.

Although scientists have been trying for decades to exploit wave power as a source of renewable energy, it remains a difficult enterprise economically because wave action is so dispersed, Staedter reports. In November 2000, however, Wavegen, an Inverness, Scotland-based company, installed the world's first commercial system to generate electricity directly from the surf. The system is capable of generating 500 kilowatts of power reliably, which is sufficient for around 400 homes. Staedter also describes the operation of the system, and diagrams detailing the structure of the system accompany the article.

Sky Power. Ed Darack. *Weatherwise* v. 58 pp30–35 November/December 2005.

People around the world are increasingly taking advantage of solar and wind energy to either supplement the existing power grid or avoid it altogether, Darack observes. The availability of solar panels, wind turbines, and supporting equipment has increased enormously, so the main question in most of the world is whether weather conditions will support the use of either technology or a combination of both. The principal barrier remains cost, but technological advances and government support are making wind and solar power more attractive in a number of countries.

Index